Veer Savarkar
Father of Hindu Nationalism

J. D. Joglekar

First Marathi Edition - 1983
Second Marathi Edition - 2006
(c) Jaywant D. Joglekar
ISBN 978-1-84728-380-1

Dedicated to the loving memory of my father and mother.

"Krishnavarma and Savarkar coupled their fiery nationalism with a vision of a scientific and secular India of the future. Intense as they were in their dedication to national independence, Gandhi believed they erred in their intention to Westernize India. A deeper nationalism, a cultural nationalism, was required." - James D. Hunt: Gandhi in London - p.151-152

"If after my death you would raise a monument over my cremation ground and would write and epitaph, I would prefer 'Savarkar, the Organizer of Hindus' to 'Swatantryaveer Savarkar; for all my efforts towards independence were intended for Hindu unity, for independent and strong Hindu nation, and for Hindusthan." - V. D. Savarkar: From the speech at Jodhpur in 1956

Table of contents

Preface

I knew Veer Savarkar from 1938 and had studied his philosophy very closely. I was considered a good interpreter of his philosophy. It was but natural that I should feel that I should write his biography. A few good friends also constantly argued me to write it as the birthday centenary year started approaching rapidly. I wanted to write the biography in English and Marathi languages. But I soon realized that the English version would take longer. Marathi being my mother-tongue, it was easy to write and publish the biography in Marathi on May 28, 1983. On that day the centenary celebrations began and my Savarkar biography was published.

Now I had to do the English version. But as happens in life, other pressing matters caught up with me and that work was put on the back burner.

But my conscience was always pricking me. Doing Savarkar's biography in English was a national duty.

Now his portrait has been unveiled in the hall of the Indian Parliament, and in the hall of the Gujarat Legislative Assembly and in the hall of the Maharashtra Legislative Assembly. Already the aerodrome in the Andamans has been named after him. His personality and services are slowly receiving attention.

Savarkar's personality needs more exposure, more so now, in the non-Marathi world. His services in the cause of India's freedom, his lone fight to keep India united, his decade old efforts to remove untouchability, his single handed effort to rouse the Hindu community and to unite it is a glorious page in national history. These superhuman efforts need to be written in golden letters. I hope, in future, Savarkar will get his Boswell who will produce a biography worthy of the subject. In the meantime, I offer my effort at his biography which will give a glimpse of that giant of a man, such of whom nature products once or twice in a century.

A number of people have helped me this endeavor. I thank them. But two persons deserved to be mentioned by names: My son, Vijay and my late wife, Dr. Mrs. S. J. Joglekar. Without their help, I could not have succeeded in my endeavor. The cover picture is by Mr. S. M. Pandit. I have reproduced it from the volume of articles on Savarkar published by Savarkar Darshan Pratishthan. I am deeply indebted to them and express my deep gratitude to them.

I am 84 years old. I am aware that mistakes may have reminded and the English version may be inelegant. I crave indulgence of the readers.

I also thank all the authors and their publishers. Their books have been useful while writing this book.

J. D. Joglekar

India After 1857

"Thus the year 1857 may be looked upon as the great divide between the two great landmarks in Indian history- that of British paramountcy in the first half, and that of Indian nationalism in the second half of the nineteenth century."[1]

When a 21st century historian reviews the first seven decades of the 20th century, he will come across the names of Justice Ranade, Dadabhai Naoroji, Honorable Gokhale, Lokamanya Tilak, Mahatma Gandhi, Pandit Nehru who had stamped their mark on some of its decades. He will also find that during these seven decades there is one person whose name on and off meets his eye. That person is Swatantryaveer Vinayak Damodar Savarkar. This is quite natural. For, by his outstanding capability he has carved his name on these seven decades. This extraordinary man's life is unique in various ways. Savarkar was a flaming patriot, a leading revolutionary, an epic poet, a historian, one of the foremost social reformers, a stoic in enduring hardships for his country's freedom, a great savant, and a leader of the likes of Lenin, Stalin, or Kamal Ataturk. Unlike them, he did not enjoy supreme power. This does not detract from his greatness. As Savarkar never came to power, the loser was the Hindu society. It lost the services of a nation-builder. The country is suffering from a number of social ills. Savarkar would have mercilessly dealt with them. For, his motto was: 'Not courting popularity, but looking to the good of the society should be the aim.' But that was not to be.

Some of the political, religious, and social events that occurred and the thought systems that were developed before Savarkar was born or during his infancy are reflected in his later life. It is, therefore, necessary to take stock of the social, religious, and political life in India in the latter half of the nineteenth century. It would, however, be useful to know something about the events of the 1857 eruption.

When the revolt of 1857 occurred, the British did not initially think that it would be so wide spread. But as it began to develop into a conflagration, they realized that this was no ordinary military mutiny and that their empire might become its casualty. Once this realization came, they struck back hard at the revolt. It became a case of hang first and try afterwards. Brigadier General Nicholson wrote to Herbert Edwards, Commissioner of Peshawar, "Let us propose a Bill for the flaying alive, impalement or burning of the murderers of the women and children at Delhi. The idea of simply hanging the perpetrators of such atrocities is maddening."

---

[1] R. C. Majumdar: British Paramountcy and Indian Renaissance - Part I - p.668

Nicholson's thoughts did not remain on paper, nor did they remain confined to him. A number of British officers actually behaved that way. A contemporary military official wrote that officers now went to court-martial declaring they would hang the prisoners whether guilty or innocent, and the provost-marshal had his cart waiting for them at the tent door. Some brought the names of the offending villages and sought permission to get them destroyed and plundered on the strength of vague reports. The fierceness of men increased every day often venting it upon the camp servants, many of whom ran away. These prisoners, during the few hours between their trial and execution, were unceasingly tormented by the soldiers. They pulled their hair, pricked them with bayonets, and forced them to eat cow's flesh, while officers stood by approving.

Godse, a Maharashtrian priest, who happened to be in Jhansi during this upheaval, wrote about his experiences as follows: "On the second day a lot of men folk died. When people saw white soldiers, they ran and hid themselves in the hay stack. The white soldiers came and set fire to this hay stack in which these people were burnt. Some seeing these soldiers, jumped into the wells. But these soldiers sat at the mouth of the well and shot at the bobbing head and thus killing a number of people. Some took shelter in the latrine. They were searched out and shot."[1] The above shows the cruelty of the British soldiers. They murdered more than ten times the number of women and children killed by the Indians.[2]

In his minutes dated 24 December, 1857 Governor-General in Council graphically describes what happened in northern India, "The indiscriminate hanging, not only of persons of all shades of guilt, but of those whose guilt was at the least very doubtful and the general burning and plunder of villages, whereby the innocent as well as the guilty, without regard to age or sex, were indiscriminately punished and in some cases, sacrificed, had deeply exasperated large communities not otherwise hostile to the Government."[3] To quell the rebellion of the Indian soldiers, the British resorted to frightful measures. No wonder Reynolds's newspaper published in Britain called the British soldiers, "English cut-throats."[4]

With the help of superior weapons and better organization, the British established law and order in India by 1858. But the events that happened during the upheaval scarred the minds of the people. Because of circumstances, the mental anguish was not often given vent to, but the pangs remained. A good example can be quoted. Lord Linlithgow came to India as Viceroy in 1936. Later he met Gandhiji to discuss the Indian political situation. Reporting to the then Secretary of State, Lord Zetland, the Viceroy wrote, "Gandhi had first talked of

---

[1] Vishnubhat Godse: Maza Pravas - p.100

[2] Dr. R. C. Majumdar: British Paramountcy and Indian Renaissance - Part I - p.600

[3] Dr. R. C. Majumdar: British Paramountcy and Indian Renaissance – Part I - p.599

[4] Edward Spiers: The Army and Society - p.131

the past, including the Indian mutiny of 1857, and was inclined to be bitter about it."[1] If a pacifist like Gandhiji, after decades, was still bitter about the events of 1857, then one can well imagine the feelings of ordinary people.

The failure of the revolt of 1857 ushered a new era in the political life of the country. It appears that in these new times, emphasis on violence had declined and people had moved to the constitutional methods. By the Act of August 2, 1858 the governance of India was taken away from the East India Company and was entrusted to the Crown. This was done to ensure better administration in India. Lord Canning remained the Governor-General in this new set-up. During his tenure of office, direct tax was imposed, Penal Code was introduced and the High Courts were established. Three years later, the Indian Council Act of 1861 came into force. It admitted non-officials and Indians to Legislative Council. This was a paltry reform. It could, however, be said that the admission of Indians to the Council, though it appeared trivial, turned out to be in the long run the thin end of the wedge.

The British dominion in India was extensive. There was a great need of personnel for operating this vast administrative machinery. It was impossible to bring in a large work force from Britain. So natives were recruited for manning the lower ranks in the administration. In addition, with the decision to make English the official language, its knowledge for this lower grade staff became indispensable. With the spread of English education, the new English knowing class began to slowly acquire knowledge of arts and sciences as also of various movements, of wars and other happenings in Britain and Europe. The upshot was that the people who had been ignorant so far about world events or who had no access to such knowledge began to learn about them. Its results soon became apparent.

There were ongoing social and political reforms in Britain. The Indians began to learn about them through their knowledge of English. The leaders of the new educated class began to feel that there should be such movements in India and that they should start them. There was nothing strange about it, because man, by nature, is imitative. During the British Raj, it became customary to establish all kinds of institutions. For starting an agitation a group of people had to come together. It was easy for such a group to establish an organization and submit its charter of grievances or requests to the government. Not only in the political field but also in the social field, a number of caste organizations began to make their appearance. Bengal, Madras, Bombay were key provinces. The ports of Calcutta, Madras, and Bombay were linked to world markets. The spread of English education and its influence became first perceptible in these cities. Here it was that a new English educated class came into being.

---

[1] John Glendevon: The Viceroy at Bay - p.72

The leaders of this new class were Prosunna Kumar Tagore, Ram Gopal Ghose, and Hurish Chunder Mukherji at Calcutta, Raghunath Rao and Madhava Rao at Madras, and Naoroji Furdunji, Dadabhai Naoroji, and Sorabji Bengali at Bombay. Through the medium of newspapers, such as, Hindu Intelligence, The Crescent, Rast Goftar, as also through the medium of institutions, like the British Indian Association, the Madras Native Association, and the Bombay Association, they had demanded before the 1857 revolt, that the quality of University education should be improved, that educated Indians should get more employment opportunities in government services, and that there should be Indian representatives in the Governor's councils. These demands were turned down. Later in 1870s The Indian Association in Calcutta led by Banerjee, the Sarvajanik Sabha in Poona led by Ranade, Chiplunkar, and Nulkar, Triplicane Literary Society in Madras led by Iyer and Chariar, championed the cause of educated Indians.

These institutions were mainly provincial. Now a need for an All India Organization was felt. After the Delhi Darbar of 1876, Sen, Banerjea, Malabari, Chaterjee, Chiplunkar and some other Indian editors tried to organize a "Press Foundation" on an all India basis. Its platform was to be utilized for the discussion of political situation in the country. This organization never came into being. The Europeans had set up an Anglo-Indian Defense Association in 1883 to oppose Ripon's liberal policy. The Association was backed both by the Anglo-Indians and the Eurasians. With such experience spread over many years, a firm idea took hold of the minds of leaders from various provinces that an all India platform to discuss the national affairs should be set up. Thus the Indian National Congress was established. Its first session was held on December 28, 1885 at the Gokuldas Tejpal Sanskrit College in Bombay. Mr. W. C. Bonnerjee presided over this session. Thus a new political power emerged in India.

The above may lead one to believe that the atmosphere in the country was peaceful and that all movements were constitutional. Such a belief would not be completely true. Now and then, India did witness somewhere some kind of insurrectionary movements. Chronologically these were: 1. Wahabi Movement, 2. Kukas' Revolt, 3. Revolt of Aborigines in Chota Nagpur, 4. Revolt in Pancha Mahals, and 5. the armed uprising of Vasudeo Balwant Phadke.

Syed Ahmad of Bareilly was the founder of the Wahabi sect. In the beginning the sect emphasized that society should lead a true Islamic life, but soon it took a political turn. As a young man, Syed Ahmad took service in the military establishment of the ruler of Tonk as Pesh Imam. His elder brother had joined that army earlier. When the ruler of Tonk entered into friendly relations with the British, Syed Ahmad left his service. For sometime he traveled and preached his doctrine in Northern India. Then he went on pilgrimage to Haj. After returning from Haj, he left Bareilly in 1826 and migrated to the Frontier Province. Here he was appointed Imam and under his guidance jihad began. As the province was under Sikh domination his fight began with the Sikhs. He was killed in the battle at Balakote.

After his death, the leadership of the movement passed on to Vilayat Ali and Enayat Ali. Under their leadership the Wahabis fought in vain against the Sikhs. Later, Punjab and the Frontier Province came under the jurisdiction of the British. The Wahabis fought them too. Finally, the British launched a campaign that destroyed the Wahabis. The various Wahabi centers in India used to send money and men to the Wahabi base in the Frontier province. The leading men in this movement were arrested and after trials, some of them were sentenced to life imprisonment and were shipped to the Andamans. This brought an end to the movement.

Dr. Ahmed thinks that the Wahabi movement was a national one. The Wahabis did not actively participate in the revolt of 1857. According to the Wahabis the battle against the British had to be fought from outside the country. Dr. Ahmed advances this plea for Wahabis' non-participation in the 1857 revolt.[1] According to Dr. Majumdar it was not a national movement, but was a movement of the Muslims, by the Muslims, and for the Muslims.[2]

Baba Ram Singh was the founder of the Kuka movement. He had joined the Khalsa (Sikh) army when he was twenty. After Ranjit Singh's death, he left the service and opened a grocer's shop. His observant eye was watching the developments around him. He had concluded that the British ascendancy in India was due to moral degradation of the Indians. Hence he laid great emphasis on ethical behavior in his new movement.

A ban on tobacco and liquor, prohibition of infanticide, opposition to caste system, and equal rights to women were the special features of the Kuka movement. It also advocated a boycott of British goods and the British courts. It supported a Panchayat system and the use of separate postal service.

In 1863, the government received information that there was a likelihood of Kuka revolt after Diwali. So Baba Ram Singh was interned in his home town and his movement was banned. Even then from 1868 to 1870 the movement gathered momentum. After the establishment of the British government, the ban on cow slaughter was abolished. So a group of Kukas attacked the butcher shops at Amritsar, Raykot, Maldhoga, and Maler Kotla. Finally, in order to liquidate the movement, the government blew from the mouth of guns 50 Kukas on the parade ground at Kotla. Later, Ram Singh was taken to Rangoon and interned there, where in 1885 he expired. Kuka movement had a wide network. Before 1872 Kukas had established clandestine relations with Nepal and Kashmir governments and in 1872 they made approaches to the Russian Government. The army of

---

[1]Dr. Qeyamudin Ahmad: The Wahabi Movement in India - p.217
[2]Dr. R. C. Majumdar: British Paramountcy and Indian Renaissance - I - p.901

Jammu and Kashmir State contained Kuka elements. The relevant papers are in the national archives.[1]

Between 1855 and 1857 the Santhal tribe rose in rebellion. It was suppressed. Still, some minor agrarian revolts occurred between 1881 and 1895. The one that deserves notice was led by Birsa belonging to the Munda tribe. He had some English education, and had become a Christian. This change of faith did not give him peace of mind and he reverted to his former faith. At the age of 21 he founded a new faith. Soon he had a large following. Even those Mundas who had become Christian earlier joined him.

When the British officers realized that the movement was aimed at subverting the British rule and establishing a Munda one in its place, they resolved to suppress it. One day, while Birsa was asleep, he was arrested. Later he was tried and jailed for two years. After his sentence ran out, he resumed his activities that received a wide public support. He now organized an armed force. The armed Mundas attacked a police station. When the government found that the movement was beyond control, it suppressed it with the help of the army. Some time later Birsa was apprehended. He died of cholera in jail on June 2, 1900.

There was a small uprising in the Panchmahal district of Gujarat in 1858. It was, however, suppressed and amnesty was declared. Nine years later, in 1867, a person named Joria declared himself an incarnation of God (Parmeshwar). He came from Vadek, a village in Jambughoda. People flocked to him. Rupa Naik, who was one of the stalwarts of 1857 revolt, joined him. Later, both plundered some villages. This created unrest in that area. So British troops were deployed who put an end to this revolt.

In 1875, Poona and Ahmednagar witnessed agrarian riots. In 1880, the aborigines in the Godavari valley rose in revolt against forest laws, but with the help of the army, the government suppressed it. In 1860, Income-Tax was imposed. This created discontent among the people. There was commotion at Surat, Bhiwandi, Thane, Kalyan, Panvel, and Shahapur. One Mr. Hunter, an Income-Tax officer, was manhandled at Vasai.

Here mention has to be made of an unprecedented event that occurred at Banaras. The British government decided to levy a house-tax in the city. People decided to organize a sit-in. Accordingly, 300,000 people stopped their business and sat outside the city limits. As a precautionary measure, the government brought in the British troops. Soon the public became weary and decided to organize a march of 10,000 people to Calcutta. Accordingly, the people assembled. It was an arduous task. In a few days, a large number of people returned home. Soon the remaining ones followed suit. The agitation had such an effect on the government that it withdrew the house-tax. This event needs to be

---

[1]Dr. F. S. Bajwa: Kuka Movement - p.129

noted. It shows that the notion that such national movements started only after 1920 is erroneous.

A number of British planters were involved in the trade of indigo. In their pursuit of enormous profits, they had ground down the common cultivator from Bihar and Bengal. This became a scandal and the government had to appoint a commission. The oppressive methods employed in the production of indigo and the discontent arising from them was the subject of editorial comment by Amrit Bazar Patrika which observed: "It was the Indigo disturbances which first taught the natives the value of combination and political agitation. Indeed, it was the first revolution in Bengal after the advent of the English. If there be a second revolution it will be to free the nation from the death grips of the all-powerful police and district Magistrate."[1]

The above gives us a glimpse of the turbulent conditions in the country. These events had no long-term effects. They happened and were soon forgotten. But the armed revolt of Vasudeo Balwant Phadke had far-reaching effects. Phadke was born on November 4, 1845. After completing primary education, he studied for two years in an English medium school. He then entered government service. While he was working in Poona, his mother fell ill. His leave application for going home was turned down. So, Phadke could not remain present during the last hours of his dying mother. This hurt him much and turned his mind to the path of revolution. He began his activities by establishing the Poona Native School in 1874.

He, however, came to the conclusion that only an armed revolt could overthrow the British government. For this armed struggle, money was required. To collect it, he began to raid houses of money-lenders. Three months later, he published a declaration denouncing the British economic exploitation of India. Afterwards he plundered the affluent. So the government announced a reward of Rs. 3,000 for the apprehension of Phadke. On July 20, 1879, Phadke was arrested. He was tried in the court of law and was sentenced to life imprisonment. He was incarcerated in Aden. Once he broke out of jail, but was later apprehended. Finally the great patriot died on February 17, 1883.

It was an uncommon thing for an unknown person to challenge the might of the British Empire. Considering the circumstances of those times, Phadke's failure was inevitable. His work must not be judged by the immediate failure. His efforts of organizing an armed uprising sowed afresh the seeds of armed revolt which in fifty years grew into a mighty banyan tree. It was he who showed the way as to how arms were to be secretly collected, how physical training was to be imparted to the youth and how by means of political dacoities funds were to be collected. An impression prevails in Maharashtra that Ranade, Phule, and Tilak had some connection with Phadke's revolt. It is impossible to say whether this had

---

[1] Dr. R. C. Majumdar: British Paramountcy and Indian Renaissance - Part I - p.935

any foundation. But it would not be wrong to say that he was the father of the tradition that produced Chaphekar, Savarkar, Hardayal, Dr. Khankhoje, Bhai Parmananda, Dhingra, Bhagatsingh, Rajguru, Dutt and other revolutionaries.

The establishment of British rule affected the political as well as the religious and social life in India. As the new knowledge acquired through the medium of English education spread, the newly educated class felt revulsion to religious rituals, blind faith, and cruel customs. In a society politically dependent and helpless, it was natural that such a reaction should occur. In addition, the British, with the backing of the state power, had introduced social reforms.

The first and the most talked about reform was the banning of the custom of Sati, that is, the burning of the widow on the funeral pyre of her husband. It is a wrong notion that this custom was prevalent throughout India. This custom had no active support of the State. It was more prevalent in Bengal. In a period of two years, that is, from 1815 to 1817, 864 cases of Sati were reported in five districts of Bengal, while in the same period in remaining part of British India only 663 cases were reported.[1] This gives an idea as to where and to what extent the custom of Sati was prevalent. The custom no doubt was inhuman and had to be abolished. Finally in 1829 Sati was banned by law first in Bengal and later in Madras and Bombay.

The second reform was about infanticide. It was customary in certain communities to kill newly born girls. Under regulation III of 1804 such killing was declared as murder. Yet the custom persisted. So the British officials, by exerting moral pressure, slowly brought an end to this custom in various native states. To effectively end this practice, an act was passed in 1870 whereby registration of births was made compulsory and a system of regular verification of female children for some years after their birth was introduced in the areas where infanticide was common.

The third reform was the remarriage of widows. Widow Remarriage had sanction in the Smritis. However, such marriages had become obsolete in practice. Before the advent of the British rule two eminent men, Raja Rajballabh of Dacca and Parshurambhau Tatya, a Maratha nobleman, tried to get their widowed daughters remarried. In both instances the custom proved stronger than Smriti. In 1856, Hindu Widow Remarriage Act came into force. Ten years later a 'Widow Remarriage Association' was started in Bombay and thirty years later Dr. Dhondo Keshav Karve founded a widow's home in Poona. Despite these efforts, widow remarriage has yet to become common.

The institution of slavery, like other countries, existed in India. When an agitation for its abolition began in Europe and America, it had its echoes in India.

---

[1]Dr. R. C. Majumdar: British Paramountcy and Indian Renaissance Part II - p.271

In 1843 it was abolished by law and in 1860 it became an offence under the Indian Penal Code to keep slaves or to traffic in them.

The reform that hurt the Hindu mind most was 'The Emancipation Act." It was enacted by the Government when Dalhousie was the Governor-General. It removed an impediment in the way of those who wanted to embrace Christianity. Henceforth even after change of religion, a person's right to property or of inheritance was to remain unimpaired. Also, the fear of the caste boycott was removed. This law cleared the way for the spread of Christianity more easily. This piece of legislation could be mentioned as one of the combustible materials that sparked the eruption of 1857.

It was because of English education that institutions for ventilating political discontent were founded. Similarly, for effecting social and religious reforms, a number of institutions were established in different parts of the country and eminent social leaders emerged. Prominent among these institutions was the 'Brahma Samaj' of Calcutta. It was established on August 20, 1828 by Raja Ramohan Roy. He was born in 1774 in a Brahmin family. When he was 16, he wrote an essay against idol worship. Subsequently he had an altercation with his father on this subject and he had to leave his parental home. Then he spent a number of years in service. Even during this time he continued his self-education. In 1815 he started an institution called 'Atmiya Sabha' for the propagation of monotheistic doctrine from the Hindu scriptures. In 1818 he submitted to the Government a petition signed by a large number of eminent men requesting it to enact the law banning the custom of Sati. Rammohan was opposed to the caste system and polygamy. He was the supporter of widow remarriage. He had broken the prohibition of sea travel by himself going abroad. Rammohan can be ranked among the foremost men who tried to bring about renaissance in India.

'Brahma Samaj' movement gave a new vigor to Hindu society. It helped considerably in educating Hindus about the importance of rationalism and of freedom of individual conscience. With the passage of time, the reforms suggested by this Samaj, became common in the Hindu society. Further the tempo of conversion from Hinduism to Christianity was arrested by the activities of the 'Brahma Samaj'. It is necessary to mention here one important fact. Rammohan Roy did consider the establishment of British rule as 'a benign act of Providence.' But it would be wrong to deduce from this that his opposition to orthodox Hindus persuaded him to support the British Raj. The British rule liberated the Bengali Hindus from the Muslim yoke and therefore Rammohan and Devandranath Tagore supported it. Rammohan wrote, "I now conclude my Essay by offering up thanks to the Supreme Disposer of the events of this universe, for having unexpectedly delivered this country from the long-continued tyranny of its former rulers and placed it under the government of the English."[1]

---

[1]Dr. R. C. Majumdar: British Paramountcy and Indian Renaissance – Part II - p.12

Keshavchandra Sen, one of the leaders of the Calcutta branch of 'Brahma Samaj' came to Bombay in 1864. He inspired some men of liberal views to establish a similar institution in Bombay. Sometime later a meeting was held at the residence of Dr. Atmaram Pandurang Tarkhadkar that was attended by Bondse, Shirgaonkar, Sanzgiri, Wagle, Bhagwat, Padval, Parmananda, Mankar, Cholkar, and Navarange. It was then resolved to found an institution called 'Prarthana Samaj' and accordingly it was founded on March 31, 1867. Dr. Tarkhadkar was its first Chairman. Justice Ranade and Dr. Bhandarkar joined it later. The burden of the work of the society was borne by Mama Parmananda.[1]

The 'Prathana Samaj' agitated for such reforms as abolition of caste system, remarriage of widows, education of women, abolition of the veil, and the prohibition of child marriage. It also ran institutions like 'Arya Mahilashram' in Poona, 'Rammohan Ashram' in Bombay, 'An Orphanage' at Pandharpur, 'Rammohan English School' in Bombay, and 'Depressed Class Mission.' But Prarthana Samaj did not have an enduring influence on the then Presidency of Bombay.

'Brahma Samaj' did inspire the founding of the Prarthana Samaj. Though it did not provide the same amount of inspiration to the establishment of the 'Arya Samaj', it appears that it was only after Dayananda Saraswati came into contact with the leaders of 'Brahma Samaj' that the idea of founding 'Arya Samaj' first occurred to him. He was a great reformer of the nineteenth century. Prof. Jordens has described him as, "Luther of India." He was born in Morvi State in 1824. His family belonged to Shaivite faith. After his traditional education was over, he requested permission from his father to go to Benaras for further studies. This was refused. Instead, the family began to talk about his marriage. So Dayananda ran away from home. He later took Sannyas and went to the Himalayas. He trekked in these mountains in search of a yogi who could show him the way to salvation. But he met no such person. So he came to Mathura where for three years he studied grammar under Virajananda, a blind scholar. When his studies were finished, Virajananda asked his pupil to give him the following type of Guru's fee, "I will devote my whole life time in propagating the books of Vedas and Vedic religion and in this mission, if necessary, and I will lay down my life." Dayananda promised this kind of tuition fee and kept his pledge till the end of his life.

In 1874, he wrote the famous treatise, 'Satyartha Prakash.' In this book, Hinduism has been heavily criticized and with the help of logic and moral science, he showed what things should be discarded from Hinduism. It was his firm belief that India's rejuvenation depended upon the spread of education in the four Varnas. He held the view that not birth but merit should have preference in social organizations. His vigorous espousal of monogamy was then a new thing in the Hindu society. He rejected the idea that going abroad was a sin. He demonstrated that the benefits of increase in trade, prosperity, and the knowledge of the world

---

[1]P. B. Kulkarni: Mama Parmananda Ani tyancha Kalakhanda (Marathi) - p.170

accrued from foreign travel. He maintained on the authority of Manusmriti that those who have no knowledge of the Vedas are all Sudras. Later, he founded the 'Arya Samaj,' and in the words of Dr. Jordens "... the organization that planted his message and his reforms firmly in the soil of North India and that had enormous influence on the later development of Hinduism and Hindu nationalism."[1]

Swami Vivekananda was another person whose name, like Swami Dayannda's, resounded throughout India. He was born in a Kayastha family of the name of Dutt on January 12, 1863. During his student days, the mystery of the universe made him restless. Later he met Ramakrishna Paramahansa who changed the entire direction of Vivekananda's life. Vivekananda became a Sannyasi. He spent time in studies and traveling in India. In 1893 he attended the Parliament of Religions held at Chicago and captivated the audience by his erudition and eloquence. Within a short period Vivekananda became a world famous Sannyasi. He felt that Hinduism, Hindu religion and Hindu society must regain their pristine glory.

Expressing his thoughts as to how the Indian history should be written he said, "The available history is in scattered form. The chronology is not exact. So far our history has been by and large written by English writers. The reading of these books is sure to depress us, because these books contain narration and analysis of our decay and failure. It is, however, true that the Europeans showed us the method as to how ancient Indian history should be researched. Now the task remains to write with reverence a lively history of the Hindu nation after independent and thoughtful study of the Vedas, the Puranas, and the ancient history. Hindus must undertake this task."[2]

When one Mr. Ashvinikumar asked Vivekananda as to what he should do for the uplift of India, the latter replied, "Crack a whip at places where you hear the love-songs of Radha and Krishna. The country is going to pots because of them." He further said, "Go to the untouchables: to Chambhars, Bhangis, and such others and tell them that they are the nation's soul; they have the capacity to revolutionize the world. Stand on your legs. Go amongst them and start school. Perform the rites of thread ceremony and give them the sacrificial threads."[3]

In April 1899 Vivekananda gave an interview to the reporter of the monthly magazine 'Prabudha Bharat'. In this interview he was asked, "Swamiji, what is your opinion about the reconversion of the Hindus to their former faith? Should they be taken back?" Swamiji replied, "Taking back? We must take them back!" Then he was lost in thought for sometime. A little later, he began to talk again, "Secondly, if they are not taken back, then our numbers will decrease. Also,

[1] J. T. F. Jordens: Dayananda Saraswati, His life and ideas - p.127

[2] V. V. Pendse: Rashtradrashte Vivekanada (Marathi) - p. 112-113

[3] V. V. Pendse: Rashtradrashte Vivekanada (Marathi) - p. 287

one who renounces Hindutva, not only reduces the strength of the Hindus by one, but also increases the enemy's strength by one."[1]

Like other Indian provinces, Maharashtra also witnessed various movements. Lokahitawadi heads the list of those eminent men who ushered in a new age in Maharashtra. His real name was Gopal Hari Deshmukh. He was born on February 18, 1823, that is, five years after the end of the Peshwa Raj. After finishing his education, he entered government service, and rose to the rank of joint judge. He is remembered today for the articles he wrote under his pen-name 'Lokahitawadi'. These articles mirror the society of his time, especially the life style of the Brahmins. He had coined a word 'Hindunashastaka' to describe the decline of India. In this article he says, "... much was made of purity in the house while forgetting to keep the country pure.... Hindus are such fools that even now they do not know when the English came, from where they came, and who they are... Priests worry only about the meal and nobles and gentlemen worry about making money."[2]

But Lokahitawadi did not indulge in criticism only. Through his articles like, 'Knowledge is valor' or 'In praise of Industry', he showed the people the way to progress. In the article, 'What the Hindus should do' he advises, "... English traders sell here glass, cloth, cutlery, furniture, watches, whips, machines, etc. Our people should learn to manufacture these things. And the products which will not have a home market, they should take to other countries and sell there. We should boycott English goods; instead we should sell them our goods. We should not purchase anything from them."[3]

On occasions his anger finds expression in the following words: "Hindus have been slaves of the Muslims for five hundred years; and now they are slaves of the English for the past hundred or hundred and fifty years. And yet enlightenment has not come to our people."[4] Because he was a patriot, he could advise, "Let us do what is good for our country... We have slept for two thousand years ... so let us wake up, have a look about and use our wits."[5]

In 1849 he wrote an article 'The fruits of the English rule'. It is good evidence of his revolutionary thinking and of his foresight. He writes, "When people will become wise, they will quietly tell the English to grant them Parliament as England has. After having served in Parliament for sometime, they will whisper to them that we have become wise like you, then why should we be denied powers? When a considerable number of the Hindus express such an

---

[1] V. V. Pendse: Rashtradrashte Vivekananda (Marathi) - p. 409

[2] S. R. Tikekar: Lokhitawadichi Shatapatre (Editor - Marathi) - p. 72

[3] S. R. Tikekar: Lokhitawadichi Shatapatre (Editor - Marathi) - p. 357

[4] S. R. Tikekar: Lokhitawadichi Shatapatre (Editor - Marathi) - p. 331

[5] S. R. Tikekar: Lokhitawadichi Shatapatre (Editor - Marathi) - p. 86

opinion, the Government will have to concede that demand. When the natives begin to run the administration efficiently, when they cease taking bribes, then they will be appointed to various posts including that of the governor; and then the English will stay here as traders only..."

"Once the people have acquired strength, they will express their gratitude to the English for sometime. Because it was through them that Hindus acquired knowledge. But if the English start making trouble or try to enforce any new regulation then, as happened in America, Hindus will free themselves. And they will tell the English to return to their country. We are now able to manage our country's affairs. We do not need your guidance. You may come here for trade. We will protect you as we protect our citizens. But we do not want your dominance. This is how the future of the country will evolve. And the new government will be better. First, ignorance will disappear. This will come to pass after two hundred years. But there is no doubt that this will happen. The past history indicates this course."[1]

One can humorously say that on three points Lokahitawadis's prophecy went wrong. The English left India in the 98th year; two, the habit of bribe-taking instead of ending has assumed gigantic proportion; three, looking to the native administration the ordinary man may be inclined to say that the British rule was preferable.

Mr. Jyotiba Phule was another eminent social reformer. He was born in 1827. After preliminary education, his schooling was interrupted for some time. However his English education began in 1841 and was completed in 1847. After studying social conditions, he acutely felt the need for social transformation. He wrote voluminously for effecting social awakening. Phule was also a social activist. In 1848, he established a school for girls. A year later, he opened two schools for the untouchables. His objective was to liberate the Shudra and the Atishudra classes from the tyranny of the Brahmins. He, therefore, laid stress on modern education till the end of his life.

In Bombay, notable men like Mama Paramananda, Jambhekar, and Shankershet were doing their best for social awakening. But the credit for reinvigorating the life of Maharashtra goes to Justice Ranade. He was born in Nasik district in January 1842. The late Mr. N. C. Kelkar did not exaggerate when he described him as the Guru not only of Poona but of India. Tilak used to liken Ranade to Hemadri or Madhavacharaya of olden times because of his monumental erudition. Though he was in government service he still helped to build finely the Indian political life. For some time he had incurred the displeasure of the government. But in course of time the British Government had to appoint him as judge in the High Court of Bombay. He either helped in founding a number of institutions in Maharashtra or nursed them. Ranade was a source of inspiration to

---

[1] S. R. Tikekar: Lokhitawadichi Shatapatre (Editor - Marathi) - p. 79 - 80

institutions like Vaktrutvasabha, Vasant Vyakhanmala, Industrial Institute, Female high-school, Prarthana Samaj, Library, Sarvajanik Sabha. And the most important thing was that though he sang praises of the British rule, he said, like Mama Parmananda,[1] that in the course of time the British would have to transfer power to India.[2]

Ranade was a man of gentle disposition. But in a few years, three men of bold temperament and aggressive spirit came forward. They were Vishnushastri Chiplunkar, Tilak, and Agarkar. Amongst them, Chiplunkar was senior in age. He was born in 1850. He took service in the Government High School in 1873. But he soon left it. A year later he began publishing Nibandhamala and ran it for seven years on his own. V. K. Rajwade, Shivarampant Paranjpe, H. N. Apte, who later became famous Marathi authors, drew inspiration for their patriotic and literary activities from Nibandhamala. Chiplunkar and his Nibandhamala have played a vital role in the nationalist awakening in Maharashtra.

Chiplunkar was one of the founders of the New English School and of 'Kesari' and 'Maratha' newspapers. In the beginning Agarkar was the editor of 'Kesari'. By temperament he was a social reformer. He resigned from the editorship of Kesari and started his own paper 'Sudharark'. In his articles he castigated the harmful social customs. His criticism angered the orthodox class who, as a protest, took out his funeral procession. Agarkar's motto was, "We will speak what is desirable and do what is possible," The flame of social reform which was lit by Lokahitawadi, Phule and Ranade was kept blazing, despite social hostility, by Agarkar.

But it was Tilak whose name first resounded in India and abroad as a leader of all India stature. Chirol described Tilak as the 'Father of Indian unrest'. This is an apt characterization of Tilak's radical political movement and its range. Tilak used more than one means in his political activities. Therefore, whether it was submitting petitions or requests to government or whether it was a terrorist movement, Tilak either openly supported it or silently blessed it. It was under Tilak's leadership that first Maharashtra and afterwards India became extremist. Hence, Savarkar has described Tilak as a 'Guru's Guru'.

Such is the political, social and religious panorama of the time beginning from 1857 and ending at the close of the century. And as Savarkar's life unfolds we find that he and he alone became the standard bearer of the revolutionary movement of Phadke and Chaphekars, of the intellectual political movement of Ranade and Tilak, of the social reform movement of Lokhitawadi and Agarkar,

---

[1] P. B. Kulkarni: Mama Parmananda ani Tyancha Kalakhanda - p.392

[2] N. R. Pathak: Nyaymurti Ranade Yanche Charita (Marathi) - p.362

and finally of the Hindu nationalism movement of Swami Dayananda and Vivekananda.

A Pledged Revolutionary

"When a man is eighteen", writes Thiebault who was one of the recruits of 1789, "He belongs to any party that will attack."[1]

Nasik, Prayag, Pushkar, Naimisharanya and Gaya are five holy places. There is no sixth. Such is the religious importance of Nasik. It is also called Western Kashi. Nasik and Panchavati together constitute the land of pilgrimage. The historical glimpses of Nasik become discernible from the times of Andhrabhrutya. Later the Abhirs ruled the land. In the sixth century Chalukyas became its overlords. Then came the Rathod rule which, in turn, was replaced by the Yadavas of Devagiri. Yadav dominion lasted till the end of thirteenth century. In the next century the Sultans of Devagiri absorbed Nasik in their kingdom. In the sixteenth century Nasik came under the jurisdiction of Bahamani Sultans. In the following century, the city became a part of the Mughal Empire. Mughals renamed the town as Gulshanabad. Not only that, they destroyed a number of temples and with stones thus obtained they built Auranga gate, Delhi gate, Jama Masjid, etc.

In 1747, the Marathas became masters of the city. From ancient times Nasik had been an industrial and trade center. During the Mughal times it suffered considerable hardships and declined. But the Peshwas gave a facelift to this city. They made it an important center, and beyond the Sarasvati Bridge they built a new area called Navapura. They rebuilt the temples destroyed by the Muslims. They constructed small stone pools in the stream of Godavari. Also, at Nasik and Gangapur they erected magnificent mansion. Gopikabai, mother of Madhavrao Peshwa, resided there. Raghobadada built a mansion in Chownghas town, which is about two miles from Nasik and named it Anandvalli. Such was the historical tradition of the city. In the twentieth century, this tradition was made richer. Savarkar founded Abhinav Bharat here and the city became a center of revolutionaries. The historic event of the assassination of Jackson took place here and because of the martyrdom of Kanhere, Karve and Deshpande, this land of salvation also became a land of martyrs.

A few miles away from Nasik there is a town called Bhagur. It is situated on the bank of Darna River. Today it has a population of over 10,000. In 1925 a municipality was established here. The town covers an area of 31 square kilometers. There are two temples in the town. The Nasik District Gazetteer while giving this information further adds, as a matter of pride, that this is the birthplace of Veer Savarkar.

---

[1] Louis Madelin : The French Revolution - p.30

Mr. Vinayak Damodar Savarkar was born on May 28, 1883. His elder brother Ganesh Damodar, alias Baba Savarkar, was born on June 13, 1879 while their younger brother, Dr. Narayan Damodar Savarkar, was born on May 25, 1888. It is not possible to trace how the family began to go by the name Savarkar. About six miles away from Guhagar, there is a stream and a dam at Palshet. Close by there is a locality called Savarwadi. According to Savarkar, the family name may have been derived from it.[1]

The two families, Savarkar and Dhopavakar, made an agreement to share gains equally and migrated from Guhagar village in Chiplun taluka to the Deccan plateau and later settled in Bhagur. Both were learned families. During the reign of Nanasahb Peshwa, both families were jointly given Rahuri village for their maintenance. Because of his great erudition, one of the members of the Savarkar family was given the honor of riding in a palanquin by the Peshwa. Savarkar's family belongs to the Chitpavan Brahmin caste and his family lineage is Vasishta. With the advent of the Peshwas, a number of Chitpavan families came to the forefront. Even after the Peshwa rule was replaced by the British regime, the members belonging to this small community considerably influenced the political, social, and religious life of the country and provided it with leadership. The names which quickly come to one's mind of men belonging to the Chitpavan community are Vasudeo Balwant Phadke, Chaphekar, Ranade, Kanhere, Karve, Chiplunkar, Tilak, Agarkar, Gokhale, Kelkar, and Paranjape. The former Governor of Bombay, Sir Richard Temple, described the temper and character of this community in the following words, "But nothing that we do now by way of education, emolument, or advancement in the public service at all satisfies the Chitpavans. They will never be satisfied till they regain the ascendancy in their country. But never have I known a national and political ambition, so continuous, so enduring, so far-reaching, and so utterly impossible for us to satisfy, as that of the Brahmins of Western India."[2]

Savarkar's grandfather had two sons; the younger son, Damodarpant, was the father of Savarkar. Bapukaka, the elder son, was fourteen years senior to Damodarpant. Savarkar was a favorite of his uncle. When Savarkar was fourteen, he spoke in a public meeting held during the Ganapati festival. When the meeting was over, Bapukaka said, "Well done! You will do honor to our family." Damodarpant also had a special affection for his son. He also nursed Savarkar's poetic instincts. He recited many poems from 'Navanit' so often that Savarkar could easily retain them in memory.

Savarkar household was running smoothly. There was plenty in the family. Considering those times it could be said that the family belonged to the well-to-do class. His mother was a very fair and handsome woman. Her temper was sweet and she was liked by all. She never showed off as a leading lady of the

---

[1]V. D. Savarkar : Samagra Savarkar Wangmaya, Vol I - p.85

[2]Dhananjay Keer : Mahatma Jotirao Phooley - p.16

town. Unfortunately Savarkar lost his mother in 1892 when he was nine years old. From that time the family began to suffer a series of calamities.

Savarkar's schooling began at the age of six. A year later his thread ceremony was performed. There were no complaints about his studies; but he was not a star student. However, from childhood his memory was strong. After his thread ceremony, he mastered the 'Sandhya' (chanting of the religious mantras) within five or six days. Also, his reading was extensive. He had read Vishnushastri Chiplunkar's 'Nibandhamala' a number of times. Not only that; in order to be able to write long and complex sentences, like the ones from Nibandhamala, he began to write essays. He used to read newspapers like 'Kesari', 'Gurakhi', Jagadithechhu', and 'Punevaibhav'. He also read books. Stories from Mahabharat, history of the world, Chatrapatichi Bakhar, Peshavyanchi Bakhar were the books he repeatedly read. Strange as it may seem, at this early age he read Homer's Iliad translated by Pope. Navanit - treasury of Marathi poems - he had learned it by heart. Savarkar was a born poet, and from childhood his mind was nurtured by great poets like Homer, Moropant, and Waman. Therefore, his poetry later blossomed so fruitfully.

As he was a born poet, so was he a born orator. But he took immense pain to develop his natural gifts as an orator. He read two books on the art of speaking when he was barely twelve. These books taught him how to open a subject, how to develop a point, how to argue for and against, how to summarize and how to conclude with illustrations from reputed authors. He studied these things closely. He did not, however, rest content with the pains he took in his boyhood. Though he was gifted with a talent for eloquence, he labored hard to give his eloquence an artistic touch. In later years he read the biographies of Demosthenes, Cicero, and Sheridan and studied their speeches. He committed to memory a number of eloquent passages from Macaulay's 'History of England.'

Savarkar's vernacular education up to the fifth standard was completed at Bhagur. Because of some domestic problems, his education was interrupted for nearly two years. Still with self-help he completed his English education up to second standard at home. His father had kept Babarao, his eldest son, at Nasik for higher education. Now at the age of 13, Savarkar was also sent there for the same purpose. He entered his name in Shivaji School which had been recently started. After preliminary tests, he was admitted in the third standard.

For the first few months, he was home sick. At this time the Savarkar brothers were staying near Kanadya Maruti. Babarao's friends used to visit this place. Savarkar's interests were different from theirs. These senior boys were a happy-go-lucky type indulging in drama or in music or in gossip by the roadside. Savarkar, on the other hand, took more interest in studies, exercise, reading, and politics. As he did not meet anyone of similar temperament, he became dejected and felt that he should return to Bhagur. In addition, he suffered from lack of home food. Boys who have to dine in hostels do miss home food. The Savarkar brothers had to put up with this inconvenience. For some time they cooked food at home. Then they started boarding out. Savarkar, by nature, was shy. Even when he was hungry, he would not ask for another helping. So his elder brother found a way out. There was a famous confectioner in Nasik. Babarao arranged that Savarkar should eat 'Jilebi' every day at the shop. Such eating out was unfashionable then. But since childhood, Savarkar considered it foolish to think that one lost caste because of eating food outside. At Bhagur, Parsuram and Rajaram Shimpi were his childhood friends. Savarkar used to eat at their house and, in turn, they would eat at his. The womenfolk from his friends' family often gave Savarkar freshly baked bhakri (bread) and garlic chutney. Savarkar has written, "I detested the caste system from childhood. The idea that they were of a tailor caste and I was of Brahmin caste appeared to me as insulting." No wonder Savarkar ate jilebi at this confectioner's shop without qualms.

Four months later, after his admission to Shivaji School, he was promoted to the fourth standard. The teachers were impressed by his neatness, sharpness, and intelligence. They were especially struck by the range of his knowledge at such a young age. When he became more familiar with them, he showed them articles written and poems composed by him at Bhagur. After reading his composition, the teachers patted Savarkar on the back and recommended his name to Khare who was the editor of Nasikvaibhav. Khare perused the composition and expressed his appreciation to Savarkar, who now thought of doing an article for Nasikvaibhav. He wrote this article under the caption 'Glory of the Hindu Culture' and sent it to the editor. Looking to the language and thought Khare doubted whether Savarkar had written the article. Savarkar's teachers, however, vouched for him. So it was published in two installments in the editorial column in the Nasikvaibhav. Brilliant thought and fiery language made the article very readable and it became the talk of the town.

Like his first article, his first speech also became the talk of the town. Vaktrutvottejaka Sabha of Nasik - an institute to help develop the art of public speaking - used to run an annual elocution competition. Savarkar decided to participate in it. Since he was late in entering his name, he was placed last on the speakers' list. After writing his speech he showed it to his teachers. On the day of the competition, after having heard the earlier speakers, the audience was tired and was about to depart from the hall, when Savarkar rose to speak. His first few sentences were enough to arrest the attention of the audience and there was a pin-drop silence as he cast his oratorical spell on the meeting. Savarkar's speech was adjudged the best. The judges at first doubted whether it was Savarkar's own speech. But Mr. Barve, editor of Lokseva, removed their doubt and Savarkar was placed first. It could be said that from that time till his last years, Savarkar retained his reputation as the foremost orator in the country.

While Savarkar was schooling in Nasik, plague broke out in Poona. The epidemic started in Bombay in October 1896. Next year it broke out in Poona and Ravivar, Bhajiaali, Lonaraali and other localities were considerably affected. Then

Tilak published two articles in Kesari written by competent doctors for public knowledge. He also blamed people for throwing garbage on the streets and for negligent behavior. Further, he advised, through the columns of Kesari, that poor people should be sent to the Government hospital.

Soon the government machinery started moving. It issued an ordinance for arming itself with special powers. Then Rand was appointed officer for overseeing the arrangements for epidemic control. A plague committee was set up for Poona which included areas like Khadki, Camp, etc. Colonel Phillips and Captain Beveridge were appointed to help Rand in his task. The appointment of military officers introduced elements of severity and coercion in the house searches. How the British soldiers conducted themselves in such searches has been described by Kelkar in the following words: "Either, through ignorance or impudence, they would mock, indulge in monkey tricks, talk foolishly, intimidate, touch innocent people, shove them, enter any place without justification, pocket valuable items, etc.."[1] This high-handedness of the government provoked the people of Poona and some soldiers were beaten in the Rastapeth locality. Gradually the force of the epidemic ebbed. On May 16, a notice, under the signature of Rand, was issued announcing that plague inspection would shortly end. This brought normalcy to the city. But it barely lasted a month. On May 23, Poona Sarvajanik Sabha passed a resolution about presenting an address to Queen Victoria on the occasion of her diamond jubilee. Tilak wrote three articles in Kesari about the jubilee hailing the Queen which appeared in the issue of the June 8, 15, and 23. In the last article he wrote about the poverty of India.

Fortuitously on June 22, 1897 an event occurred whose reverberation was felt in Maharashtra for a long time. On that day at night a reception and state banquet was held to celebrate the diamond jubilee of the Queen at the Governor's bungalow in Ganeshkhind. The function came to a close at midnight and the guests began to depart in their horse carriages. In this group were Lieut. Ayerst and Mr. Rand. Lieut. Ayerst was riding in the first carriage. Balkrishna Chaphekar jumped on it from behind and fired a shot. Rand was riding the next carriage. Damodar Chaphekar jumped on it from behind and discharged his revolver. In these shootings Ayerst was killed instantaneously, but Rand died after eleven days.

These murders started a spate of rumors. Eventually from information provided by Dravid brothers, Damodarpant was arrested. He confessed. Damodarpant wanted to join the army and had made some efforts in that direction. He had told the army officers that if he was taken in service, he would recruit a battalion of four hundred Brahmins. This suggestion bore no fruit. So his youthful energies found other outlets. In his confession he said that he had thrashed reformers like Patwardhan, Kulkarni and converts like Thorat and Velinkar. He had tarred the statue of the Queen in Bombay and to take revenge for atrocities committed by the British soldiers in Poona, he and his brother, Balkrishna, had

---

[1] N. C. Kelkar : Lokamanya Tilak Yanche Charitra, Vol I - p.529

shot Rand and Ayerst respectively. Subsequently a trial was held and after conviction Damodarpant was hanged on April 18, 1898. On December 17 Balkrishna was arrested. Then on February 8, 1899 Vasudeo Chaphekar and Ranade shot Dravid brothers. These brothers had given information to the police about Chaphekars for obtaining the reward of Rs. 20,000. Soon trials were held and, being found guilty, the three were sentenced to death. Then on May 8, 1899, Vasudeorao mounted the gallows, followed by Ranade on May 10 and then by Balkrishna on May 12. Such an extraordinary event happened in Maharashtra.

Kesari and other newspapers were carrying the news of these proceedings. While reading them, Savarkar was overcome with grief and tears rolled down his cheeks. If anyone called Chaphekar a madman, Savarkar would retort that he was a patriot. The matter, however, did not rest there. Savarkar began to think that someone must carry forward the mission of Chaphekars. If so, then why should he not shoulder it?

He was agitated by this question. He had read about the hanging of Chaphekars and Ranade, and had passed the subsequent days in mental agony. The thought that he should carry forward the mission of Chaphekars had often crossed his mind. At last, Savarkar went into the room where the family deity was kept. He worshipped the deity and then he took the following vow: "For the freedom of my country, I will conduct an armed fight and in it either I will perish like Chaphekar or like Shivaji become victorious and celebrate my country's freedom." This incident of pledge-taking occurred in 1899 and not in 1898 as Savarkar mentions in his reminiscences. For, Chaphekar brothers and Ranade were hanged in 1899. At this time Savarkar was 16 years old. It is true that Savarkar had no active role to play in the celebrations of India's independence. He, however, witnessed the birth of freedom in India. That in itself was a great fortune. Very few revolutionaries are blessed this way. Therefore, in his retirement, he often spoke about the coming of freedom with a contented mind.

The plague epidemic did not afflict Poona only. Its tentacles also reached Nasik and especially it played havoc in the Savarkar family. The first victim was his father. One day he beckoned Savarkar to come near him and then said, "I am a plague victim and now what is to happen to my children?" Savarkar's temper was such that the greater the calamity the higher rose his courage. He told his father not to worry; he would bring medicines from the local physician. Then the treatment began. Soon his younger brother was afflicted by the disease. In the mean while his father died and a few days later his uncle also died. The younger brother was taken to the government hospital, and to keep him company, Babarao, the eldest brother, stayed with him there. Soon Babarao himself became a plague victim. As usual, Savarkar came to the hospital door with a Tiffin box. Babarao did not come out to get it. Savarkar was greeted with the news that he was suffering from plague. This was a thunderbolt to him. But Savarkar's family was spared further trials. Both brothers recovered and returned home.

Now there was no elderly person in the family. It fell to Babarao to become its head. In view of the change in circumstances, Babarao decided to settle in Nasik. Accordingly, he came to stay as a neighbor of Datar household. The schools had closed during the epidemic. Since the nationalist Shivaji School had no facility to teach beyond the fourth standard, Savarkar enrolled his name in the fifth standard at the Nasik High School in 1899. A year later, having passed the fifth standard, he was promoted to the sixth standard.

While he was schooling, Savarkar continued his public activities. In fact, he became more active. Earlier he had taken a pledge to carry forward the mission of Chaphekars and that he would raise the standard of armed revolt and fight till death. Now action had to follow his oath. He had struck up friendship with Mhaskar, Page, Datar, Vartak, Abba Darekar alias Govind Kavi, and some others in Nasik. Now after prolonged discussion with Mhaskar and Page he decided to form a secret society for armed revolt. Its name was Rashtrabhaktasamuha. He also thought that there should be another organization for conducting open activities. So another institution was founded. This was the famous Mitramela. Savarkar, Mhaskar, Page, Bhide, Date, Vartak brothers, Datar brothers, Ganpat Nhavi were its members. Its weekly meetings were held and various subjects were discussed and debated. Savarkar spoke mainly on the subjects of politics and revolution. 'Independence was the object and armed revolution was the means' was the central theme of his talks.

Mitramela was founded sometime in January 1900. Shivaji Jayanti was the first festival celebrated by Mitramela. It was followed by Ganesh festival. In these celebrations songs composed by Govind Kavi were first sung. Also, the slogan 'Victory to Goddess of Liberty' came in vogue. Naturally Mitramela cast a spell on the people of Nasik. Next year the Ganesh festival was held on a bigger scale. Govind Kavi composed special songs for this occasion and also started a 'Mela' to sing them. Its spell on the Nasik public remained for a long time. Govind Kavi gave beautiful poetic form to the thoughts and subjects about which Savarkar spoke in the weekly meetings of Mitramela. The Mela became popular in Maharashtra because in its rank were boys who with histrionic ability melodiously sang songs. This Mela played an important part in fanning the flames of patriotism in Maharashtra.

Looking to Savarkar's nature, the activities of Mitramela could not have remained confined only to Nasik. Also, if the idea of armed revolt was to spread all over India, then the branches of Mitramela had to be opened wherever it was possible. Tilak's activities had led to a considerable public awakening in Maharashtra about the Indian conditions. Thus the atmosphere was very favorable to the activities of Mitramela. The first branch of Mitramela was opened in Kothur. As Nasik was affected by plague, Savarkar had shifted to his maternal uncle's house at Kothur. Here with the help of Tatya Barve and Balwantrao Barve a branch was opened. The Barves were a leading landholder family. One of the girls from this family was married to the Peshwa. In the latter half of the Peshwa rule, this family was involved in conducting political affairs in Delhi.

The next branch was opened at Bhagur. On one occasion, Savarkar had gone to Bhagur. There he met with his childhood associates and talked to them about the making of a revolution. After administering an oath to them, he started a Mitramela branch there. Another branch was established at Trimbakeshwar. Savarkar's sister was married into the family which lived there. So Savarkar used to visit this town either as an escort to his sister or for some other work. He utilized his visit to establish a branch there. His elder brother Babarao's brother-in-law, Anna Phadke, his younger brother and other youngsters helped Savarkar in his task. When one reads about these activities one question inevitably occurs to one's mind: How is it that Savarkar succeeded in attracting so many young men to his way of thinking? For, mere lectures or discussions on patriotism excite people temporarily but do not activate them. Knowledge, sacrifice, and character attract people. Not only at this time but in the latter part of his life also it was with his exceptional erudition, Savarkar inspired people to action. While he was in matriculation class in 1901, the extensive reading that he did was amazing. 'The Story of Nations' was an historical series in English. The then Baroda state published in Marathi a series based on it. From this series, he read books on Ancient Akkad, Babylon, Assyria, Moors in Spain, Turkish Empire, etc. He also read books on Iranian Empire, the revolt in Netherlands, and biographies of Mazzini and Garibaldi and gave talks on these subjects in the Mitramela meetings. He read the poetry of Moropant, and he was a regular reader of Kavyetihas and Kavyasangraha. His introduction to Spencer's Works also occurred this year; but it was through Marathi versions of Dabholkar. Savarkar has said that he had read all the books that the Nasik city library contained. He not only read the books, he also took notes from them. He had named this collection of notes as 'Sarvasarasangraha.' In addition, he kept tab on all the books read each year in his diary. This mental discipline helped him immensely in his public speaking and writings. Savarkar naturally insisted that his associates and followers should follow his example in order to develop their intellectual capacity. So he had prepared a list of books which was a required reading for every member of Mitramela. There were about twenty-five titles in his list. The important books were on revolution, biographies of leaders like Napoleon, Indian history, physical exercise, and the works of Vivekananda and Ramtirth. In addition, articles appearing in Kal under the caption 'The Young Italy', etc. giving information about European revolutionary societies, were read in the weekly meetings of Mitramela.

Mr. Shivarampant Paranjape's articles appearing in the Kal were fiery and were to Savarkar's taste. An article had appeared in Kal under the caption 'Chaphekar and Ranade', and in it they were described as martyrs. Savarkar was naturally more attracted to the Kal. From that day onwards, he never missed articles from the Kal. In fact, he read some articles repeatedly. If anyone disapproved of Kal or objected to its line of thought, Savarkar promptly came to its defense. This was natural. The language of the editor of Kal was elegant, vivid, and provocative. Kal used to justify the idea of armed revolt and to show the direction it should take. It was inevitable that the repeated readings of the Kal articles should influence the language and the thought of Savarkar who was a pledged revolutionary. Savarkar, therefore, calls the editor of Kal, Paranjape, and his guru who inspired him to revolutionary activities. But at the same time he makes it quite clear that this credit is only for inspiration and not for action. For, in those days the ideas of revolution were just sprouting. Phadke died in the year in which Savarkar was born. When Chaphekar was hanged, Savarkar was in his teens. After Phadke and Chaphekar, it was Savarkar alone who made the idea of armed revolt popular in Maharashtra. Such being the case how could he get a Guru for himself? At every time and in every action he had to lead the way. The thoughts of revolution are in themselves scalding. So, those who did not approve of Savarkar's thought called him a wild person. Paranjape, however, never spoke disparagingly about Savarkar or stood in his way.

Savarkar was very much influenced by Kal. Under the circumstances one may wonder what his feelings were regarding Tilak and the Kesari. For, Tilak had already become 'The Lokamanya' in Maharashtra if not in India. Savarkar's devotion to this great man was total. To quote him: 'Guru's Guru was Kesari, - Lokamanya Tilak only.' According to Savarkar, the revolutionaries had done their utmost to translate into action the politics and preaching of Lokamanya and had resolved to enter the actual field of combat. What Tilak thought, the revolutionaries gave loud public expression to it. Tilak, being the leader of the nation, was only a step ahead of the society. But in order to clear the path for the future armed revolution, Savarkar tells, "We revolutionaries became the sappers. Tilak was the hilt, while we revolutionaries were the steel blade. The hilt can never become the blade, but the blade flashes only with the help of the hilt."

Savarkar says that Tilak was imbued with the Shivaji tradition. The political language of Tilak was of the previous generation, but his political soul belonged to the Shivaji family. He was never loyal to the English in his heart. He maintained that the British rule might have conferred some benefits; but the harm it had done was far worse. His politics, however, was confined to the constitutional methods and his ideal was political reform.

Of course, if independence could be had by petitions made by moderates or by protest and legal resistance, or by swadeshi, by boycott, by non-payment of tax, or by unarmed fight, as advocated by nationalists, then revolutionaries would have welcomed it. Also, these movements were necessary to prepare the public mind for an armed revolution. But the revolutionary party held a firm view that the country would not achieve freedom without an armed revolution. That is why the song 'No one wins freedom without a battle' was composed.

But how to fight a mighty and well-armed enemy like the British? This question was bound to occur to anybody. Savarkar had answered this question for himself. It is better to quote him: "Abhinav Bharat, whose activities of the last two years have been narrated here, then advocated the guerrilla method. This method was adopted by Mazzini in Italy for a revolutionary war. It was being practiced in similar circumstances by the Irish and Russian revolutionaries, and which was practiced by India in 1857. This guerrilla warfare would probably help and succeed in India during an armed revolt. To propagate the idea of revolution in the army and police and fill their ranks with revolutionaries, to join hands with foreign powers like Russia and others, to adopt guerrilla warfare, to attack individually the English centers of power and its representatives, to collect arms in the Indian states and beyond Indian borders, and wait for an opportune moment to enter British India, from time to time stage small revolts, which will help the country to know how to make revolutions, how to die and by showing the capacity to die, to make running of administration dangerous and difficult for the enemy, and when the British empire was locked in a deadly struggle with another stronger power resulting in the diminishing of the British power, India would become free by declaring armed revolt; if it failed, then to make another attempt at rebellion, and continue fighting till death; this was the plan of action of our armed revolt. We never had the credulous notion that the English would pack off because few of their people were killed."[1]

Savarkar was talking and planning in this manner about the revolution. Though he was engrossed in this kind of work he did not neglect his studies or his regular physical exercise. He understood the importance of both these things. He, therefore, exhorted that every member of Mitramela should be keen on doing both the things. In order that public activities should not interrupt the educational career of a member of Mitramela, a rule was made that every member must pass his school examination. Also, to endure jail, starvation, beating, torture, hard labor, and to build a soldier's hardihood, heavy physical exercise was made obligatory for every member. Savarkar himself used to take heavy exercise like dips, sit-ups, wrestling, and Malkhamb. Later, when he entered college, he used to do five hundred dips and a thousand sit-ups.

In 1901, Savarkar passed the sixth standard examination and entered the matriculation class. At this time the family was in straitened circumstances. To lighten the financial burden of the family, Savarkar began to think of entering service. In order to have at hand a sure means of getting service, he decided to appear for public service examination. Those who passed this examination used to get employment in Government district offices. Savarkar studied at home and passed this examination. Naturally, his relatives advised him that now it would be better if he entered service. But Babarao did not approve of this idea. The idea that his brother should serve for 20 rupees never occurred to him. He had vowed that he would suffer every kind of hardship in order that Savarkar's education was not interrupted.

---

[1] V. D. Savarkar : Samagra Savarkar Wangmaya Vol I - p.255

Savarkar himself had resolved that in spite of difficulties he would take higher education. He, therefore, decided that he would work as a domestic in Poona, he would beg for food but there would be no interruption in his education. Mhaskar wrote to the editor of Kal, Paranjape, as to what could be done about Savarkar's higher education. Savarkar himself wrote a letter to Paranjape. In it he said that he was willing to work as a sweeper, compositor or domestic at his or any other person's house. But this bore no fruit. One incident tells us how keen Savarkar was about getting higher education. While he was in matriculation class, he fell ill with typhoid and one day his condition worsened. In delirium he asked Babarao what would happen to his higher education. Babarao answered, "You will be educated. I will do anything; if it is necessary, I will beg for food. But I will not fail in educating you."

Fortunately Babarao was spared this ordeal. One day their maternal uncle came and said, "Tatya's marriage had been fixed." Looking to the problem of higher education, neither Babarao nor Savarkar could agree to this marriage proposal. It was discussed in the family circle. Finally Savarkar laid down a condition that if Bhaurao Chiplunkar was ready to bear the expenditure of his higher education, then he would give his consent to the marriage proposal. When Chiplunkar heard the condition, he said "Oh! Tatya's education? I don't have to give a promise to anyone about the education of my son. Same is the case. It is my duty." In view of this assurance from Chiplunkar, there was no discussion about dowry and Savarkar was married sometime in March or April of 1901.

Public activities and marriage had occupied a large part of Savarkar's year. Matriculation examination was only a month away. So in order to have some privacy for studies, Savarkar decided to go to Bombay. But before he left, a meeting of Mitramela was held and the line of action was agreed during his absence. Then Savarkar came to Bombay to study. He stayed in Angrewadi. When the examination was over, he went back to Nasik. Since the plague was raging there, he went to his grandfather's place in Kothur. Kothur is on the banks of the Godawari. Savarkar was captivated by the beauty of the river and on its bank, in solitude; he composed a long poem about it. After it was completed, he read it over to the gentry of Kothur. It was appreciated by them and Savarkar's name became familiar in Kothur as a poet. Then the local minstrels importuned Savarkar to compose some ballads for them. At the desire of his maternal uncle, Savarkar composed some ballads. At this time an essay-competition was announced in the magazine 'Karamanuk' of Mr. Hari Narayan Apte, the great Marathi novelist. The subject of the competition was, 'Who was the greatest Peshwa?' Savarkar wrote an essay for the competition. It was adjudged the best. It got a prize and was published in 'Karamanuk'.

Sometime later Savarkar came back to Nasik from Kothur. Two days later, that is, on November 19, 1901 a wire was received announcing Savarkar's success at the matriculation examination. Now the question of college education became urgent. So Savarkar wrote a letter to his father-in-law, Chiplunkar, inquiring what was to be done about his going to college. Chiplunkar came to Nasik, and told Savarkar to apply for college admission. Accordingly, Savarkar applied to The Fergusson College for admission. When the news spread that Savarkar was to go to Poona, members of Mitramela felt elated. They held a public meeting and gave him an affectionate farewell.

Revolutionary Web Spreads

"To know how to say what other people only think, is what makes men poets and sages; and to dare to say what others only dare to think makes men martyrs and reformers."- Elizabeth R. Charles[1]

Poona had become the center of Indian politics at the beginning of the 20th Century. The episode of Rand's murder had occurred three years ago. A little later Tilak was prosecuted for treason and sentenced to rigorous imprisonment for eighteen months. Similarly newspapers like Punevahibhava, Modavrutta and Pratoda were also prosecuted for treason. The editor of Punevahibhava, Kelkar, tendered apology and he was freed. The editor of Modavrutta, Lele Shastri, was sentenced to imprisonment for nine months, and Kashilkar, the editor of Pratoda, published from Islampur, was sentenced to rigorous imprisonment for one year. The three Chaphekar brothers and Ranade were earlier hanged for the murder of Rand, Ayerst and Dravid brothers. One can imagine from this how hot was the political temperature in Maharashtra. And Tilak was, of course, the leader of this politics. After he came out of jail, he began his political activities by writing an editorial in Kesari under the caption 'Once Again'. Strangely in the issue of January 7, 1902, Tilak indicated that the format of Kesari would change. Its size was to remain the same; but the number of pages was to double. Such an issue came out on February 4. It seemed that Kesari was undergoing transformation both externally and internally. During this period a series of newsletters on China were published, under 'nom de plume' Poona traveler.

Such was Poona. Savarkar came to this city for higher education. On January 24, 1902 he enrolled at the Fergusson College for a major in arts. Sir Raghunathrao Paranjape, who had become Wrangler of Cambridge University only a year earlier, had decided to teach at Fergusson College. The college was renowned for its self-sacrificing teaching staff. Paranjape's joining this institution enhanced its reputation.

Tilak was always drawn to the student world, and when he was teaching in the New English School and Fergusson College, the students were attracted to him. The public awakening he had effected through the columns of the Kesari and the physical hardships he had undergone in his struggle with the Government had made the younger generation Tilakite. Speaking about the student world of that time, Kelkar has said that, if a political opinion poll was taken, the result would have shown that the students had become nationalist. Students of Maharashtra, (Old) Central Province, Berar, and Karnataka naturally used to flock to Fergusson College for higher education. Savarkar had entered this student world. By his

---

[1] John Bartlet : Familiar Quotation

eloquence, skilled arguments, and abundant knowledge for his age he attracted to himself a large section of the students. He selected the right type from amongst them and in 1902 he founded the branch of Mitramela at the Fergusson College. Ranade of Sholapur, Joglekar of Junner, Athani, Oak, Godbloe, Daji Nagesh Apte, Pense, and Thatte were the young men who took the pledge, and joined this branch.

Savarkar stayed in the hostel. Some part of this hostel was reserved for senior and bright students. Savarkar humorously called them 'North-wing aristocracy'. He had joined the First Club for dining, and soon he became the leader of it. The Club used to take out a hand-written monthly. Savarkar wrote a poem in it. During a feast on a Dassera festival, a dispute occurred. Mohaniraj Pradhan had earlier published a poem in this magazine. In it he had referred to gourd as a good means to swim the sea. Savarkar raised an argument by saying that strong arms were better than gourd. Soon Savarkar left his place and sat in front of Pradhan to convince him. During this argument hot words were exchanged. Finally a complaint was lodged with principal Paranjape, whose attention was already drawn to an inflammatory article written by Savarkar in the magazine. Paranjape entrusted this complaint for inquiry to two senior students, Bhide and Kanitkar. Thereafter Savarkar, with some of his friends, left this club and joined another one called the Fourth Club. There are always a few students, who are studious, and peace loving or who liked to be left alone. Such students found Savarkar and his friends a bit of a nuisance. Savarkar's group would meet at night in one of the rooms in the residency for a talk. On many occasions, forgetting the time of night, the discussion would get too loud and senior students, like Kanitkar, had to tell them to stop the discussion or lower their voices.

Soon after his arrival in Poona, Savarkar started visiting Paranjape, the editor of Kal. His son Krishanajipant was of Savarkar's age and had struck up a friendship with him. As their acquaintance grew, Paranjape discovered that Savarkar possessed intelligence, imagination, and eloquence of a very high order. Later Savarkar's poems began to appear in the Kal. Now Paranjape and Savarkar began to discuss about revolutions, literature, history, and other such subjects. Savarkar also went to see Tilak. But the age difference between them was considerable. Also, Tilak was a busy person and naturally Savarkar did not often visit him.

One incident of this time reveals Savarkar's aggressive temperament. Tilak was involved in litigation in connection with the Tai Maharaj case. Savarkar and his friends went to the court to witness the hearings. They were prevented from entering the courtroom by the peon. But Savarkar brushed him aside and saw the court clerk. He informed the latter that they had come to witness the proceedings quietly, and thus secured admittance to the court room. On another occasion he showed the same temperament. There used to be yearly elections to the college Gymkhana and senior students were customarily elected. Savarkar decided to put an end to this exclusive privilege and to see that good sportsmen from junior classes were elected to the official positions. In this he succeeded. Savarkar had a variety of interests. He used to compose poems. In the latter half of his life he wrote plays. It would have been a surprise if such a person did not act in a drama on a college day. In 1902, he acted in the play 'Tratika'. He probably had a minor role. However, in 1904 the play 'Zunzarrao', the Marathi version of Othelo, was staged. Savarkar played Iago in it.

Though Savarkar was participating in college activities, he still stuck to the routine he had formed in Nasik. Every day he went to the gymnasium for heavy physical exercise, which included working out with dumbbells. Occasionally he played soccer. As he gave special attention to his physical development, he also saw that his intellectual pursuits kept the same pace. He found time for extra reading. He read Sardesai's historical works, many books from Dabholkar's translation series, all epics in English and Sanskrit, Macaulay's essays and history, and the history of Italy. Such extensive reading was reflected in his speeches and writings. At this time, he wrote an essay entitled 'Ramayana and Iliad'. Professor Patwardhan had a word of praise for it. Later Savarkar took part in a debate on the subject of Italian history presided over by Principal Rajwade. Savarkar's profound knowledge of Italian history pleased Rajwade. He, however, did not approve of Savarkar's linking that subject to Indian politics and told him to refrain from making such speeches in future.

Savarkar seems to have composed a lot of poetry while in college. There was a picture of Shivaji in the dining hall of the club of which Savarkar was a member. Every Friday, after the worship of this picture, a devotional song, composed by Savarkar was sung. Later Savarkar wrote a poem under the caption, 'What is permanent in the universe?' It was published in Kal in 1902. The poem shows how deeply Savarkar had read history. In the same year, he wrote a poem describing the hardships of widows. Sir Balchandra Bhatawdekar had announced a verse competition on behalf of 'Winter Lecture Series' run by Bombay's Hindu Union Club inviting poems on hardships of widows. A prize of Rs. 20.00 was to be awarded to the best poem. Savarkar entered his name for this competition. In all sixteen entries were received. The judges selected two poems which they declared of equal merit. One was Savarkar's and the other was of Majumdar of Dapoli. So the prize was increased to Rs. 30.00 and was distributed equally to both the successful competitors. In 1903 he composed 'Hymn to Liberty', a poem which has become very popular since 1962 and which has often been broadcast on All India Radio. Two years later he composed the celebrated ballads of Sinhagad and Baji Deshpande.

The ballads were sung by a group belonging to Mitramela. There were three bright boys who use to sing them. Their names were Dattu, Shridhar, and Bal. These boys later became well known as Prof. Dattopant Ketkar, Advocate Shridharpant Vartak, and Dr. Narayanrao Savarkar. These ballads were first sung in Nasik and became popular. Very soon they became well-known in Maharashtra. At the instance of Savarkar, Paranjape, the editor of Kal, invited this group to

Poona. Because of their popularity, this group was invited to perform before the Ganesh Idol in Gaikwadwada. Tilak praised the performance of the group and ranked it first amongst the competitors and gave them a gold medal.[1]

Sometime afterwards Shivaji festival was celebrated on the Raigad fort. It was presided over by Daji Abaji Khare a well-known Bombay lawyer and a friend of Tilak. As the ballad singing progressed, its inflammatory ideas made Khare uneasy. Later the ballad of Baji Deshpande began. When the refrain began to be sung, the audience had become so enthralled that it joined in. So, Khare advised Tilak to close the show as he did not wish to bear any responsibility for this unconstitutional activity. Tilak, therefore, informed the audience that the chairman was a little tired by the journey and hence both would like to retire. But the performance would go on under the chairmanship of Paranjape, the editor of Kal.[2] These ballads were printed by Babarao Savarkar in May 1906. This enabled a large number of people to learn them by heart. Three years later, proscribed them.

Not much of the prose writing of Savarkar of this period is available. The centenary of Nana Phadnavis was celebrated at Velas, and an essay competition on the subject, 'Why should the celebration of historic personalities be held?' was announced. There were hundred entries. Savarkar's was one of them. It was awarded the first prize. There is an article in the Kal issue of September 19, 1902, written under the pen name 'Vinayak'. Its caption read 'Duralabham Bharate Janma Manushyam Tatra Durlabham'. According to Karandikar this article was written by Savarkar.[3]

Dr. V. M. Bhat matriculated in 1902 and next year he joined the Fergusson College. The mothers of Bhat and Savarkar were cousins. Bhat had been a best man to Savarkar when the latter was married. According to Bhat, it was at that time that Savarkar administered to him the pledge of Mitramela.[4] So when Bhat came to Poona, he and Savarkar roomed together. And Bhat began to take part in Savarkar's public activities.

Reference has already been made to the founding of the branch of Mitramela in 1902 in the Fergusson College. The members of this branch used to meet on the hillock adjacent to Chaturshringi or on a hill which was behind Fergusson College. Generally a discussion or debate on an important subject was held at such a meeting. A hand-written magazine was also produced in the Fourth Club to help members to learn the art of writing. The names of the persons who were administered oath by Savarkar have already been mentioned earlier. Bhat has also mentioned the following names: Shrikrsihna Paranjape - son of the editor of

---

[1] Dr. V. M. Bhat : Abhinav Bharat - p.26

[2] V. D. Savarkar : Samagra Savarkar Wangamaya Vol. 3 - p.53

[3] S. L. Karanandikar : Savarkar Charitra - p.107

[4] Dr. V. M. Bhat : Abhinav Bharat - p.14

Kal, Chinchalkar, H. B. Bhide, Moholkar, Antrolikar, Sant, Kaka Kalekar, Thatte, Tarkhadkar, Risbud, Gokhale, Patankar, and a few others.

Some Furgussonian members of Mitramela were staying in the city. They started branches of Mitramela in their localities. There was a vernacular training college for teachers. A large number of students in this college were from Satara. One of them was Krishnaji Maruti Kalambe. A facility was available at the Deccan College whereby students in junior B.A. class could keep terms for first year LL.B. class. So Savarkar and Bhat began attending lectures there in the evenings. And soon they opened a branch in that college. Babasaheb Khaparde, Randive, Pande, Senapati Bapat, Devbhankar, and Sir (later) Gurunath Bevoor were inducted in this branch.

By now there were many branches of Mitramela flourishing in Maharashtra. In order to know the extent of the work done, the mistakes committed, and the difficulties encountered, a meeting of selected members was held once or twice a year. In 1903 the first meeting was held in the house of advocate Randive at Dhule. It lasted for two days. About 70 members attended this meeting and they came from Poona, Nasik, Kothur, Trimbak, Bhagur, and Berar. Two members, Babasaheb Khaparde and Veer Wamanrao Joshi, became well-known in later life.

In 1904, at the instance of Savarkar, about 200 members of Mitramela assembled at Bhat's residence in Nasik. They had come from Bombay, Poona, Sholapur, Khandesh, Berar, etc. Savarkar addressed their gathering. He first spoke about 'Mazzini' and 'Young Italy' and then announced that he was changing the name of Mitramela to Abhinav Bharat. Thus was founded the celebrated organization 'Abhinav Bharat'. A number of people spoke at this meeting and all of them emphasized the importance of armed revolt.

In 1905, the yearly meeting of Abhinav Bharat was held at Kothur. Next year it was held in Sion. During this year, advocate Babasaheb Khare and Bhat went to Calcutta. There they met the leaders of Anushilan Samiti, Swadhin Bharat, and other organizations and established links with them. During the meeting it was decided that a simultaneous armed rising by all should be staged in India. In 1907 the revolutionary group from Calcutta came to attend the Congress session at Surat. Amongst them were Arvindbabu Ghosh and his brother Barindrakumar Ghosh. Here Chidambaram Pillai was initiated as a member into Abhinav Bharat. About 200 to 300 persons had come from all over India to attend the secret meeting of the revolutionaries. This indicates how and to what extent the revolutionary ideology was spreading in India.

Now wherever a member of Abhinav Bharat went, he propagated the idea of armed revolt. If he felt that the atmosphere was favorable, he would then establish a branch of Abhinav Bharat. In Nasik district, branches had been opened at Trimbak, Bhagur, Ozar, Kothur, Nifad, Yavale, Igatpuri, Vani, Dhodap, etc. But now the pace quickened and branches of Abhinav Bharat were opened at Junnar, Bombay, Pen, Satara, Nagar, Sholapur, Dhule, Kolhapur, Baroda, Indore, Gwalior, Aurangabad, Hyderabad, and some other places.

Marathe, Bapat, Kolhatkar, Jog, and Gokhale belonged to the Pen branch. Tonape, Barve, Joshi, Trimbakseth Gujarati, and Shivram Seth Sonal belonged to Yavale branch. Anant Kanhare, who later shot Jackson, was administered oath by Tonape. Hyderabad branch was headed by Tikhe. Bombay branch included men like Bhat, Former Chief Minister Balasaheb Kher, Dr. Gune, Chandawarkar, Murdeshwar, Gundil, Dr. Sonapar, Solicitor Thatte, Dr. Thatte, Engineer Ghate, Patankar, Gore, Bhate, Chiplunkar, and some others. The Vasai branch had Dr. Parulkar, Wagh, Gokhale, Bhate, and Dr. Athalye who later went to Satara. The Gwalior branch had about 40 to 50 members amongst them was Dr. Divekar, and Desai. The Baroda branch included, amongst others, Barrister Deshpande, Prof. Kelkar, and Rajaratna Manikrao. There were a few more secret societies similar to Abhinav Bharat. Their objectives were identical. Their members met one another on occasions.

Each branch of Abhinav Bharat was autonomous. The branches were linked only through the heads. In a way it was a federation of secret societies. The work of Abhinav Bharat was conducted on the lines of secret societies of Ireland and Russia. So all the members were not known to one another. In fact, such intimacy was avoided. This rule was rigorously observed. The benefit derived there from, in the words of Bhat, was "a number of institutions, thousands of members and cache of arms were later saved."[1] The above information has been given in an unbroken form here with a view to give a complete picture of the activities of Abhinav Bharat.

Lokamanya Tilak attended a meeting of the Nasik branch of the Abhinav Bharat. He had come to Nasik in 1906 to attend the thread ceremony of his grandson. The branch leaders decided to invite Tilak for a discussion. In response to this invitation, Tilak attended the meeting. He was given a poetic address composed by poet Govind. Later Hari Anant Thatte gave him an account of the secret society and about the collection of arms. Tilak patiently heard this account. Then he said, "There is nothing wrong with the basic approach of Abhinav Bharat. But, before the decisive means for gaining independence become available, any hasty step will defeat our objective. Nothing will be gained by ordinary means. We have gone through this process in our time. My experience tells me to advise you to be patient and to be alert till you are fully prepared. When your preparations are complete, then I will become your leader."[2]

For the Ganapati Festival of 1905, the Nasik branch of Abhinav Bharat decided to invite Paranjape, the editor of Kal, as the guest of honor. Paranjape was

---

[1] Dr. V. M. Bhat : Abhinav Bharat - p.32

[2] S. R. Vartak : Bharatiya Swatantrayache Ranazunzar - p.39-40

once heckled in Karnataka on assumption that he was competing with Tilak for leadership and popularity. So Paranjape was in two minds about this invitation. But when Savarkar clarified the matter, he accepted the invitation. He stayed for two days in Nasik and delivered six discourses, each one was better than the previous one. Paranjpe was presented an address at the hands of Savarkar who was also the main speaker at this function. After this function was over, Savarkar proceeded to Kothur. There he addressed a public meeting along with Barve. In this meeting the Bengalis were congratulated for opposing the partition of their province and a resolution was passed calling upon people to use locally manufactured cloth.

From there, Savarkar came back to Poona; and then an event, unheard of before in the Swadeshi movement, occurred. A meeting of Poona students was held to support the movement opposing the partition of Bengal. Kelkar presided at this meeting. One of the speakers was Savarkar. He advocated in a forceful language that a bonfire of foreign clothes be made to intensify the boycott of foreign goods.

On the day this meeting was held Tilak was out of Poona. When he came back, Savarkar and his associates met him and told him about their idea of making bonfire of foreign clothes. Tilak told them that at least there should be a cart-load of foreign clothes for making such a bonfire; otherwise it would not create any impact. After hearing Tilak's view, the students supporting Savarkar's idea, began to collect foreign clothes. They were helped in this labor of love by students of the 'Maharashtra Vidyalaya', an institution run by Bhopatkar brothers. Savarkar addressed a public meeting to help the collection of clothes. By the Dassera day enough clothes had been collected.

In the evening, these clothes were loaded on a cart and red powder sprinkled on it. Then the cart procession began with a band leading it. Paranjape and Bhalakar Bhopatkar were in the procession from the beginning. Tilak joined it near Chitrashala. The procession terminated in the vicinity of the Fergusson College. Then the clothes were unloaded in a nearby farm and a bonfire was made of them. Tilak as usual spoke well, but Paranjape really excelled. He took out from the burning heap a jacket which was still intact and held it before the audience. Then he felt for the pockets and derisively described how India was being drained of its wealth through trade. He ended by saying that he was committing such a jacket to the flames. It was about 9 p.m. when the meeting ended.

At this time haystacks were stored at a place near the road leading to Fergusson College and opposite to Deccan gymkhana. If a police agent were to set fire to the haystack bundles, organizers of the bonfire would be held responsible for it. To avoid this eventuality, Tilak advised Savarkar and his associates to keep a watch on the bonfire till it was burnt out. So Savarkar asked Bhat and Thatte to keep such a watch and he returned to the hostel. It was probably at the instance of Savarkar that a similar bonfire was made in Nasik.

The news that Savarkar, who was residing in the college hostel, had been the leader in this bonfire affair disconcerted the moderate management of the Fergusson College. In addition, the government asked the management to penalize Savarkar. So bowing to government pressure, the management fined Savarkar Rs. 10 and asked him to leave the hostel. Immediately Savarkar went to see his colleague, Ganpatrao Joglekar who came from Junner. He offered to pay the fine. However, the students had already collected some amount. So Savarkar paid the fine and donated the remaining amount to the Paisa Fund. Tilak was enraged by this affair. He wrote a strong editorial under the caption 'These are not our gurus' and attacked the management of the Fergusson College. A student meeting was held in Sarvajanik Sabha hall under the chairmanship of Paranjape. Bhalakar Bhopatkar, Harendranath Mitra, and Ghamendabuva spoke at this meeting and students were congratulated for paying the fine. Joglekar, to whom Savarkar had first approached, was also turned out of the hostel. The irony is that the student who was turned out from the Fergusson college hostel for unlawful activities was admitted by Principal Benn in his Deccan College. It was this Joglekar who later administered the oath of Abhinav Bharat to Acharya Kripalani who, in his later life, became the Congress President.

Savarkar came to stay with Haribhau Risbud in the city after he left the hostel. The final examination for B.A. degree was not far away. It was Savarkar's habit to study very hard in the last few weeks and pass the examination. So now he shun all public activities and concentrated his attention on his studies. Later he appeared for the examination and came out successful. The results were declared on December 21, 1905. A year earlier he had passed the first LL.B. examination. So at the beginning of the New Year Savarkar shifted to Bombay for his final law degree examination. Bhat followed him there and enrolled his name in the Wilson College. At this time both were staying at Sukha Niwas Lodge which was off the Girgaum Tram Terminus.

In Bombay, Savarkar's prolific pen got a very good opportunity. The publisher of Vivekananda and Ramtirtha series, Bhaskar Vishnu Phadke, was a member of Abhinav Bharat. He was now running Vihari, a weekly, founded by Phatak. Savarkar began to contribute to this weekly and because of his fiery and forceful articles the weekly soon became very popular. According to Bhat some of the articles were outstanding and Savarkar's poetic imagination had a free play in them. Once an article had become long. So Savarkar was told to reduce it. Savarkar simply tore up three or four column written material. As Bhat remonstrated, Savarkar said that he would write off hundred such articles.

Along with this newspaper work, Savarkar and Bhat began in earnest the propagation of Abhinav Bharat's philosophy of revolution. They developed new acquaintances and discussed with them the country's political situation. Those who showed willingness to take part in the activities of Abhinav Bharat were administered the oath. Then meetings of old and new members began to be held either at Sukha Niwas Lodge or in Shastri Hall or in Chikhalwadi tenements or at some other places. The young leaders of Abhinav Bharat wanted all educational institutions to be pervaded with revolutionary philosophy. Accordingly, its members began their intensive propaganda work in all institutions where higher education was imparted, such as, the Elphinstone college, Wilson college, Medical colleges, Law School, Victoria Technical Institute, Gujjur's Laboratory, Art School, etc. If revolutionaries are serving in the government, it becomes easy to keep watch on government activities. This is essential from the point of view of organizing a revolution. Hence revolutionaries had secured posts in the Railways, the Posts and Telegraph department, Customs, High Court, Secretariat, Weather Bureau, Haffkine Institute, etc. Regarding the extent of this preparation, Bhat writes, "If our plan to rise in arms simultaneously all over India had not miscarried, we would have heralded the coming of that revolution by throwing bombs and by murdering British officers all at one time. We had collected enough arms to make life difficult for the British Government, especially the officials. The bomb factory at Vasai was a secret school where trust-worthy revolutionaries were taught the art of bomb making."[1]

At this time one person, answering to the name of Agamya Guru was staying in Poona. He advised the students to collect funds for the liberation of the country. He further told them that he would discuss future plans with their leaders. So the students sent for Savarkar who came to Poona and discuss the political situation with Agamya Guru. During the discussion, Savarkar took the measure of the man and later told his colleagues to ignore him. Savarkar's estimate of the Guru proved correct. When the Guru was in England, he tried to be fresh with his maid. This resulted in a court case wherein he was sentenced to four months' imprisonment. The Sedition Committee Report states that Savarkar was initiated into revolutionary activities by this Agamya Guru. This statement is baseless and childish. This shows what happens when implicit faith is put in Police reports. The incident is not worth mentioning in Savarkar's biography. But as reference has been made to it in the Government report it becomes necessary to demonstrate the worthlessness of that statement.

After exposing the sham patriotism of Agamya Guru, Savarkar returned to Bombay. A few days later, he came across the issue of the 'Indian Sociologist' edited by Shyamaji Krishnavarma. In it Shyamaji had announced a few scholarships to promising and patriotic young men for studying abroad.

Shyamaji Krishnavarma is one of the gems from the ranks of Indian revolutionaries. He was born on October 4, 1857 in Mandavi in Kutch State. He lost his parents in childhood. So he came to Bombay where he had both traditional Sanskrit education and English schooling. In 1879 he went to England and in 1883 he graduated from Oxford. A year later he was called to the Bar. He then returned to India. In the following nine years he acted as Diwan in Ratlam, Udaipur, and

---

[1]Dr. V. M. Bhat : Abhinav Bharat - p.49

Junagad states. At Ajmer, he practiced law for three years. The money he earned in service and in legal practice, he invested in shares and thus made provision for a permanent income.

Shyamaji had attraction for politics. During this time he became acquainted with Tilak. But Rand's murder, Tilaks' conviction for sedition and other happenings persuaded him that the Indian atmosphere was not conducive to preaching his philosophy. He, therefore, decided to settle in England and left India permanently in 1897. In England Hume, Wedderbern, and Dadabahi Nawrowji were exerting themselves to rouse public opinion about the Indian question. But Shyamaji felt that he could not work with them and so decided to go his own way in 1903. After the death of Herbert Spencer, he announced a donation of 1,000 pounds for establishing the Spencer Lectureship at Oxford. It was accepted by that university and was utilized for arranging lectures by eminent scholars on philosophy.

Shyamaji began to publish a monthly called 'The Indian Sociologist' in 1905. It was priced 1 pence. For propagating new political ideas this monthly became useful to Shyamaji. The same year he founded the Indian Home Rule Society. Its object was to obtain Home Rule for India by all means. Its office bearers were as under: Shyamaji Krishnavarma, president; barrister Rana, vice president; and J. C. Mukerjee, secretary. Shyamaji also decided to open a hostel known as 'India House'. Its purpose was to enable Indian students, travelers, and leaders to stay together in a free and patriotic atmosphere. Accordingly he purchased a spacious and beautiful house in the Highgate area. Later this India House became a center of revolutionary activities. He also established contacts with 'Gaelic American', a newspaper, published by Irish Republican Party from New York.

Savarkar began to feel that he should take advantage of the scholarship announced in the Indian Sociologist. But he realized that the scholarship amount would be insufficient for his entire stay in England. So, he met his father-in-law Chiplunkar and requested him to give him supplementary assistance. Chiplunkar agreed. Savarkar then applied to Shyamaji Krishnavarma. In this application, Savarkar dilated upon how he took part in the Swadeshi movement and thereby incurred displeasure of the college management, and how Tilak and Paranjape had sympathetically treated him. In the end he wrote: "(Independence and liberty) I took upon as the very pulse and breath of a nation. From my boyhood, dear Sir, up to this moment of my youth, the loss of independence of my country and the possibility of regaining it forms the only theme of which I have dreamt at night and on which I mused during the day."

Savarkar hurriedly sent the application, as considerable delay had already occurred. Later on he sent Tilak's and Paranjape references. Shyamaji had received about 150 applications. As Tilak came to know this fact, he wrote in his reference that in view of a large number of applications received by Shyamaji, it would not be proper to recommend only one name. Still he would like to draw attention to one applicant. He is from Bombay and his name is Savarkar. He graduated last year. He is a dynamic young man and had been in the forefront of the Swadeshi movement. Because of that he had incurred the displeasure of his college authorities. He does not wish to enter government service and has an excellent moral character.

Though he had decided against joining government service, still Savarkar knew he would practice law. He, however, did not wish to give anyone an opportunity to say that practicing law amounted to helping the government. So he made his position clear to Shyamaji in another letter.

At the beginning of May 1906 Savarkar came to know that he had been awarded the Shivaji Scholarship. The scholarship amount was of Rs. 2,000.00 and the recipient was to get it in five installments of Rs. 400.00. The applicant had to enter into agreement with Shyamaji about scholarship. Such an agreement was signed by Savarkar on May 20, and the deed was witnessed by Daji Nagesh Apte and Krishnaji Prabhakar Khadilkar. In the case of dispute between Shyamaji and Savarkar, Tilak was to act as an arbitrator according to a condition in this agreement. On May 25, Tilak informed Shyamaji that he had paid Savarkar Rs. 400.00 who was leaving by a steamer the next day. He added that he was sending the stamped-deed as an enclosure.

But Savarkar could not leave for London by S. S. Macedonia the next day as stated by Tilak. A reception was arranged in his honor in Nasik before his departure. This was held in the Bhadrakali temple. It was presided over by Harishastri Garge. Savarkar's speech, thanking the people, captivated the audience as usual. He said that he was proceeding to England to discharge the debt of obligation to the motherland. After this reception, he came to Bombay. A large number of relatives and friends were present on the pier to wish him bon voyage. Amongst them were his wife and an 18 months old son. After bidding them good-bye, he embarked on June 9, 1906 on S. S. Persia for his passage to England. Soon the ship weighed anchor and sailed out. Savarkar has graphically described this parting scene.

"The ship that was carrying me to England left the shores of Bombay and began to roll and pitch as it sailed towards the open sea. Soon my relatives and friends who had gathered on the pier to bid me loving good-bye slowly went out of sight. As the shore receded, the picture of my friends that was cast on my mind began to dance before my eyes. Looking at it, my mind, hurt by the separation, began to ask itself piteously 'Will I safely come back to India at least after three years? Will I be able to meet all my relations?'"[1]

---

[1] V. D. Savarkar : Shatruchya Shibirat - p. 1

Answers to these questions were shrouded in the womb of time. And it was a good thing so far as Savarkar was concerned.

In the Heart of the British Empire

"The all India program of Abhinav Bharat could be effectively accomplished by me only after I arrived in England. That was one of my main aims in going to England." - Savarkar[1]

A voyage to England on a ship is a unique experience. For those 15-20 days the ship becomes a small world in itself. And human passions, such as love, friendship, likes, dislikes, joy, and anger have a free play. Queer incidents also happen. New relationships are developed, some of them become lifelong, and others turn out to be ephemeral. Savarkar had now stepped into this world. It was natural that he should feel depressed and that he should stand in a dejected mood, looking at the vast expanse of the sea. But this condition could not last long. Finally he accosted an officer and requested his help to find his cabin. This officer directed a Goanese lascar to show Savarkar his cabin.

As Savarkar entered his cabin, he found a young Sikh arranging his baggage. He was delighted to meet Savarkar. He felt comfortable when he saw that he would have an Indian co-passenger. Looking to those times, it was a natural reaction. The name of the young Sikh was Hernam Singh. Soon after the voyage began, Hernam Singh became sea-sick and felt that he should return home. Then Savarkar reminded him of the life of Guru Govind Singh. This had a salutary effect and Hernam Singh gave up the idea of returning home from Aden. It may be mentioned here that Herman Singh's friendly relationship with Savarkar did not turn out to be ephemeral.

During this voyage Savarkar persuaded two more persons to join Abhinav Bharat. Savarkar has mentioned their nicknames in his autobiographical piece 'In the camp of the enemy'. These were Keshavananda and Shistachari. Both were influenced by the biography of Mazzini Savarkar gave them to read. Later they took the oath of Abhinav Bharat. However, Shistachari at the outset made it clear that he would not openly participate in any activities. But Savarkar has testified that Shistachari gave financial assistance to the revolutionary work, helped to dispatch books, brochures to various centers in Punjab, and remained present with a group of 10 or 20 people at a meeting for defending Savarkar in case of need.[2]

Savarkar, whose life was dedicated to the liberation of his motherland, had to spend a large part of his day in public activities. But by temperament he was a poet and philosopher. Such a man enjoys solitude. It was, therefore, not unnatural that Savarkar longed for privacy. He satisfied this urge at night. At that hour he would go on the deck and sit in a corner. He had read about oceanography and astronomy. But for the first time he was having the sight of these natural

---

[1] V. D. Savarkar : Shatruchya Shibirat - p.42

[2] V. D. Savarkar : Shatruchya Shibirat - p.24

elements. Their beauty, which he saw while sitting in open air, was bewitching. But instead of their apparent beauty, their magnitude made a greater impact on his mind. He has described in the following words what thoughts crowded into his mind at that time: "What is the purpose and object of this ceaseless change of creation and destruction? Or it has no purpose? For what reason this evolution is going on in this universe? Or is it a blind-man's buff?"[1]

Countless stars twinkle in the blue sky at night. There is a heavy wind. A strange sound is heard when the ship ploughs through the water. At this time a number of passengers routinely stand at the deck-railing and enjoy the beauty of nature. Not all of them, however, are poets. But if one is a poet, then the atmosphere surely proves inspiring. Savarkar was enthralled by the sight. He had a poetic inspiration and he wrote a most delightful poem 'After looking at stars'.

The ship sailed via Aden, Suez, and Port Said and reached Marseilles. Savarkar disembarked. There was still considerable time for the train to London to depart. Two things made Marseilles attractive to Savarkar. One was the French national anthem - Marseillaise; the other was Mazzini who after his deportation from Italy, had stayed in this city for some time and had founded here 'Young Italy'. So, Savarkar got hold of a guide and went round the city searching the house where Mazzini had stayed. Despite considerable effort, the search proved fruitless. Finally they made inquires at a newspaper office. They were told to go to Italy to make inquiries about the house address; for, it was there that they might get it. Savarkar comments, "If because of ignorance, the guide or the people were unable to show me the house, the fault was not theirs. It was improper on my part to have made this inquiry." Of course a traveler, once in a while, goes through such an experience.

Savarkar seems to be laboring under some misconception about the song Marseillaise. He writes that the war-song was composed by one Rouget, a poet, in Marseilles during the excitement of the French revolution. This is not correct. It was composed by him in Strasbourg for the army of the Rhine. Later the volunteers from Marseilles sang it continuously while marching towards Paris and thus made it popular. After many decades, it became a national anthem. The stirring story of this song has been narrated by Stefan Zweig in the essay 'The Genius of One Night.'[2]

By the time Savarkar had done the city, the time for departure of the train had arrived. Savarkar boarded the train and it pulled out. Savarkar said good-bye to this historic Marseilles at this time. He could not have imagined then that in 1910 there would occur on the pier of this city an historic event. From Marseilles Savarkar came to London. Some residents from Shyamaji Krishnavarma's India House were present at the station to receive him. His co-passenger, Hernam Singh,

---

[1]V. D. Savarkar : Shatruchya Shibirat - p.26
[2]Stefan Zweig : The Tide of Fortune - p.101

also decided to go to India House on Savarkar's advice. Then all of them came to the hostel.

Savarkar seems to have reached London sometime in the last week of June, and he left it as a prisoner on July 1, 1910. Thus his stay abroad lasted for nearly four years. During this time he performed a variety of tasks. These could be divided into three parts. One, the writing; two, organizing public meetings and functions; three, conducting secret revolutionary activities. All these are intermixed in point of time. Of course these could be narrated chronologically. But it was felt that if narration is done subject wise, it would be more convenient to the reader. And hence that method has been adopted.

After settling down in London, Savarkar began to send newsletters to India. His first newsletter is dated 16 August 1906 and the last one is dated 25 November 1909. These newsletters occupy 122 pages of the fourth volume of Savarkar's collected works. He also decided to do a book on Mazzini. Mazzini, Garibaldi, and Cavour, the then contemporary Italian leaders, had made a deep impression on the English knowing Indian generations. It was under the leadership of Cavour that the movement for liberation and integration of Italy was nearly completed between 1850 and 1861. It was but natural that the biographies of these great men should prove powerful attraction to the freedom-loving youths. Mazzini's biography had cast a spell on Savarkar. When he was 17 years old, he had first read Mazzini's Marathi biography by Ghanekar. Savarkar had also perused the articles written by Paranjape in the 'Kal' giving account of the recent revolutionary wars, of secret societies, and of revolutionaries who took part in them. Later he read the English biography of Mazzini which told him that there were collected works of Mazzini in English. But only when he arrived in London could he see these works. Here with the help of Mukherjee, the manager of India House, he secured the collected works. At the end of July, he began his work on the book 'Joseph Mazzini's Biography and Politics", and completed it on September 28, 1906. It seems incredible that he completed the translation work and wrote an explosive 25 page preface to it while simultaneously attending to work of correspondence, of propaganda, of writing newsletters and doing his studies.

The following account will show how explosive this preface was. The book was dedicated to Lokamanya Tilak and Paranjape. But Babarao showed the manuscript to Tilak to avoid any possible trouble to the latter. After reading the preface, Tilak said it would be dangerous to publish it. Naturally Babarao thought it advisable to ask Tilak about the dedication. Tilak replied that Babarao might do what he thought was best and that he had no objection. In June 1907 the book was published. It was priced one rupee and a half. The first edition of 2,000 copies was sold in a month. This shows its instant success. There are a few writers in Marathi who quibble about the actual number of copies sold. According to their research the statement that all copies were sold was incorrect. So be it. But small minds are always attracted to useless details. However, it is interesting to mention here that after independence the book has run into four or five editions. Then, the book, like a holy book, was taken out in procession. And its preface was memorized by a large section of youth. This celebrated preface is now useful for understanding Savarkar's strategy of revolution.

At the beginning of the preface Savarkar says, "Italian people had solved one question at the time Mazzini was born. The county would not prosper by begging." Then what was the way out? Savarkar quotes Mazzini, "Italy would not prosper unless the old machines were melted and new ones forged. The material for the new machine was the youth. For, new situation demands new men."

But what was the machine? Secret Societies. Savarkar writes, "All European nations aspiring to freedom have had recourse to secret societies... Men could be well trained for freedom struggle in a secret society. With very little strength the foreign power could be distracted, and battle preparation could be made."

Italians had no arms. Nor were they permitted to bear them. Savarkar writes, "Italy was not put out by these difficulties. The young and brave Italians went to Spain, America, Germany, Poland, and such other countries and learnt the art of war."

But how arms are to be procured? Savarkar says, "Arms were to be purchased from countries like Germany and were to be stored near the borders and when there was tumult in the country, then revolutionaries were to rush in." Savarkar adds, "But the most important artifice Mazzini and the Italian patriots employed was to spread disaffection in the army. All the officers commanding the Italian units in the Austrian army had been administered the oath of young Italy."

The most important part of the preface has been quoted succinctly. If the word Italy is replaced by the word India, one gets an idea of the strategy of revolution that Savarkar wanted to adopt for India.

When he finished the work of translating Mazzini's autobiography, Savarkar decided to collect material for writing a book on the Indian War of Independence, 1857. Mukherjee, who had helped him to get Mazzini's works, now procured for him the first volume of Kaye's 'History of Indian Mutiny.' When he read the first volume, Savarkar became depressed. Because the volume did not contain any description of the stirring events or of battles. But at the end of the first volume there was a note, that succeeding five volumes have also been published. Savarkar entreated Mukherjee to procure the remaining volumes for him. In a week's time Mukherjee bought the entire work of Kaye and Malleson and gave it to Savarkar. Though this work contained disparaging remarks about the Indians, still it gave Savarkar enough insight into the magnitude of the revolt of 1857. Not only that; from the notes and references given therein, Savarkar realized that the English have produced massive material on that subject. So Savarkar inquired of Mukherjee where he could find these books to read. Mukherjee told him that these books were available in the India Office Library, and that he would need a letter of introduction for admission there. Later, Mukherjee obtained a reader's card for Savarkar.

Savarkar, accompanied by Mukherjee, went to the library with his reader's card. The librarian took Savarkar to one wing. Savarkar thought that all material stocked there might not be in connection with the revolt and he expressed his doubt to the librarian. But the librarian told him that the books and the documents were full of evil deeds perpetrated by the ferocious soldiery. These remarks annoyed Savarkar. But at the same time he was overjoyed to know that so much material was easily available. Savarkar also admired the administrative excellence of the English in providing such facilities to scholars.

Next day at 11 am. Savarkar went to the library. There he saw the list of books and documents. The librarian advised him which books he should read first. But as Savarkar had decided to read all the literature about the revolt, he took out one book after the other to read and to take notes from each book. He followed the same method with the files. The librarian was pleased with the industriousness of Savarkar, and began to discuss the subject with him. In such a discussion, he used to praise the British and disparage the Indian soldiers. Savarkar did not controvert him. For that would have revealed his design. As he continued to read, a conviction grew in him that the revolt of 1857 by the Indian soldiers, rulers, and the people from the various provinces was a far more extensive and pre-concerted plan than what was thought of to be. Though it failed, it gave a rude shock to the British Empire. Also, it set up an excellent example for future generations as to how revolts could be planned. Savarkar wrote his book in Marathi on the basis of his conclusions.[1]

Savarkar began to lecture on the events of the revolt while the book was being written. The detectives learnt about it and they submitted a report to the superiors who informed the India Office librarian to bar Savarkar's entry into the library. Naturally its doors were closed to Savarkar. But the book was already written. The only job that remained was to check the excerpts quoted. This task was efficiently performed by V. V. S. Aiyar.

The Marathi version was completed some time in April 1908. Two chapters were pilfered. It was then said that the Scotland Yard was behind it. Be that as it may. However, the manuscript was surreptitiously brought into India avoiding police surveillance. One of the members of Abhinav Bharat, Limaye, who owned a Press in Sholapur, decided to print it. In the meanwhile police came to know about the printing of the book and the search began. A patriotic police officer gave prior warning to Limaye. He, therefore, returned the manuscript to Babarao who sent it back to Paris.

---

[1] V. D. Savarkar : Shatruchya Shibirat - p.199

Finding it difficult to print the Marathi book in India, efforts were made to print it in Germany as Sanskrit literature was printed there. But that effort also failed. Then it was decided to print it in English. But then an English version of the book became necessary. This job was seen through by Savarkar with the help of Koregaonkar, Phadke, and Kunte. But new difficulties cropped up in having the English version printed in England. So the manuscript was sent to Paris. There also difficulties were encountered and arrangements had to be made to print it in Holland. Later copies of the book were received in Paris and were stored in Barrister Rana's house. Considerable expenditure was incurred in printing this volume and Savarkar has stated that Khaparde and Karandikar had lovingly donated a goodly sum towards the printing cost.[1] Later copies were wrapped in the jackets of Pickwick papers, Scot's works, Don Quixote and mailed to India. Sir Sinkander Hayat Khan, who afterwards became the premier of Punjab and a leader of the Muslim League, was then a member of Abhinav Bharat. While returning home from England, he brought with him a parcel of this book. In the meantime, the Government of India got inkling that the book was being published, and it issued an order banning its importation in India. When Savarkar learnt about it, he wrote a letter to the London Times protesting against that order. The Times published it and criticized the action of the Government. Since then the book ran into May editions and was also published in other languages. There is an interesting story about the Marathi manuscript.

Dr. Coutinho was a Goanese. He became a member of Abhinav Bharat in London. Savarkar had handed over to him the first draft of the manuscript for safe-keeping. Later Dr. Coutinho moved to Lisbon from London. From there he went to the United States and settled there. After India became free, Dr. Coutinho gave the manuscript to Gohokar who brought it back to Savarkar in 1949. Such was the circuitous journey of the manuscript.

While he was writing the history of 1857, he came across references in books and articles about the armed uprising of the Kukas. Based on this information, Savarkar delivered a lecture on the life of Guru Ram Singh in the India House.[2] While he was conducting his revolutionary activities in London, Savarkar had on one occasion discussed with a Sikh colleague, how to create national awakening amongst the Sikhs.[3] Punjab was the recruiting center of army personnel. Savarkar used to talk how the revolutionary idea of armed uprising could be disseminated in this center. In December 1908, he spoke on the life of Guru Gobind Singh. He had studied the Gurumukhi script. Further, he had read the books from Adi Granth to Gobind Singh's 'Vichitra Natak.' Thus he had collected enough material about Sikh history. The only thing that remained was to turn this material into a book.

---

[1] V. D. Savarkar : Samagra Savarkar Wangamaya - Vol IV - p.392

[2] V. D. Savarkar : Samagra Savarkar Wangamaya - Vol I - p.38

[3] V. D. Savarkar : Samagra Savarkar Wangamaya - Vol I - p.544

Savarkar by now had spent three years in writing books, doing propaganda work, and conducting secret revolutionary and other ancillary activities. This pressure broke his health. Soon he came down with pneumonia. In order that Savarkar should be looked after well, Dr. Muthu took him to his sanitarium in Wales. When he recovered sufficiently, the doctors gave him permission to do a little reading and writing. So Savarkar began the writing of Sikh history. Looking to Savarkar's speed of writing, it is probable that the draft was ready while he was convalescing in the sanitarium. Later, he went to Paris where he edited this draft and prepared the final manuscript. According to Karandikar, three copies were made from it. One was mailed to India which was lost in transit or was seized by the police. One copy was entrusted to an Indian artist when he was on his way to India. During the voyage, he learnt that a strict search was made of passenger's baggage in the port. Fearing that he would get into trouble if this copy found in his baggage during a search, he threw it into the sea. Karandikar suggests that the third copy was probably in Madam Cama's possession.[1] What happened to the original manuscript still remains a mystery. Savarkar dedicated the book to his son Prabhakar who had died in India when Savarkar was in England. In order to make his first-born immortal with the help of a literary piece, Savarkar had dedicated the book to him. But the book itself was lost before it could see the light of the day. So Savarkar wrote a poetic epitaph in 1912. He said "where it was felt that fire, and hurricane would not touch you, there the fire and hurricane of revolution have touched you?"

So far we have surveyed the literary activities of Savarkar during his residence in London. We will now proceed to his public activities. A reference has already been made to Savarkar's writing of newsletters from London to 'The Vihari' and 'The Kal'. Savarkar now began to contribute articles against British Imperialism under the pen-name 'Vinayak' to Gaelic American published from New York by the freedom-loving Irish. Also, he prepared a plan for a simultaneous uprising by the Irish, Egyptian, Chinese, Indian, and Turkish secret societies against the British and tried to give a concrete shape to it. Further he got articles about Indian affairs written out. Then he had them translated into French, Portuguese, Chinese, and Russian languages and arranged for their publication in the respective languages to help win world public opinion to the Indian cause. Another thing that he did was to write revolutionary brochures and made secret arrangements to dispatch them to army centers in India to prepare the minds of Sikh soldiers for an uprising. In addition, he began weekly meetings, like the ones he used to have in India. Later, he founded the 'Free India Society' to serve as a platform for his public activities, and appointed Gyanchand Varma as its secretary.

During his London stay, Savarkar organized public meetings from 1907 to 1909. The fist one was held on May 11, 1907 to celebrate the 10th May day. Shyamaji's brother-in-law, Nitin Sen Dwarkadas, was staying in Acton. His

---

[1] S. L. Karandikar : Savarkar Charitra - p.332

residence was named 'Tilak House'. Here a small function was held which was presided over by Savarkar. Gyanchand Varma was the principal speaker. About twenty people attended, amongst whom were Gowrishankar Bhatnagar, Deepchand Jhaveri, and Yerulkar. Thus was celebrated the fifteenth anniversary of the 1857 eruption.

The next function was held in the following year. It was Shivaji festival. It was celebrated on May 2, 1908 on behalf of the Free India Society. The main organizers were Deshmukh from Nagpur and Ratnabhu from Madras. V. V. S. Aiyar delivered the principal address. Yerulkar who was a Jew and Master who was a Parsee also spoke at this meeting. Savarkar was in the chair and gave a rousing speech at the end.

A week later a magnificent festival celebrating the occasion of the War of Independence of 1857 was held. Its echoes resounded in England for quite some time. The celebration was held on Sunday, May 10, 1908 at 4 p.m. in the India House, 65 Cromwell Avenue, Highgate, North. Barrister Rana was in the chair. That the event of 1857 would be celebrated on a large scale was talked about in London's Indian community. Earlier small meetings were held to emphasize its importance. Because of that, the enthusiasm of Indian youths had keyed up. They had specially decorated the hall in the India House. At the back of the platform a huge red cloth was hanging enlaced with flowers of variegated colors; and between them was displayed in green, white, and red colors the names of Bahadur Shah, Shrimant Nanasaheb Peshwa, Rani Laxmibai, Moulavi Ahmad Shah, Raja Kunwar Singh, and other warriors, who fought in 1857, in grateful remembrance. Also, the pictures of various patriots were displayed. The hall was full of burning incense sticks. The melodious tunes of harmonium and the stirring singing of Varma created an inspiring atmosphere. There was an unprecedented attendance and some guests had to stand outside the hall in the street. For this festival Indians had come from Cambridge, Oxford, Sorencester, Reading, and other places. Aiyar sang the national prayer. Then Savarkar spoke about Bahadur Shah and Nanasaheb Peshwa and explained the true character of the revolt of 1857. Next, Khan spoke about Raja Kunwar Singh, Das spoke about Rani Laxmibai, Master, Yerulkar, and Raipen, who was a Christian, spoke in praise of other warriors. Rana read out Madam Camas's message which he had brought with him and made a concluding speech.

Then the vows of sacrifice were taken by old and young men and women and these included doctors, pleaders, barristers, editors, graduates, and businessmen. Special badges of remembrance were prepared for the month of penance. These were worn by all. At this time, some vowed to fast for a month, some gave up smoking, some vowed to abstain from liquor, while some others decided to shun play-going. The money saved by these methods was to be given to the fund which was being specially raised for the warriors of 1857. Also, a goodly number of people volunteered to go from house to house and collect donations. For this fund Madam Cama gave Rs. 75.00 while Rana gave a month's income to this fund. Afterwards Mrs. Dutt sang patriotic songs. Then chapattis were distributed as 'Prasad'. Finally Vande Mataram was sung.

In this celebration, a brochure 'Oh Martyrs' was distributed. Looking to the language and thought, there is little doubt that it was written by Savarkar. It said: "Today is the 10th of May! It was on this day that, in the ever memorable year of 1857, the first campaign of the War of Independence was opened by you, Oh martyrs, on the battlefield of India....... All honor be to you, Oh Martyrs; for it was for the preservation of the honor of the race that you performed the fiery ordeal of a revolution..."

"We take up your cry, we revere your flag, we are determined to continue that fiery mission of 'away with the foreigner', which you uttered, amidst the prophetic thundering of the Revolutionary war - Revolutionary, yes, it was a Revolutionary war......"

"No, a Revolutionary war knows no truce, save liberty or death!.... Indians, these words, must be fulfilled! Your blood, Oh Martyrs, shall be avenged!"

"Vande Mataram."

Later Savarkar arranged to have copies of these brochures secretly sent to India for distribution all over the country.

Savarkar and Aiyar each contributed 25 shillings weekly during the month of penance. Further, Savarkar with Aiyar and Dr. Rajan collected donations from eminent people. They saw Mr. Dutt, who belonged to the first batch of Indian Civil Service, and Honorable Gokhale and discussed with them the events of 1857 and the present Indian political situation. In the end Dutt conceded that the revolt of 1857 had a national character as maintained by Savarkar. Gokhale neither accepted that proposition nor contributed any money to the fund.

This London festival of 1857 produced some awkward consequences. Hernam Singh and Khan were studying in the agricultural college at Sorencester. They went to the college wearing these badges when the college principal called Nanasaheb and Rani of Jhansi as murderers. This angered both of them and they left the college. For their self-respecting behavior both were given a dinner party. Mrs. Dhandevi, a Punjabi lady, presided at this party and awarded Yar-e-Hind title to both of them. What a great intellectual transformation had taken place in the Indian community is revealed by this incident!

On October 16 two functions were held. One was to show sympathy to the Indian settlers in South Africa. The other was Rakhi-bandhan. In the first program a meeting was held under the chairmanship of Sir Mancharji Bhavnagari in which Lala Lajpat Rai, Parekh, Bipin Chandra Pal, Savarkar, Khaparde, and

Raipen spoke in support of various resolutions. After it was over, another meeting was held at the same venue. First Lajpat Rai spoke; he was followed by Kumarswami, Dadasaheb Karandikar, and Khaparde. Then the ceremony of tying silken thread - Rakhi Bhandan - was held. The meeting was rounded off by a rousing speech by Bipin Chandra Pal.

After an interval of two months, a meeting was held on December 29 in Caxton Hall to celebrate the birthday of Guru Gobind Singh. It was held with great éclat. What was not happening in India happened in London. On the platform was hoisted a big banner in roseate color and on it were written three words 'Deg, Teg, Fathe'. Also, under the line 'Honor to the sacred memory of Shree Guru Gobind Singh', the words 'Prophet, Poet, and Warrior' in different colors were written. Flowers, smell of incense, and banners gave the hall a look of a temple.

Bipin Chandra Pal presided over this function. At the beginning two songs were sung, 'Amar Desh' and 'Priyaker Hindusthan', the latter was composed by Savarkar. This was followed by prayers which were recited by two Sikhs from the sacred writings of Guru Nanak. Then Prof. Gokulchand Narang read his spirited essay on Guru Gobind Singh's life. This was followed by speeches of Lala Lajpat Rai and Bipin Chandra Pal. Then the audience clamored that Savarkar should speak. So Bipinbabu compelled him to address this meeting. Savarkar revolved his speech around the words on the banner that was fluttering in the hall. He said, "Deg means doctrine, Teg means sword, and Fathe means victory." As doctrine is lame without arms, Gobind Singh drew his sword and the Hindu party triumphed. Leading papers like 'Times', 'Daily telegraph', 'Daily Express', took notice of this function in their columns. 'Daily Mirror' carried a picture.

The last big public function was held in November 1909. It was the 'Dassera' festival. On this day a banquet was arranged for the Indians in Queens Road Hall. The subscription for it was Rs. 3.00 per person. A large number of doctors, businessmen, professors, and students attended it. Gandhiji presided over this function. The beautiful rows, the fragrance of frankincense, in the center the national flag displaying the words 'Vande Mataram' and the melodious tunes of national songs - all these things made the show impressive. Gandhiji spoke first. He said that he was gratified to see doctors, professors, and such other people working as volunteers and to observe the attendance of Parsis and Muslims at this function. Finally he said that whatever differences of opinion there might be, he felt honored that he got an opportunity of sitting beside Savarkar. May our country enjoy the sweet fruits of his sacrifice and patriotism. Speaking on this occasion, Savarkar said, "When people forget Rama, India's soul is lost. Hindus are the heart of Hindustan. However various colors in a rainbow do not mar but heighten its beauty. Similarly, by accepting the best elements from the Muslim, Parsi, and Jewish culture, Hindusthan will brightly shine in the course of time." As chairman, Gandhiji made a concluding speech. He exhorted the audience to remember forever Savarkar's speech and fulfill his plea for sacrifice made at the end of that rousing speech.[1] Incidentally it is creditable to Savarkar that he could bring prominent communities on the stage on a Hindu festival.

Up till now we have surveyed Savarkar's literary and public activities. Now we shall proceed to his third field of activity. From the time of founding of Mitra Mela, Savarkar had divided his revolutionary work in two parts, namely, open and secret. After arriving in London, he founded 'Free India Society' for public activity. Similarly in December 1906, that is, six months after his arrival in London, he decided to launch his secret society 'Abhinav Bharat' and collected a group of like-minded students.

After some time one of the members of this group, Bapat, who later became renowned as Senapati Bapat, went to Paris. Here, along with Hemachandra Das and Mirza Abbas, he mastered the technique of bomb-making with the help of Russian revolutionaries. Now the London group of revolutionaries began to discuss the ways and means of spreading the knowledge of this technique in India. Then the Russian manuscript was translated into English and its copies were made. Later some of these copies were sent with Hemachandra Das and Hotilal Varma to India. One of these copies was given to Lokamanya Tilak by Varma.

The London group of revolutionaries was not satisfied with sending the copies of the manuscript to India. They made experiments to find out whether the formulas were correct. On one occasion Bapat threw the papers on which the drops of picric acid had fallen into the coal fire. There was a loud explosion, and some people gathered outside to find out the cause of it. Savarkar offered some plausible excuse which satisfied them. On another occasion, at night, an experiment was being conducted. The time came to take the flask off the burner as it was getting too hot. But Savarkar had no pincers with him. Savarkar wondered what he should do when Dhingra lifted the flask by his bare hand and put it down. But in doing so his palm was scalded.

To organize revolutionary bands in different parts of the country, to teach the technique of bomb making, and to collect arms, Das, Varma, and Bapat had proceeded to India. At about this time a gentleman who went by the name of Varahaneri Vankatesa Subramania Aiyar reached London. He had practiced law for some time in Rangoon. Now he had come to London to study law and to be called to the Bar. Initially he was enamored of the European way of life. But when Savarkar and he met, the former convinced him that dancing and singing were a waste of one's energy. Then Aiyar began to attend the meetings of the Free India Society. Here he once heard Savarkar speaking on the subject, 'Are we obliged to British rule?', and this changed him. Later he became so involved in revolutionary activities that he became the right hand man of Savarkar.

---

[1]V. D. Savarkar : Samagra Savarkar Wangamaya Vol IV - p.146

After the month of penance, which was part of 1857 celebrations in 1908 was over, Savarkar went to Paris. About this visit Yajnik writes: "... Nay more, he even went to Paris, and incredible as it might seem, and all that Shyamaji wrote on the subject notwithstanding - scored such a personal triumph that he actually persuaded hard-headed Indian businessmen to take solemn vows in the service of his new society. He further secured the manuscript of a bomb manual that Hemachandra Das had secured with the help of some Russian revolutionaries."[1] The manuscript was of 20 pages. After Savarkar's return to London its cyclostyled copies were prepared in his room. Later these were secretly sent to various centers in India.

In July of 1908 a meeting of the inner council of the London branch of Abhinav Bharat was held in Barrister Gyanchand Varma's house which was located in Warwick Street. At this time Varma, with a revolver in his hand, uttered the vow which was repeated by Dhingra, Koregaonkar, Savarkar, Baba Joshi, Sen, Hernam Singh, Khan, Jayaswal, and some others. Later, Savarkar was elected as chief of the organization.

It was necessary to create a certain atmosphere for an uprising against the British. With that end in view, Savarkar had written books on 'Mazzini' and 'War of Independence-1857', brochures like 'Oh Martyrs', 'Choose! Oh Indian Princes', and 'Two historic documents', etc. and all this literature was sent by him to India through various agencies. Also, as part of the program of collecting arms, he had arranged to send revolvers to India. Some were carried by Sir Sikander Hayat Khan. These reached the destination safely. One revolver and 50 cartridges were sent with one Chanjeri Ram Rao. But these were detected in the customs. Savarkar had sent some revolvers with an Italian lady. These also reached the right places in Hyderabad state. There was a cook named Chaturbhuj at the India House. He learnt the trade of a tailor. He was admitted as a member of Abhinav Bharat. With him Savarkar and Aiyar sent 20 revolvers and a few thousand cartridges in a bag with a false bottom. Gopalrao Patankar received them and sent them to Pen.

Further, Savarkar made repeated attempts to build a world-wide revolutionary conspiracy against the British in cooperation with Irish revolutionaries, Egyptian nationalists, German officials, and Turkish revolutionaries. Moreover at his instance an Indian revolutionary got himself employed in Scotland Yard to find out what true information it had received and also to supply it with false information. M. P. T. Acharya was the name of that employee. He was paid 5 pounds as a police informer. The then Bombay government also decided to find out what was transpiring in the India House. For that purpose it selected a person whose name was Kirtikar. He came to London under the pretext of studying dentistry. He secured accommodation at the India House. But very soon Aiyar and Dr. Rajan found out his real mission. One day at

---

[1]Indulal Yajnik : Shyamaji Krishnavarma - p.262

night Savarkar and Aiyar entered his room. Under the threat of using a revolver, Aiyar made him confess to all his activities. But Kirtikar was not thrown out of the India House. It was ensured that every document that Kirtikar gave to Scotland Yard was first scrutinized by Aiyar.

The 'Evening Standard' was the first to come out with an accusation that the Indian students were seditious. Then it stated that the students were instigated by Savarkar. To this Savarkar's friend sent a strong and threatening reply. Then the reporter of the paper visited the India House. In addition, the reporters of 'Daily Mail', 'Manchester Guardian', and 'Dispatch' also interviewed Savarkar and published their reports. Savarkar in one of his London letters quoted some paragraphs from the report which was carried in the 'Sunday Chronicle' after its reporter had interviewed him.

The reporter wrote, "It may be that my eyesight is not good! It is a house of mystery. Mr. Shyamaji Krishhavarma works for the independence of India. If he does not approve the assassinations of British officials, who accidentally or incidentally suffer thereby, he excuses them. He has offered rupees towards a fund of Indian Martyrs' Memorial for the men hanged in Bengal. Any how the shadow of Krishhavarma is on India House. That is to be fair and to say the least. Now what is the answer? I had an opportunity of a long friendly discussion with Mr. V. D. Savarkar, who seems to be not only the spokesman for the students but the spokesman for Mr. Shyamaji Krishhavarma. He is a young Grey's Inn Law student, 23 years at a guess. He has a clear olive complexion, clear deep penetrating eyes, a width of jaw, such as I have seen in few men. His English is excellent. If I mistake not Mr. Savarkar will go far - I hope he will go far in the right direction."

The reporter further adds, "Let me state a fact before an impression. The fact is Mr. V. D. Savarkar believes in India for Indians, in the complete emancipation of India from the British rule. He says India has nothing for what to thank the English, unless it be the denationalization, as he calls it, of the Hindus."

Finally the reporter concluded, "Mr. Savarkar said, 'We do not mind detectives watching outside and following us, if the climate suits them!' That last is a quite English touch. It shows how the British hand has molded the intellect of young India. It has even breathed into it the British joke..."

Nearly three years' residence in England had made Savarkar, to use his words, an up-to-date person.

Dhingra's Martyrdom

"Perhaps there is no happiness in life so perfect as the martyr's" - O. Henry.[1]

Savarkar, as said earlier, reached London in the last week of June in the year 1906, and in a few months started organizing his public and secret revolutionary activities. In a short time these assumed an inflammatory character. With so much of incendiary talk going on, it was no wonder that an explosion occurred in London.

In India, the revolutionary movement had also grown very strong. The 'Abhinav Bharat' was a manifestation of the revolutionary activity in Maharashtra. The partition of Bengal created a new upsurge in that province and revolutionary organizations had sprung up there. The leaders of the revolutionary movement were knowledgeable men. They were well aware of what was happening around the world. The Marathi daily, the Kal, carried stories about Italian revolutionaries in its columns; similarly the Yugantar, a Bengali newspaper, wrote an article about Russian experience in which the following information was given. "There is another very good means of acquiring strength of arms. Many people have observed in the Russian revolution that there are many partisans of the revolutionaries among the Czar's troops. These troops will join the revolutionists with various arms. This method succeeded well during the French Revolution. The revolutionists have additional advantages where the ruling power is a foreign power, because the latter has to recruit most of its troops from among the subject people. Much work can be done by the revolutionists very cautiously spreading the gospel of independence among these native troops. When the time arrives for a practical collusion with the ruling power, the revolutionists not only get these troops among their ranks, but also the arms with which the ruling power supplied them. Besides, all the enthusiasm and courage of the ruling power can be destroyed by exciting a serious alarm in its minds."[2]

It would have been a surprise if the Anglo-Indian bureaucracy did not take cognizance of the newspapers publishing such literature. The press where 'Yugantar' was printed was attached. Still the paper came out. So the editors were prosecuted. One editor was sentenced to a year's imprisonment in July 1907. Yogi Arvindbabu was arrested in the month of August for an article published in the 'Vande Mataram'. The publisher of 'Hari Kishore', which was published from Yavatmal, was prosecuted. The editor of 'Vihari', B. V. Phadke, was sentenced to imprisonment for two years. This was the paper in which Savarkar had earlier written articles and was sending newsletters from London. Bramhabandhav Upadhyaya, the editor of 'Sandhya', a paper as popular as 'Yugantar', died in jail.

---

[1] John Bartlett : Familiar Quotation - p.800

[2] Sedition Committee 1918 Report - p.22

This considerably agitated the Indians. Further, the Viranwali episode aggravated the matter. Viranwali was a young girl of seventeen. She left the house after a quarrel with her in-laws. She got off at Rawalpindi station where the station-master, Moore, and his Muslim servant raped her. In the court Moore pleaded in defense that he had paid her for the pleasure. The court accepted this plea. When the girl found that aspersions had been cast on her character, she committed suicide. This led to popular indignation against the British Government.

Hemachandra Das had brought the bomb manual to India and soon attempts of bomb-throwing were made. But these did not have much success. However, the one that was thrown in Muzaffarpur on April 30, 1908 did explode. Instead of killing the intended victim the District Magistrate, Kingsford, it killed Mrs. Kennedy and her daughter. In this connection, Khudiram Bose and his colleague Prafulla Kumar Chaki alias Dinesh Chandra Ray were arrested. But Ray escaped and shot himself. Khudiram was convicted and hanged. Now the police investigation started in earnest, and they found a small library in Maniktola gardens. Here the manual for the manufacturing of bombs was found. So 34 young men, including Hemachandra Das, Barindra Kumar Ghosh, Indubhushan Rai-Chowdhari, were arrested.

In Maharashtra the government also took stern measures. On May 15, 1908 Dhondopant Phadke, editor of 'Arunodaya' from Thane, and Rambhau Mandlik, the editor of 'Vihari', were arrested, tried, and jailed. Paranjape, the editor of the 'Kal', had written an article on the episode of bomb throwing at Muzaffarpur. He was arrested for it and sentenced to 19 months of imprisonment on July 6, 1908. Lokamanya Tilak was also arrested and on July 23 was sentenced to six years in exile. Because he was Savarkar's brother, Babarao was under police surveillance. During Paranjape's trial, Babarao was in Bombay. While the police were trying to control the crowd, angry words were exchanged between them and Babarao. So the police prosecuted him and he was jailed for a month. The police had got wind that revolvers sent by Savarkar from London would reach Babarao. So when he came to Bombay, he was arrested in the room of Dr. Bhat in Madhavashram on February 28, 1909. Later he was tried for publishing verses in the 'Laghu Abhinav Bharat' series and the book on 'Mazzini' and was sentenced to life imprisonment. His property was also forfeited. The date of this sentence was June 8, 1909.

And 23 days later Madanlal Dhingra shot Colonel Curzon Wyllie in London creating a great furor for a time in the capital of the British Empire. Dhingra was a Punjabi youth. His father was a police officer. Dhingra was a clever lad, but would not bend to his father's wishes. So, he left Lahore College in the first year and took employment in Settlement Department. During his service, he experienced rudeness from some English officers. Dhingra did not talk much about himself. But, according to Koregaonkar, Dhingra had been to Australia and had worked in Assam for some time and had also gone to Turkey on a ship as a

Coaler.[1] Later his family decided to send him to England for higher education. On May 29, 1906 he sailed to England. His cabin-mate was Koregaonkar.

On reaching London, Dhingra enrolled his name in the University College. Being happy go lucky fellow he soon had a circle of friends. However, gradually he was attracted to the group gathering around Savarkar. But, Dhingra had no faith in the meetings of 'Free India Society' where speeches were made or discussions took place. Still he identified himself with all the work that Savarkar was doing.

The experience Dhingra had during his government service and when he worked on a ship made him hate the English. In addition, when he read the articles from 'London Opinion', such as, 'Colored Men and English Women', or articles from Cassel's Weekly, such as, 'Babu Black sheep' against the Indians he would go off the deep end. In one meeting, Dhingra proposed to dynamite a P & O liner. But Savarkar thought that it would be better to assassinate either Lord Curzon, or Asquith, or Morley.

Once during a talk on Russo-Japanese war someone spoke highly about the Japanese and derided the Hindu nation and the Hindu youth. Dhingra angrily retorted 'My Hindu nation is as brave and adventurous and people will sing praises of our bravery.' This sparked a dispute. In order to test his endurance, someone pushed a needle in Dhingra's hand. As the needle went through, blood spurted out. But Dhingra remained calm. Another such incident occurred when the Nepalese premier visited London. The revolutionists decided to send a letter to him. This letter was to be signed in blood. Dhingra stabbed his finger and gave blood for the signatures.

On October 11, 1908, Khudiram Bose was hanged. Dhingra felt depressed for doing nothing when men like Khudiram Bose were becoming immortal by dying. To reduce his depression, he began to indulge in music and dance. During the last days of the year 1908 on one occasion Savarkar got angry with him. While a discussion was in full swing, melodious tunes wafted from the adjoining room, and on the street a bevy of girls had gathered. When Savarkar came out to see who was causing this disturbance, he saw Dhingra. So Savarkar, while chiding him, said, "What is all this! You talk of action and martyrdom. You avoid meetings by talking highly of martyrdom. Are these the signs of martyrdom? Do not attend meetings if you please, but at least stop being noisy." Savarkar's reprimand had an effect and an abashed Dhingra went back to his quarters.

A few days later he came to see Savarkar. Feeling that Savarkar would still be angry with him, Dhingra met him outside his room. But Savarkar began to talk in a jolly way with him as if nothing had happened earlier. After some time Dhingra asked him the question which was on his mind: "Has the time for

---

[1] Mukund Sonpataki : Daryapar - p.49

martyrdom come?" "If the martyr's mind is resolved and if he is ready to face all the consequences, it might then be said that the time for martyrdom has arrived," replied Savarkar. Later, there were further meetings between the two. In these meetings Savarkar told Dhingra about the precautions to be taken to ensure that nothing would go wrong. Koregaonkar was present at these meetings.

Soon Dhingra secured a license for a revolver, and bought a six-chamber colt revolver. Then he enrolled his name in the school which gave lessons in shooting. It was run by one Mr. Morley at Tottenham Court road. Then he became a member of 'National Indian Association', a Pro-British Institution, and began to supply bits of information to senior British officers regarding the revolutionary activities going on in London. Dhingra's conduct naturally caused misunderstanding and a demand was made by others that this traitor should be removed from the Free India Society. Savarkar, of course, could not disclose the plan. So to play for time, he said that Dhingra was our old colleague. It would not be fair to summarily eject him. We should wait for some time. I would keep a watch on him and, if there was no noticeable change in his behavior, we would then see what should be done.

Though he was equipping himself to carry out his design, Dhingra was studying hard for his engineering examination. He was also telling his friends that he would go home after the results were announced. Further, he continued to visit his English friends. Once he met Curzon Wyllie at the latter's invitation. Wyllie, on this occasion, told Dhingra to shun the India House. But Dhingra explained that he went there to collect information which he provided them.

Soon the examination was over. Dhingra's one objective was achieved. Now the thought of how to achieve the next one made him a little solemn. In the meanwhile on June 8 news arrived that Savarkar's elder brother Babarao was sentenced to life in exile. Considering Dhingra's mental condition it was but natural that this news considerably agitated him. At once, he made his decision. That evening there was a talk under the auspices of Colonial Institute on 'Indian Aspirations' by Bengal's ex-Governor Sir Bramfield Fuller. Lord Curzon was to preside at this meeting. Dhingra went to the meeting, hoping to shoot either of them. But he was late and the doors of the hall were closed. Naturally in a depressed mood, he returned home.

Dhingra now resolved that his next attempt had to succeed. The annual celebrations of the 'National Indian Association' were scheduled on July 1 at the Jahangir Hall in the Imperial Institute. Dhingra collected all information about this function. On June 30 he met Savarkar who directed that Koregaonkar and Varma should also attend this function. On July 1, Dhingra, after taking his lunch, told his landlady that he would not be home for dinner in the evening. Later he visited the shooting school and practiced for a while. In the evening, he came home and armed himself with three revolvers, one dagger and one knife. Then he put on his best clothes and went to the meeting.

It was eight in the evening. In hour and a half all the invitees had gathered. Due to an earlier engagement, Curzon Wyllie and his wife came a little later. The program continued till 11 at night. Then the crowd began to disperse. Wyllie fell to talking with those Indians with whom he could not speak earlier during the program. In this group was Dhingra. When the crowd in the front thinned, Dhingra stepped forward and began to whisper to Wyllie. While the intimate conversation was going on, Dhingra whipped out a revolver. Seeing it, Wyllie stepped back. But Dhingra pulled the trigger and pumped bullets into Wyllie who collapsed on the ground and died. When the first two bullets were fired, Dr. Kawas Lalkaka rushed to Wyllie's assistance. Dhingra also fired at him and Lalkaka fell down. In all Dhingra had fired five bullets. When his attempt to fire the sixth one at himself failed, he tried to take out another revolver. At that moment Sir Leslie Probin caught Dhingra's right arm from behind. There was a scuffle. One Indian student Madan Mohan Singh rushed to help Sir Leslie, and after removing the revolver from Dhingra's hand, he threw him on the ground. In that condition, Dhingra smiling said, "Allow me to collect my spectacles which have fallen down."

The noise of the revolver shots brought people back to the hall. Amongst them were Dr. John Buchanan and Dr. Thomas Nevil. They examined Wyllie and declared him dead. Dr. Lalkaka was still breathing. He was rushed to the hospital. Then doctors examined Dhingra's pulse. It was beating normally. Soon police arrived on the scene. They took Dhingra and all his belongings in their custody including Dhingra's statement. From here Dhingra was taken to Wolton Street police station, and was locked up. In a few minutes, Dhingra was fast asleep.

In the morning Inspector Draper carried out a search of Dhingra's residence. There he found another copy of the statement. He confiscated it. Inspector Charles Glass asked Dhingra if he had any message to send to any of his friends. "My friends will come to know everything by and by. There is nothing special that has to be conveyed to them in a hurry." In the afternoon Dhingra was produced before the Magistrate in the Westminster Court. When he was charged with two murders, he said that he had not killed Lalkaka intentionally. The magistrate ordered that he be kept in police custody for a week.

That this deed would be condemned by all was obvious. Dhingra's father sent a wire to Governor-General Minto expressing his profound sorrow. When the news of Curzon Wyllie's murder spread in the city, a hostile atmosphere developed against the Indian students. Savarkar was then staying with Bipin Chandra Pal. A crowd gathered in front of the house. But nothing untoward happened. However, because of public commotion, Bipin Chandra Pal announced that Savarkar was staying with him as a paying guest only and beyond that he had no connection with him. On July 2, Prime Minister Asquith, in a public speech, stated that Wyllie's murder was part of a conspiracy. Next day prominent Indians met in the New Reform Club to condemn the deed. In this meeting Sir

Surendranath condemned the murder, but also objected to Asquith's statement about the conspiracy. Bipin Chandra Pal said that it was too early to say whether it was a political deed. However, he added, if anyone tried to connect this foul deed with the nationalist movement, then such action should be condemned.

On July 5 a meeting was held in Caxton Hall to censure Dhingra. Its proceedings caused some sensation for a few days. Aga Khan presided over this meeting. Maharaj Kumar of Kutchbihar, Syed Hussein Bilgrani, and K. C. Gupta, member of India Office, Sir Dinsha Petit, Fazalbhai Karimbhai Ibrahim, and Surendranath Banerjee were present. Mancherji Bhavnagari was the convener. Indian students in large number were present in the hall. Savarkar, Varma, and Aiyar were sitting in the front rank. Acharya was behind them.

After condolence messages were read, the first resolution, saying that this meeting shared the grief of the families of Wyllie and Lalkaka was moved by Bhavnagari. He criticized Dhingra. To some extent Amir Ali did the same while supporting the resolution. The second resolution condemned Dhingra. While the resolution was being read by the chairman, Theodore Morrison of the India Council came on the stage accompanied by Dhingra's younger brother. This boy, as coached, said that his brother had disgraced their family. This created a little stir in the meeting. Observing this, the chairman put the motion to vote on the ground that the time was short. And when he saw a large number of hands had gone up in support, he declared that the motion was passed unanimously. At once Savarkar loudly said, "Not unanimously; there are opposition votes." All eyes turned to Savarkar. While Savarkar was explaining the reasons for his opposition, Mancherji Bhavnagari descended from the stage and began to shout, 'hold him'. Naturally this created a commotion in the meeting. Then one Barrister Palmer hit Savarkar under the eye and blood began to flow. So a large number of people became annoyed. Sir Surendranath left the meeting, complaining about the assault on Savarkar. Acharya, who was sitting behind Savarkar, hit Palmer on the head with his stick. So a Sikh tried to take Acharya by his throat. Aiyar nearly took out his revolver to fire at Palmer. But Savarkar restrained him with a wink.

Soon the police arrived on the scene. They took control of the hall. As the meeting came to an end, the crowd began to disperse. Savarkar was taken home by his friends. There a discussion began whether Palmer would prosecute Acharya. Savarkar found a way to thwart Palmer. He sent a letter to 'The Times' and other newspapers explaining his conduct. He said, "... When the President put the resolution before the meeting and asked those in favor of the same to raise their hands, he acknowledged the right, in accordance with the invariable practice in all public meetings of everyone who was present to vote according to his choice. The resolution was explained by those who proposed and seconded it, presuming the criminality of the man who is accused of having committed the murder. It seemed to me an encroachment upon and assumption of the authority of the Law Courts to declare a man, who is still under trail, to be a criminal. The man accused of the murder has made no confession. So, it seemed to me more just and appropriate to omit the words 'crime' and 'criminals'' from the resolution. As the proceedings had advanced too far to affect this, I simply voted against the resolution as it stood and wanted to bring to the notice of the President the fact that the resolution could not be declared as passed unanimously. But, some exited spirits forgot themselves so much as to shout 'eject him' etc. and even went so far as to threaten me with physical force. I stood perfectly calm, simply asserting my right and without giving the least provocation. In a minute or two, one man, Mr. Palmer by name, reached to the place where I was standing and attacked me while I was actually in the act of explaining the meaning of my opposition in clear terms, though they were drowned in the cry of the exited few. The man who committed this unprovoked assault upon one who simply insisted upon either being heard or ejected will soon be brought before the courts. Meanwhile, I hasten to write this letter to you to explain my conduct at the meeting and to prevent any misunderstanding or misinterpretation." But Acharya's belaboring of Palmer exposed his identity. In order to save him from police harassment, he was sent to Gibraltar from a not much frequented English port.

On July 10, the preliminary hearing of Dhingra's case took place in Westminster court. When the statement of Madan Mohan Singh was read out in the court, Dhingra called him a traitor. Further, when he saw that the statement he had with him on the day of assassination was being suppressed, he made a short statement explaining the reasons of his action. Then his case was committed to sessions court for a trial.

Varma was the first person to meet Dhingra in jail. Dhingra gave him a list of things he needed. He also told him to send a mirror to help him dress properly. Later, Koregaonkar met him. Savarkar saw him a day before the trial. In this meeting Dhingra expressed three desires to him. One, his body should be cremated according to Hindu rites; two, his dead body should not be touched by a non-Hindu or his brother; three, a Brahmin should light the funeral pyre. He also told Savarkar that there were books and clothes in his rooms and that these should be sold and the money realized there from should be donated to the National Fund. In view of the speech made by his younger brother in the Caxton Hall meeting, Dhingra refused to see him.

On July 23, the court proceedings began. A hundred Indians had come to attend the court. But admission was refused to them. Then the proceedings began. Dhingra admitted that he had murdered Wyllie. But he said that he would like to read a statement the police confiscated from him. To this the judge replied that he was not concerned about what was in Dhingra's pocket. Whatever Dhingra wanted to say he could say it in the court. Dhingra declined. So the jury was told to return its verdict. The jury found Dhingra guilty as charged. Then Dhingra said, "I do not accept the jurisdiction of this court. But a time will come, when we will become a sovereign power." After the death sentence was pronounced he said, "I am proud to have the honor to sacrifice my life for my motherland," and then with a smile on his face he marched out of the court with the police.

The revolutionists had imagined that Dhingra's statement would be read in the court and that it would get world-wide publicity. But due to police action and also due to the court's refusal to interfere in the matter, the possibility of the statement being published ended. But Savarkar was not the one who would throw in the towel. Six days after Dhingra was convicted, Savarkar went to Brighton and he summoned Varma there. A copy of Dhingra's statement was with Savarkar. He decided that it should be printed in Paris and mailed to newspapers in Europe and in America. He entrusted this task to Varma who perfectly executed it. Not only that, the statement was also published in London's Daily News. Garnett has narrated this incident in his autobiography in the following words. "When Dhingra came before the magistrate, he asked to be allowed to read aloud a statement. This was refused. I met Savarkar shortly afterwards and he gave me a copy of Dhingra's statement and asked me if I could get it published. That was easy. I took my first and only journalistic scoop to Robert Lynd then on the staff of the 'Daily News' and it appeared in that paper next morning. Savarkar was extremely pleased."[1] This was natural. For, Savarkar had seen to it that Dhingra's statement at least saw the light of the day. It appeared under the caption 'Challenge'. It said, 'I admit, the other day, I attempted to shed English blood as a humble revenge for the inhuman hangings and deportations of patriotic Indian youths. In this attempt I have consulted none but my own duty; I have conspired with none but my own duty. I believe that a nation held in bondage with the help of foreign bayonets is in perpetual state of war. Since open battle is rendered impossible to a disarmed race, I attacked by surprise; since guns were denied to me, I drew forth my pistol and fired.'

When Dhingra's statement appeared in the 'Daily News', it created a stir in the government quarters. 'Daily Mirror' challenged the government to publish the original statement of Dhingra if the one which appeared in the 'Daily News' was not authentic. 'The Times' commented on all this in the following words: 'There is every reason to believe that Dhingra did not compose the statement but that it was composed by those who egged him on to commit murder. The statement found in Dhingra's room was at once taken possession of by the police; it remains in their possession and it has been shown to none outside the official circle. Yet, none the less, copies of the statement have been given to various persons and to one newspaper. These circumstances, it is pointed out, afford proof that the statement found in Dhingra's room was the copy of a document, the original of which is in the hands of others. Moreover, the style of the composition of the statement is entirely unlike the style of Dhingra's statement before the magistrate. Copies of the document, it is stated, have been received by some persons in this country from Paris.' Garnett has written 'I guessed who the author of it was.' But he has not mentioned Savarkar's name.

---

[1] David Garnett : The Golden Echo - p.148

Dhingra was intelligent. His studies in college were excellent, and he had stood first in the examination. He had completed his 3-year course and had come out with flying colors in the final examination. In two months' time he was to return home. Mr. Stead, editor of Review of Reviews, took pains to have Dhingra's sentence of death commuted. A memorandum, signed by a large number of people, requesting that the body of Dhingra be handed over to them, so they could cremate it with religious rites, was submitted to the government. This was turned down. On August 17, Dhingra walked to the gallows with firm steps, and at 9.00 a.m. he was dead. His body was examined in the presence of Mr. Master, a Parsi gentleman. Later, a reporter of 'Daily Mirror' asked him, "Will he be considered as a martyr by the Indians?" Mr. Master replied, "Certainly. He has laid down his life for his country's good. Whether his idea of 'this good' was right or wrong is a matter of opinion."

The Indian students fasted on the day Dhingra was hanged. As the body of Dhingra was not handed over, no religious rites could be performed on it. But on the 10th day, Gyanchand Varma performed all the religious ceremonies by having his head shaved. The revolutionists issued a statement glorifying the martyrdom of Dhingra. Lloyd Gorge expressed to Churchill his highest admiration of Dhingra's attitude as a patriot. Churchill felt that Dhingra's last words were the finest ever made in the name of patriotism.[1]

In the first issue of 'Vande-Mataram', Hardayal wrote, "Dhingra, the immortal, has behaved at each stage of his trial like a hero of ancient times. He has reminded us of the history of medieval Rajputs and Sikhs, who loved death like a bride. England thinks she has killed Dhingra; in reality, he lives forever and has given the death-blow to English Sovereignty in India."

"In time to come, when the British Empire in India shall have been reduced to dust and ashes, Dhingra's monument will adorn the squares of our chief towns, recalling to the memory of our children the noble life and noble death of him who laid down his life in a far-off land for the cause he loved so well."[2] Poor hapless Dhingra and dreamer Hardayal! The British Empire has disappeared. However, when Hardayal's dream will come true, is yet to be seen!

When the Dhingra affair was going on, Savarkar had to face an inquiry in the court of Gray's Inn. Savarkar had passed the bar examination. The authorities of Gray's Inn raised the question whether he should be admitted to the bar. Before admission, the applicant had to secure recommendations from two benchers. In this connection Savarkar saw some people. But they told him that they would do nothing without first seeking advice from the India Office. Finally two benchers gave him recommendations. Then the matter came to a head. And Savarkar was served with a notice in which he was charged with instigating bloodshed and war,

---

[1] W. S. Blunt : My Diaries, Part II - p.288
[2] S. L. Karandikar : Savarkar Charitra - p.298

and advocating India's complete independence, etc. Later the documents, submitted during the trial of his elder brother, were produced and new charges were added. He was subjected to severe cross-examination by seasoned barristers. He was asked to explain the Caxton Hall incident. But in view of Savarkar's letter to 'The Times' the charges could not be sustained. Finally, the decision was announced. It said the charges had failed; Savarkar was a member of the Grays' Inn. But because of the atmosphere of suspicion, he should not be permitted to practice for the time being.

Babarao's sentence of life in exile, the inquiry in Gray's Inn, the Dhingra affair, and the Caxton Hall incident - all this told on Savarkar's mind and his health was broken. Since April, he had left India House and was staying as a paying guest at Bipin Chandra Pal's house. On November 13, 1909 a bomb was thrown at Viceroy Lord Minto. In that connection, his younger brother was arrested. Eight days later his elder brother's appeal was rejected, and the sentence of exile was confirmed. Being assailed with tides of misfortune his sister-in-law wrote a letter to him. In reply, Savarkar wrote a poem, 'Consolation', and sent it to her. At the end of December Savarkar had an attack of pneumonia. So he was removed to the clinic of Dr. Muthu in Wales. Here he got news of Jackson's murder. When Savarkar recovered considerably, he was sent to Paris by his friends.

In Paris Savarkar stayed for two months. He was putting up with Madam Cama. Even though he had come for convalescence, he would not remain idle. As Chitragupta has said, "The center of revolutionary activity had shifted from London to Paris."[1] Here he wrote articles for 'Talwar' and created awareness in the Indian community about Indian Independence and organized it. He also tried to recruit members for Abhinav Bharat. Further, he read an essay on 'How to make a revolution?' The theme of the essay was how to secretly help the revolutionary movement in spite of being in Government service. But there was a disagreement on this point. It has already been stated in the earlier chapter as to how he had sent a copy of the manuscript of Sikh history with an Indian painter and revolvers with an Italian lady. While all these activities were going on, he received letters which told him how his relatives and colleagues were being subjected to police harassment and torture. He also realized that he could be arrested on the strength of the statements made by Chaturbhuj and Koregaonkar.

This was a testing time in Savarkar's life. His mind was agitated with one question: What was his real duty? If he left his Paris refuge and went to a place where the British could reach him, it was likely he would lose his liberty.

Savarkar was the moving spirit behind the organization of the revolutionary party in India and in England and whatever that party had achieved.

---

[1]Chitragupta : Life of Barrister Savarkar - p.78

If he stepped aside or if he was put behind the bars by the government, the movement was sure to collapse. Like others, Savarkar was also aware of this fact.

Yet the matter had become complicated. Shyamaji Krishnavarma used to support the revolutionary activities thorough the columns of the 'Indian Sociologist'. Chattopadhyaya had written letters to 'The Times' saying that Shyamaji's activities were conducted from the Paris sanctuary.

Savarkar naturally thought that the same charge would be leveled against him after some time if he stayed in Paris. Dr. Bhat has mentioned that, when the conspiratorial activities of Abhinav Bharat were going on, Savarkar's critics used to complain that he only lectured and did not involve himself in any action.[1] In the early stage the leader has to face the danger personally to establish his primacy. Shivaji did not ask his followers to kill Afzulkhan or attack Shahistekhan. He carried out those tasks himself. Bajirao personally went to see the Nizam in his camp. Sometime the leader has to put his life in danger. It is a gamble. But great captains must have a gambler's instinct.

On doctor's advice Savarkar used to take morning walks daily in the gardens of Paris. One bright sunny morning, when the sky was clear, he went for a walk in the park. From time to time he came across ponds wherein swans, ducks, and other aquatic animals were floating about. Water lilies had bloomed. The scene was delightful to the eye. Here Savarkar reclined on the lawn and glanced through an Indian newspaper. It said that the first chapter of the Nasik conspiracy was over and that Kanhere and his colleagues had been sentenced to death. He reread the news again to see if his brother's name was there. Then he got up. The surrounding natural scene was soothing to his eyes. But suddenly he felt a mental jolt. His colleagues and followers were rotting in jail. Were they enjoying the pleasures of the garden, the sunny atmosphere, this beautiful natural scene? If they were not getting such pleasures, he felt it immoral to roam in this garden. He felt that he must, at least, run a risk of going to England. Savarkar used to preach that one must face jail, torture, or death for the freedom of the country. He thought the time for that test had come.

Savarkar returned home in an agitated state of mind. Later he got his colleagues together. He showed them the item of news from the paper, and explained to them why his return to London was necessary. He also showed them the letter Aiyar had written to him asking him to return to London within 4 to 6 weeks. Shyamaji Krishnavarma, Madam Cama, and barrister Rana tried to persuade him from returning to London. But Savarkar remained steadfast in his resolve.

On March 13, 1910 Savarkar left Paris. He crossed the English Channel and then took a train to London. Savarkar soon realized that he was being watched

---

[1] Dr. V. M. Bhat : Abhinav Bharat - p.72

from the stations along which the train passed. As he got off the train at Victoria Station, the police surrounded him and then took him to the waiting room. There he was served with a warrant and then locked up. Lack of warm clothing and the English cold woke him once or twice. Otherwise he slept like a log.

Next day the court proceedings began. Varma, Aiyar, and Chattopadhyaya began organizing his defense. Savarkar Defense Committee was formed under the chairmanship of Guy Aldred. Savarkar was now kept in Brixton jail. Some schemes to rescue him from jail were made from the time of his arrest. According to one scheme, some one was to stay behind in his place and Savarkar was to flee. But it did not work out. Another scheme was to attack the car in which Savarkar was being taken to the court and to rescue him. In this scheme the Irish revolutionaries were to help. But the car which was attacked was not carrying Savarkar. Garnett has mentioned in his autobiography another such attempt. After its failure, Garnett met Savarkar. Garnett writes about this meeting: "The moment he saw me he knew that the plan had miscarried. But as I told him the details, he was already trying to console me for my failure. There was not a single sign in him of reproach or bitterness, or even of shock... Then Savarkar said something like this: 'You have done wonderfully and there was no reason why you should have done anything at all. Do not worry about me. I shall escape somehow. I have a plan worked out already in case your plan failed.'"[1] The words 'I have a plan' are most significant. His Marseilles attempt shows what he meant.

On the first day when Savarkar was produced before the court, the proceedings were adjourned to March 21, 1910 as both the prosecution and defense were not in possession of all the relevant papers. On that day, the court was informed that the police officers, who were coming to take Savarkar to India, would reach London on April 9. The case was adjourned to April 13. On that day a bail application was made on behalf of Savarkar on the ground that the proceedings would be prolonged. It was rejected after a week. Later the issue, whether Savarkar should be sent to India or not, was argued. Finally the decision was given that he should be sent to India. Later on May 24 a Habeas Corpus petition was made on his behalf. This too was rejected. Appeals were made against both these decisions. These too were rejected. So the decision to send Savarkar to India received legal sanction. During this period Savarkar wrote a letter to Aiyar. In it he said that his weight had increased by two pounds and that but for the sentence of life in exile only change of clothes was necessary.

Levin, the biographer of Field Marshall Wavell, has written, "his choice of poems for other 'Men's Flowers' illuminate his mind: a mind which, on his own confession, drew on them for sustenance in battle, in perplexity, in times of stressful decision."[2] Savarkar's case appears to be similar. In times of crisis the

---

[1] David Garnet : The Golden Echo - p.160
[2] Roland Levin : The Chief, Field Marshall Lord Wavell - p.247

poet in him would come alive. 'My testament', 'Murti Duji Ti', and 'Farewell' were written during this imprisonment.

Savarkar was put on the S. S. Morea on July 1 after the court's decision to send him to India was delivered. When the ship left the harbor, Savarkar began to think seriously. By going to London he had shown that he was ready to face any kind of extreme danger. No one now would accuse him of saving his skin. To die on gallows or to rot in jail might be inevitable in certain circumstances. But surely it could never be a desirable thing. Savarkar had entered the lion's den and had twisted its tail. Now to escape from this den would also be a coup de grace. Shivaji had gone to see Aurangazeb at Agra. He had escaped from the latter's clutches by a stratagem. It was but natural that a man of Savarkar's adventurous spirit should feel that he should enact in his way that historic event.

The British government felt that, if Savarkar was taken to Marseilles by train, the Indian revolutionists might attempt to free him or Shyamaji might seek the help of French court. To avoid this contingency, the government decided to send him to India directly from London.

The voyage from London to Bombay was a long one. Savarkar guessed correctly that the ship would berth at one of the European ports for loading coal or for unloading goods.

Madam Cama, Aiyar, Shyamaji, Rana, and other revolutionists were in France. To put them and Savarkar off track, it was given out that the ship would not touch Marseilles. But whichever port the ship might touch, Savarkar had decided to jump it. He had suggested this indirectly to Garnett to which reference had been made earlier.

Coincidentally, while crossing the straits of Gibraltar, the ship developed some mechanical defect and was diverted to Marseilles. On July 7 at about 10 in the morning, the ship was moored alongside the quay in the dock. Savarkar seeing the port naturally felt that his colleagues would attempt to rescue him. But no such thing happened. On the other hand, Henri Leblias, a French police official, came on board the ship. He had with him an official letter addressed by the Commissioner of Police, London, to the Chief of Police, Paris. He showed the letter to inspector Parker. It said that precautions should be taken to prevent any demonstration or attempt on the part of Savarkar's friends residing in France to interview him or to facilitate his escape during the time Morea remained at Marseilles. Leblias promised every kind of help.

Savarkar felt that once the ship left Marseilles he would not get another opportunity to escape; in fact, such an attempt would become more difficult. So putting his fate in the lap of the gods, he decided on a bold attempt to escape. Accordingly, in the morning, he informed the sentry that he wanted to go to the toilet. So he was taken to the water closet. When he entered it, he flung his dressing gown on the glass window, thereby partially blocking the inside view and thus making it difficult for the sentry to know what was going on inside. Then he made a dash for the port-hole and wriggling his body out of it, he dived into the sea. Once in the water, he began to swim towards the quay. When he heard shots, he dived, and in a few minutes touched the quay. His first attempt to scale the wall failed. But the second one succeeded. He then began to run towards the city. His luck had held so far. But so far only!

Now he found that the police were pursuing him and shouting 'thief, thief'. It was about a mile-long pursuit. Tram-cars were running parallel in the direction Savarkar was running. Since he did not have a penny to buy a ticket he could not board them. At last he decided to seek the protection of the French police and he accosted one whom he saw first. Savarkar told him in broken French his plight and requested him to take him to the French Magistrate. Soon the British police came there. They greased the palm of the French police who handed Savarkar over to them. They dragged him to the ship. There some one hit him on the back of his head. With a violent jerk, he freed himself and leapt at the police who had hit him. He told him, 'Remember, before I die, I will kill one of you.' Then the pummeling stopped. Once on board, he was locked up in his cabin with extra security.

Madam Cama and Aiyar had rushed post-haste from Paris to Marseilles. But when they came to the quay, they found that Savarkar had freed himself, but was caught and locked up in a cabin on the ship. Then Aiyar and Madam Cama informed 'L'Humanite' about this event by wire. Later, both, along with Shyamaji, met the French Socialist leader Monsieur Jaures. It was because of his demand that the Savarkar issue was submitted the Hague Arbitration.

S. S. Morea, after hurriedly completing the repairs, left Marseilles on July 9. Now the police officials began to behave and talk rudely to Savarkar. So Savarkar told them, 'I have set fire to my house. I am now dead to myself. But remember that I will not die unless and until I have killed at least one of you.' Then there was a change in the attitude of the officials. Afterwards Savarkar said to them, 'In the circumstances in which we both are, our mutual interests are in conflict. You are dragging me to the gallows and I am trying to escape from your clutches'. Then the atmosphere cooled down a little. To reduce his mental tension, Savarkar as usual, composed a verse, 'Anadi mi, Avadhya mi, Anant me Bhala'. In course of time, Morea reached Port Said. There he came to know from one of the cooks that the Marseilles affair had made a commotion in the international world and its echoes were resounding in the European newspapers.

When Morea reached Eden, the passengers, the luggage and the post was transferred on to S. S. Sasti. In the next stage of the voyage, Savarkar suffered considerable physical discomfort because of heat and a confined place. This physical hardship and mental depression nearly tempted him to commit suicide. Soon the sea became rough and Savarkar thought how wonderful it would be if the ship was to sink. He also prayed for it. "O Sea! Once I prayed to you to take me back to my motherland. Now I pray that you take me in your womb. Let not my enemies exult over me." In some such words he prayed.

But no such thing occurred. S. S. Sasti anchored in Bombay. A launch took Savarkar to the quay. There a car was waiting for him. It brought him to Victoria Terminus. Here he was put on a train which reached Nasik in the afternoon. From the station he was taken to jail and was locked up.

Assassination of Jackson

"Blood of the martyrs is the seed of the Church" - Tertullian[1]

Savarkar had founded Abhinav Bharat to make a revolution in India. To organize the pledged young men of this organization, to start new branches at different places with their help, to propagate the idea of revolution in the ranks of the army and police, to collect a cache of arms in the Indian States and other places, and to await a favorable moment for an uprising was the plan of Abhinav Bharat. The activities of the organization continued after Savarkar went to England. According to the plan some pistols, guns, daggers, spears, etc. were collected by the local revolutionists. Also the overseas revolutionists had secured a bomb manual in Paris. After it was brought to India, hundreds of copies were made from it and distributed all over the country.

From a copy of this manual, K. G. Khare made some bombs and experimented with them at Pen. However, he did not write anything about his experience probably for one of the following two reasons. "He was not publicity-conscious, or he felt frustrated for suffering ten years of rigorous imprisonment without achieving anything."[2] But he had taught a number of young men the art of bomb-making. The process was simple. Any layman could learn it and then after observing the process on a few occasions he could make a bomb anywhere he liked. Damodar Chandratre, Aba Gaidhani, Vinayak Deshpande who was hanged alongside with Kanhere, Shankar Soman who was later sentenced to life in exile, Shridhar Barve, Trimbak Marathe, Ramachandra Bhate were among Khare's disciples.

Attempts to manufacture bombs according to the manual were made at Pen, Nasik, Kothur, Aundh, and Poona. But the attempt at Vasai deserves a special mention. Bhate, whose name has been mentioned earlier, got a job of an art teacher at Vasai. Here after sometime, he started the branch of Abhinav Bharat. Dr. Parulkar, Nathu and Sidhukaka Marathe, Bapurao Wagh, Advocate Thakur, Mukund Desai, Gopal and Gangadhar Gokhale, and others were members of this branch. Gopalrao Patankar went to Vasai sometime after the branch was started. He had a copy of the bomb manual. A meeting was held when Bhate introduced selected members to Patankar. In their talk it was decided that Bhate and Dr. Parulkar would bring material from Bombay for the manufacturing of bombs, and that Patankar would provide the money for it. But further financial arrangements were to be made by other members of the Vasai branch. Thus the bomb factory was started. Twice, the manufactured bombs were taken away by Patankar in trunks. In addition, a trunk-full of bombs were received by Anna Karve.

---

[1] John Bartlett : Familiar Quotations - p.69

[2] Dr. V. M. Bhat : Abhinav Bharat - p.73

The copy of the bomb-manual received in Maharashtra was thus utilized. Also, pistols sent by Savarkar and secretly brought by Chaturbhuj to Bombay were handed over to Patankar, who hid them at Pen. A few of these were used for assassinating Jackson. That these should fall in the hands of Kanhere appears to be an irony of fate! K. G. alias Anna Karve was first a member of Abhinav Bharat. But due to differences of opinion, he left it and started another secret organization. He held the view that revolutionary activities should be conducted secretly and that the organization should keep away from people who participate in public activities. Patankar sold some of the pistols brought by Chaturbhuj to Karve. The reason was this: A large quantity of chemicals and some instruments were needed for the bomb manufacturing factory at Vasai. These could be bought in Bombay for which money was needed. Once Patankar sold his family's ornaments. Again the need for money was felt. Karve wanted to kill Justice Davar. So he asked Patankar where he could buy pistols. Because of paucity of funds, Patankar went to Pen and from there he bought a few pistols and cartridges. Then, he told Karve that if he was paid Rs. 150.00, he would give Karve a few pistols and cartridges. So Karve paid that amount and collected the pistols. Soon Bhat came to know about this transaction. He then met Karve and it was decided between them that no precipitate action was to be taken. But without Karve's knowledge the web was being woven for the assassination of Jackson. Karve kept these pistols with Ganu Vaidya at Nasik.

Kashinath Tonpe was a member of the Abhinav Bharat branch at Yavale. He was a money-lender. His business brought him in contact with one Gangaram Rupchand of Aurangabad. Ganu Vaidya had gone to Rupchand to find out if arms could be procured. There he met Anant Kanhere. Talking to Ganu, Kanhere said, "When so much repression is going on in Nasik, why don't you revolutionists kill officials by way of revenge?" Ganu excused himself by saying that his people were not yet ready. To this Kanhere replied that if they were not ready to assassinate, he was ready to do that job. Ganu informed Kanhere's readiness to Deshpande, Soman, and Joshi who were members of the Karve's group. Later Kanhere came to Nasik and saw Jackson in his office, and finalized the details about his assassination. Then Ganu panicked. He told Kanhere that, if the police were to beat him, he would make a full confession. Kanhere, therefore, should refrain from such an action. He should put forward two conditions, namely, that two pistols should be provided to him and an associate should accompany him. Kanhere spoke accordingly. So Karve was summoned from Bombay who vetoed the idea of an assassination. As Kanhere was not getting an associate, Karve felt that the former's life should not be put in jeopardy. Kanhere then went back to Aurangabad.

Kanhere, however, became restless as he wanted to perform a memorable deed like Madanlal Dhingra. He informed Wamanrao Joshi that he alone was prepared to assassinate Jackson. Karve was in Nasik at this time. So with his consent Deshpande went to Aurangabad to fetch Kanhere. On December 21, 1909 Kanhere arrived in Nasik.

Now Karve sent for two Browning pistols from Ganu Vaidya. Later he felt that he should also be armed along with Kanhere. So he sent Soman to Ganu to procure a third pistol. Karve gave, through Soman, some poison to Kanhere to commit suicide in case he felt nervous after the act of assassination. Karve also suggested to Kanhere through Deshpande that in case of need he should use the second pistol to end his own life. Kanhere was a lad of 16 and he would not be able to explain why he had committed the act of assassination. So Karve wrote out for him a statement under the caption 'Killing for revenge'. He also warned Kanhere not to disclose his real name but to say that his name was Ramprasad Tiwari and that he was a resident of Kashi.

Jackson was working as the Collector of Nasik since 1907. He was a mild mannered man. He knew Sanskrit and Marathi extremely well. He was, therefore, playfully called 'Pandit Jackson' by some people. Knowing Marathi, he spoke with the local people in their native tongue. He used to say that he must be a Shastri of Nasik in his previous life in view of his fondness for the natural beauty of the Godavari River and of his attachment to Sanskrit literature. He felt that his carrot and stick policy had changed the atmosphere of Nasik. In the afternoon of the day on which he was assassinated, he had said that he felt gratified that he was instrumental in removing prejudices from the minds of both the government and the people. He was transferred because his term of office had come to an end. But he was responsible for issuing orders to prohibit meetings in Nasik, for arresting and prosecuting Babarao Savarkar, for taking bond from advocate Khare, and for releasing William, an engineer who had killed a coachman, for lack of evidence. So, according to the Karve group, it was justifiable to assassinate him.

As Jackson was leaving Nasik, a number of programs for giving him a hearty send-off were being arranged. At that time the Kirloskar Company was at Nasik. Bal Gandharva's acting in the play 'Sharada' was riveting. Jackson had good knowledge of Marathi drama. He was very keen to see the play. So, for his convenience its show was fixed on December 21. At about 8 p.m. Kanhere came to the Vijayanand Theater armed with two pistols. Jackson was delayed owing to other engagements. He came at about 9:30 p.m. and was proceeding hurriedly to his chair when Kanhere whipped out a pistol and shot Jackson in the back. Kanhere did not stop at that. He came in front of Jackson and fired a few more shots at him. Then to shoot himself, he put his pistol to his temple, when deputy collector Khopkar seized his hand and one Mr. Jolly seized his other hand. Then Kanhere stood there calmly. Jackson was dead.

It had been agreed that Kanhere was not to disclose his name. And yet he gave his true identity to the police who quickly spread their dragnet. Ganu Vaidya was arrested. In the search of his house, one Browning pistol and some bottles of acid were recovered. When asked who gave him these things, he mentioned Karve's name. Under police torture, Karve disclosed Patankar's name who too was arrested. To save the small bomb factory at Vasai, Patankar confessed that Chaturbhuj gave him the pistols. When Chaturbhuj learnt that Patankar had blown the gaff, he told the police that he had bought these pistols from Savarkar and that he had been to see Bhat and Thatte on Savarkar's instructions and that he had handed over the pistols to Patankar on Bhat's directions. He also volunteered to become a state witness. "Thus the chain of Jackson assassination began with Kanhere and ended with Savarkar in London."[1]

A number of people were arrested in connection with Jackson's assassination and all had to face rigorous police investigation. Few could stand the police torture. Guider was specially appointed for this investigation. He had ordered that the pistols and other material must be secured from the accused, even if they were to die in the process. For collecting evidence, the police tortured both the accused and the witnesses. The police atrocities were not published. Under new regulations, the accused could not see a lawyer. They could not complain to their relatives or friends. For, such complaining would only have increased their anxiety. And even if the news could reach the newspapers, none would have dared to publish it.

Even in these circumstances some police officers were helpful. One of them was Inspector Sadavarte. He first sent for Bhat for an interrogation and in the process gave him tea. He then asked him if he knew Rambhau Datar. Bhat said that he knew him. Then Sadavarte said that he was very friendly with Datar and Ganapatrao Phadke of Poona. Naturally Bhat asked him why he could not help them. "What help do you need?" asked Sadavarte. "I want to see Patankar," replied Bhat. Then Sadvarte sent for Patankar and then told both of them: "You decide amongst yourself what statement you both would like to make. We want pistols... When we get them, I will ensure that your other activities are covered... In this matter I will give you every help you need.... It will be better if you trust me... No one is going to help you."[2] Sadavarte kept his word; and no one came to know anything about the bomb factory at Vasai and all the members of Abhinav Bharat from that place remained safe.

There is another such instance. Bhat and Nagpurkar, after their arrest, were brought to the Police Commissioner's office in Bombay. Then the Commissioner told his subordinate to beat them and see if they would make a confession. That officer took both of them to the lock-up and said, 'you only shout, I will not touch you at all. Your shouting will convince that rascal that I am beating you severely.' After some hours, he informed the Commissioner that both were tough and had refused to confess. Then the Commissioner left both of them alone.[3]

The investigating authorities collected all the evidence by means of torture, intimidation and inducements, but found it was not possible to involve all

---

[1] Dr. V. M. Bhat : Abhinaav Bharat - p.146

[2] Dr. V. M. Bhat : Abhinav Bharaat -p.102

[3] Dr. V. M. Bhat : Abhinav Bharaat -p.154

the accused in the Jackson assassination. So, they instituted a separate case against Kanhere, Karve, Deshpande, Soman, Wamanrao Joshi, Ganu Vaidya, and D. P. Joshi charging them under 302 I.P.C. The case was tried and the first three accused were sentenced to death, the next three were sent for life in exile and the last D. P. Joshi was sentenced to 2 years' imprisonment. Kanhere, Karve, and Deshpande were hanged on April 19, 1910 in the Thana Jail. Incidentally it may be mentioned here that after Jackson's assassination, Savarkar wrote an article in 'Talwar,' which was published in Paris, under the caption 'Martyrs of Nasik.'

After the Jackson case was over the Government started proceeding against the remaining members of Abhinav Bharat. They were charged with conspiracy to wage war against the British Government, and committing offense under the Explosives Act. First, the government wanted to charge all the accused with waging war, but it was found that the charges were unsustainable and so these were dropped. Then the Special Tribunal decided that except for 121-A, of I.P.C., the other charges were not sustainable. The Special Tribunal had 2 cases before it. The first case involved 38 accused including Savarkar. In the other only Savarkar was involved.

In the first case Savarkar contended that he did not accept the court's jurisdiction as he was illegally arrested on the soil of France. He further contended that his case was pending before the International Tribunal at The Hague and therefore he could not take part in the proceedings till that Tribunal delivered its judgment.

How did Savarkar's case go before Hague Tribunal? To find the answer to that question, we have to go back to the incident at Marseilles. In the previous chapter we saw how Savarkar had jumped the ship at Marseilles and had landed on French soil. But he was caught and brought on board the ship and taken to India. Madam Cama and Aiyyar had visualized that Savarkar would try to get off the ship at Marseilles and had dashed there to help him. But unfortunately there was a delay and Savarkar and his rescuers missed each other. But having known that Savarkar had landed on French soil and that he was being forcibly taken back to India, Madam Cama, Aiyar, and Shyamaji began to bring pressure on the French government.

Madam Cama sent the following wire to Barrister Baptista: "See immediately professionally Savarkar arriving Bombay Steamer Morea. French government demands his return. Choose your solicitor. Letter follows."

In France the Paris edition of 'Daily Mail' carried a small news item buried down in the columns mentioning Savarkar's bold attempt at escape. But this small item proved a spark. The socialist leader Monsieur Jean Jaures took up the issue. Also, Jean Languet, the grandson of Marx, commented in his paper 'Humanite' as under: 'This abominable violation of the right of asylum was effected in absolute secrecy. Had it not been for a telegram published yesterday in the Paris 'Daily Mail', we should still have been ignorant of the incident. But, it is quite impossible that the matter can be allowed to rest there.' In England it was Guy Aldred who took up cudgels for Savarkar. Newspapers in anti-British countries, like Germany, found an excellent topic to snub Britain. Jean Jaures and other prominent French leaders put such pressure on their government that it had to take cognizance of the matter. Being convinced that Savarkar had landed on French soil, the French government requested the British government that, in view of the fact that Savarkar actually landed on French soil, it should suspend the trial, till full reports of the case were received.

There were foreign embassies in India. It was but natural that people should be curious to know their reactions about the Marseilles affair. Reporters interviewed some embassy officials. The Spanish Charge d' affairs Monsieur Pierron said that the French police should have handed Savarkar over to his superiors. In handing him over to the British police, they had committed a grave error. The French demand that Britain should hand over Savarkar to France was reasonable. The Paraguayan ambassador Monsieur Jambon said that the French policeman who handed over Savarkar to the officials from the S. S. Morea had no knowledge of the law. He was not a judge; his action therefore could not be viewed as though it was an act of the French government. 'Pioneer', a newspaper, quoting Walker, an authority on international law, said, "That the surrender of a fugitive must be a national act. A surrender by local authorities is invalid unless local authorities are expressly authorized by their government to give up a criminal."

In the controversy that was raging in the newspapers in France and England, a novel issue was introduced. It was this: Savarkar's case could not be decided according to international law only. There were treaties between England and France signed in 1876 and 1896 governing these matters. These also had to be taken into consideration. The Daily Mail wrote an editorial about this controversy. "The illegality of Savarkar's surrender is so plain that the only defense so far attempted has been to suggest that the British government can not be responsible for the errors of a French policeman. That argument is utterly fallacious because the error and the offense were committed by the French policeman in conjunction with British officials and would have been impossible without the co-operation of British officials. We need not dwell upon the fatal consequences if we insist in not returning Savarkar to French custody and taking chances under the extradition treaty. Having ourselves maintained the legitimacy of our action, we should be unable to protest, if a British policeman were, in the future, to hand over a fugitive Garibaldi or Kossuth to a foreign government. The right of asylum, instead of being under the protection of the law, would be at the mercy of the arbitrary caprice or the corruptibility of the meanest police constable."

'Morning Post' conceded 'that a British political prisoner, who has just stepped on foreign soil frees himself from the jurisdiction of the British government.' On September 6, 1910 a session of the International Socialist

Congress was held in Copenhagen. The British Labor leader, Keir Hardie, was present at that session. He moved a resolution that a person seeking safety in a foreign country should have a right of asylum and that right should be treated as sacred by all and according to that right Savarkar should be handed over to the French government.

However, there were protests. When the news was published that without waiting for The Hague decision and rejecting Savarkar's plea that the court had no jurisdiction to try him, the proceedings against him had been started. 'Justice', a liberal newspaper, wrote: "In order that Savarkar might not have a fair trial, defended by counsel and safeguarded by public opinion in England, he was sent back to India where, innocent or guilty, his condemnation could be officially secured."

Now France and Britain signed an agreement to refer the issues pertaining to Savarkar's case to the International Tribunal at The Hague. This agreement was signed by Paul Cambon on behalf of France and by Edward Grey on behalf of Great Britain. L'Humanite warned that it was a mistake to handle Savarkar's case in such a superficial manner. The president of the Tribunal that was to be constituted according to the agreement was M. Beernaert the former premier of Belgium. His colleagues were to be Mr. Graham of Norway and Mr. Lohman of Holland. The British representative on this Tribunal was Earl of Desert and the French representative was Louis Renault. The agreement consisted of six articles.

Though the dispute referred to The Hague Tribunal was between France and England, its decision was bound to affect Savarkar's fate. Hence it was necessary that he should have been called before the Tribunal to plead his case. But this was not done. M.P. T. Acharya wrote that Jean Longuet pleaded for Savarkar at the instance of Jean Jaures.[1] The proceedings of this Tribunal were held in camera except for the opening and closing days. Naturally the justness of its decision became suspect in the public eye. The proceedings were to start on February 14, 1911, but there was a delay of two days. Within a short period of one week the Tribunal gave its award. It said in conclusion: "Whereas while admitting that an irregularity was committed by the arrest of Savarkar and by his being handed over to the British police, there is no rule in international law imposing, in circumstances such as those which have been set out above, any obligation on the power which has in its custody a prisoner to restore him because of a mistake committed by the foreign agent who delivered him up to that power."

'Post' the German newspaper, while criticizing this award, said that it had side-tracked the main issue. 'Manchester Guardian' said that the award would shock the public. 'The Daily News' said: "The judgment reduces the right of asylum to very narrow limits. According to the judgment, to put the matter in its

---

[1] S. L. Karandikar : Savarkar Charitra - p.409

extreme form, a Prince Kropotkin might conceivably be kidnapped by Russian agents in collusion with British police and without the knowledge or consent of the British government and no rule of international law could be invoked for his restoration." This award angered Shyamaji Krishnavarma. He said, "The decision of the International Tribunal at The Hague has shattered all faith in the maintenance of the rights of political refugees as ordinarily understood and it is sad to observe that the nations hitherto most conspicuous for their love of liberty are slow to recognize these rights when they are beset by political consideration."

But this criticism had no effect on the British Government. The adverse award of The Hague grievously hurt Savarkar. Now he had to undergo the penalty of fifty years of imprisonment given to him before The Hague award was announced. It is now necessary to return to the account of the cases in which Savarkar was convicted.

After Savarkar was taken to Nasik and confined there, Barrister Baptista began his efforts to see him as instructed by Madam Cama. First, he sought permission from the police Commissioner and then from the Home Department. But he drew a blank. An application was sent to Montgomery, the first magistrate at Nasik, through the solicitors Daftary, Pereira, and Dewan. It was rejected on the grounds that under the new ordinance, no advocate could meet Savarkar, that he had not asked for such a meeting and Madam Cama had no locus standi in this case. The solicitors sent another application. In it they stated that they had received the papers concerning the case from Mr. Vaughan, who was Savarkar's solicitor in London, and that they were seeking an interview with him on behalf of his family. They also added that Baptista wanted to see Savarkar to tell him that France had demanded his return. From the day that Savarkar was brought to Nasik about six weeks had passed in the police inquiry. Here Savarkar got full details about the local happenings from some of the accused. So he advised all the co-accused that, if the gravity of their offense could be mitigated and thereby they would get lighter sentences, they should freely lay the blame on him. Savarkar showed the true quality of leadership by assuming full responsibility for all that had happened.

When the prosecution's case was prepared, the preliminary hearing began before the first class magistrate, Montgomery. He completed the hearing and committed the case to the sessions court. The government had by then promulgated the Special Tribunal Act. Under this act it constitutes a Special Tribunal consisting of Chief Justice Sir Basil Scott, Justice Narayanrao Chandavarkar, and Justice Heaton. It was before this Tribunal that the case of Savarkar and other co-accused began on September 15, 1910. Already Savarkar had been brought from Yerwada jail and lodged in Dongri jail.

The news of this case had created quite a stir amongst the people. But ordinary people were barred from the court. The High Court building was surrounded by the police, and the police commissioner was personally supervising the security arrangements in the court. Except for the reporters of 'The Times of India', 'Sanj Vartaman', and 'Induprakash' no other reporters were allowed. As the number of accused was considerable, a large dock with benches was constructed to accommodate all of them. The accused were seated on these benches. Savarkar was brought to the court in a closed van before the judges occupied their benches.

Savarkar had an imperial presence. And at this time he was in his late twenties. He was attired in European clothes. With his fair skin, he looked very smart in these clothes. When he was brought in, there was applause. Savarkar was startled. He quickly looked around. The court room was empty. And then his eyes turned to the dock. The accused sitting in it had clapped. Now Savarkar was taken there. As he stepped into the dock, the other accused welcomed him. It was a touching scene. Savarkar took his seat amongst them and then the test began as to whom he was able to recognize. Savarkar's younger brother Narayanrao was 22 years old. Savarkar could not recognize him immediately as he had changed considerably. Before the proceedings began, the court suggested to Savarkar that he could take a seat amongst the advocates. But Savarkar politely declined this offer, and said that he was more comfortable amongst the co-accused.

The prosecution was led by Advocate General, Mr. Jardin, Mr. Weldon, Mr. Velinkar, and Mr. Nicolson. The accused were represented by Mr. Rangnekar, Barrister Gadgil, Barrister Chitre, and Barrister Baptista. On September 15, the proceedings began. Jardine opened the case by giving its background and then suggested that all the cases should be conducted together. The defense objected to this suggestion and asked for an adjournment for studying the papers. The case was, therefore, adjourned for eleven days. On September 26, the proceedings began again. At this stage the court's permission was sought to submit an application to both France and England on behalf of Savarkar. This was turned down. Then the defense argued that all accused and all the charges should not be tried together. When the court asked Savarkar what he had to say in this connection, he replied that, as he did not wish to participate in the proceedings, he had no comments to offer.

The court gave its order that all the accused and all the charges should be tried together. So the prosecution continued. The prosecution withdrew the charge of waging war against the Emperor. Later the examination of the witnesses began. After one witness named Gosawi was examined, the court asked Savarkar if he had any questions to ask. To which he replied: "It is my rightful demand that France should give me its protection... I went there in the hope of getting asylum. But the British police forcibly brought me back. Hence this court has no jurisdiction over me and so I do not wish to take part in the present proceedings." Later the court, giving its decision, said that though an illegal action might have taken place at Marseilles in arresting Savarkar, still that did not affect the jurisdiction of the Indian court.

Then Parker, the Scotland Yard official who had accompanied Savarkar on his voyage on board the Morea, was examined. He narrated some of the incidents from Savarkar's life in London, such as, Savarkar's utterances that 'Sikhs should revolt' made during Guru Govind Singh festival, things that were found with him when he was arrested at Victoria Station and about the pistols used in Jackson's assassination. Then Inspector Favel from Bombay C.I.D. was examined. He deposed about the articles found with Chanjeri Rao when he was searched.

The key witness was Ganu Vaidya. He was sentenced to life imprisonment in the Jackson murder case. He was the state's witness in the present case. He first deposed about the constitution and functioning of the revolutionary organizations in Nasik. Then he narrated how the arms and funds necessary for their purchase were collected. He further added as to how pistols were received and distributed, and how experiments were made for the manufacture of bombs. After the deposition of Ganu Vaidya, the other state witnesses, namely, Ankushakar, Joshi, and Kulkarni were examined. Then police inspector Ballal from Nasik was examined. He deposed that when the house of Savarkar brothers was searched he found along with the copies of Mazzini's biography the following books: Science of War, Infantry Sword Exercise, and Military Engineering. As these books give an idea of what Savarkar had read in his study of the 'Art of War', a reference to them has been made here.

At this stage, the court discharged three accused, namely, Shankar Vaidya, Barve, and Fulambrikar. Then the search witnesses, Deputy Collector Palshikar, Khopkar, and others were examined. Inspector Zarapkar deposed that in his search at Dhule two Browning pistols, two cartridges, one bullet, a manual for the operation of Browning pistols were found. Inspector Kokje deposed how he recovered pistols from Konkar and Davare. The cross examination of some of the witnesses revealed how the police had tortured the accused. In his cross examination Assistant Collector Montgomery admitted that some of the accused had complained that the police had tortured them for obtaining their confession, but that he did not inquire into their complaint.

After the prosecution rested, the Chief Justice told the accused that they could make statements if they wished to do so. Nearly all the accused stated that their earlier statements were false. After he heard them, the Chief Justice told Savarkar to make his statement. To this Savarkar replied: "I am completely innocent ... I took part in court proceedings in London... Because those courts are not founded on brute force. The situation of the Indian Courts is different... I do not recognize the jurisdiction of this court. Hence, I decline to make any statement." When the defense informed the court that it would lead no evidence, the Advocate General Jardine began his arguments for the prosecution on December 3, and ended them on December 10. On behalf of his defense, Baptista argued for four days, Rangnekar for two days, Gadgil for three days, and Chitre and Sethna for two days.

December 24, 1910 was fixed as the Day of Judgment. As the danger began to cast its ominous shadows, the poet in Savarkar came alive. On the previous day he composed a poem: 'Pleased be Thou Mother! To acknowledge this service of thy children' under the caption 'First Installment'. He had composed it in order to tell his compatriots that he was making a part-payment of the debt he owed to his motherland.

The Day of Judgment proved dramatic. The accused in the dock were indulging in witty conversations. They had playfully fixed classes for the examination results. One who got a sentence for life in exile was considered as passed in first class; one who got a little lesser punishment was considered as passed in second class; and one who escaped with lighter punishment was considered as passed in third class; and one who was acquitted was declared failed.

The judges came and took their seats. The witty conversations stopped. The examination results began to be announced. The first name announced was that of Savarkar. He was sentenced to life in exile and his property was forfeited. Savarkar rose a little from his seat to indicate the acceptance of the sentence and loudly said 'Vande Mataram'. Then the others were awarded various sentences: Chandwadkar 15 years; Marathe, Khare, and Patankar 10 years each; Nagpurkar 7 years; Bhat, Gohre, Chandratre, Dandekar, and Dharap 5 years each; Shidhaye, Palande, Paranjape, and Bhave 4 years each; Kelkar, Tonpe, Konkar, Davare, and Gokhale 3 years each; Tikhe, Barve, and Kashikar 2 years each; Manohar Rupchand, Ambdekar, and Narayan Savarkar 6 months each. Eight other accused were acquitted; three others had been acquitted earlier.

These were terrible sentences. There were no facilities of class 'A', parole, etc. available to these accused. If there was an expectation that these sentences would cow the accused, it proved false. The judges rose. The others rose in deference to them. The accused also stood in the dock. But they stood to shout the slogan 'Hail thee, Goddess of Independence.' This slogan shouting startled all. The police rushed. The Commissioner lost his temper and shouted, 'Hold them, beat them, they are prisoners now'. Even then slogan shouting continued. Police turned their attention first to Savarkar. They hand-cuffed him and brought him out of the dock, As he moved out of the dock, he took off his hat and waving farewell to all, walked away.

On January 23, 1911, the second case against Savarkar began before the same Tribunal. In this case he was charged with the abatement of Jackson's murder. His friends and relatives tried hard to persuade him to defend himself in this case as it was likely that he might be awarded the death penalty. But as Savarkar had abstained from participation in the first case, it would have looked inconsistent if he were to participate in the second case. So he stuck to his decision of non-participation.

After he was charged, he was called upon to make his statement. Savarkar informed the court that he considered himself to be under the jurisdiction of France and hence was not willing to participate in the proceedings. Then witnesses were examined and their evidence was recorded. After the prosecution rested, Savarkar said that he wanted to make a submission. So he was taken out of the dock and brought to the table of the advocates. Then Savarkar said: "I still maintain that I have no connection direct or indirect with Jackson's murder. I am in a quandary and hence have to abstain from taking any part in the proceedings against me. If I were to participate I would have proved that the first charge was not tenable. No evidence had been brought on record that would connect me to Patankar or that would show connection between Patankar and Karve. The only evidence brought forward to show that I abetted the murder was the booklet 'Vande Mataram', found from Chanjeri Rao. But that booklet could not be linked with the Jackson murder as the evidence showed that the booklet was sent after the murder of Jackson."

On January 30, 1911, the court gave its verdict. It held that it had been proved that the accused was involved in the Jackson's murder and hence was being awarded the sentence of life in exile. When Savarkar heard the sentence, he rose and uttered the following inspiring and memorable words: "I am prepared to face ungrudgingly the extreme penalty of your laws in the belief that it is through sufferings and sacrifice alone that our beloved Motherland can march on to an assured, if not a speedy, triumph." After his above utterance, he was hand-cuffed and taken out of the court. While he was on his way to jail, he was humming the lines of the poem he had recently composed.

Exile for life

".. got some papers concerning Savarkar brothers' case to read. At this time he (Tilak) began to talk to himself about the inhumanity of punishment. 'It is better to kill a man who has been working only for the good of his country, instead of sending him to life imprisonment. He has to suffer a lot of mental anguish while spending his life in jail.'" - Lokamanya Tilak[1]

Savarkar was told that the decision of the International Tribunal at The Hague had gone against him and that the sentence of 50 years had now begun to run and that henceforward he would get only convict's food and clothing. Then he was given an iron badge on which was carved 1960 as the year of his release. During the process of giving the badge, one officer with gallows humor said, "The merciful government will certainly release you in 1960." The sentence of 50 years would have stunned anyone. But even in that situation Savarkar's ready wit did not forsake him. He retorted, "Death is more kind. It may release me earlier!" The officer understood. Then all of them went away. Now alone in that gloomy cell Savarkar sat trying to bear the blow of the sentence of 50 years. Charles Dickens in his novel 'A Tale of Two Cities', while writing about the man, who had been incarcerated in the Bastille for eighteen years, has used the words 'Buried alive'. Whenever reference is made to Savarkar's two sentences of life imprisonment, Dickens' words 'buried alive' begin to ring in my ears. Savarkar has described his horrible prison life in his classic book 'My Transportation'. Its reading is a horrifying experience. This book is of about 430 pages and can easily command an honorable place in world literature.

The sentences passed against Savarkar began to run in March 1911. At this time he was in the Dongri jail. Commenting on the award of The Hague Tribunal, one Anglo-Indian newspaper wrote. "The rascal has at last met with his fate." When an officer told him this comment, Savarkar remarked, "Is that all? In Europe, they call me martyr. Here I am called a rascal. So praise cancels abuse and my original standing remains as it was." Savarkar's brother-in-law and his wife came to see him in these early days after the sentence had commenced. This meeting was like a thunderbolt. But Savarkar made light of it. Consoling his wife he said, "to procreate and to nidify is what is called domestic bliss then such a life is led by sparrows and crows. But if a higher meaning is to be given to life then we have fulfilled our duties. We have broken our few cooking utensils in order that in times to come fortune probably will smile on thousands of people." One wonders whether men who are now enjoying the perquisites of power after independence are really aware of the hardships Savarkar suffered for his country.

Later Savarkar was shifted from Dongri jail to Byculla jail. Here Savarkar made two applications: one, he should be given milk; two, he should be

---

[1]V. S. Bapat : Lokamanya Tilak yanchya athawani va akhyaika, Vol 1 - p.91

given books to read. The first request was rejected. As for books, he got the Bible to read only after the day's labor was over. Earlier Savarkar had submitted an application requesting that his sentences for life in exile should run concurrently. He had argued that a sentence for life meant the active period of a man's life. In India, it is calculated as between 20 to 25 years. Hence his two sentences for life should be combined. This application was rejected while Savarkar was in Byculla jail. From here, he was shifted to Thana jail. Here he came to know that his younger brother was in one of the nearby cells. Both were able to communicate with each other on a slate with the help of a kind warder.

One day in the month of June 1911, Savarkar was taken from the Thana jail in a car to the railway station. There he was put in a special compartment whose windows were closed. With the exception of one station, the windows of the compartment remained closed at all stations. At last the train reached Madras. The accompanying British officer, before bidding good-bye, said, "I think with the grace of God you will be released at the time of Coronation in December. The impression created by your dignified courage will never be effaced from my mind."

The name of the ship that was to carry Savarkar to the Andamans was 'Maharaja'. It was an apt name for a ship transporting a prince of revolutionaries. All kinds of thoughts were bound to surge in a prisoner's mind embarking on this ship. Savarkar has expressed his feelings in the following words: 'To embark on that Maharaja Ship by a lifer was just like being tied to a bier while alive.' When he came on board the ship, he was taken to the lowest deck and was locked in the cellar. Here Savarkar found it difficult to breathe and he began to have chest pains. Then he was allotted a place near the bar where he could get some fresh air. When the ship steamed out, some convicts wailed because they were cut off from home. The filth in the cellar made Savarkar very uncomfortable. But remembering the story of Ramakrishna Paramahansa and the verses of Saint Ramdas, Savarkar passed the days during the voyage. The traders on this ship gave a dinner of rice, fish, and pickles to all the prisoners with the permission of the ship's captain to express their respect for Savarkar.

On July 4, 1911 the Maharaja docked at Port Blair in the Andamans. Then the prisoners disembarked. Other prisoners were first taken towards the jail. Then in the custody of the English officers Savarkar began to march in the same direction. The climb was a little steep. On the way a thought crossed Savarkar's mind: "I am walking up on the road that leads from the sea to the Andamans. Will I ever in this life walk back on the same road to the sea to go to India from the Andamans?"

The climb ended. The door of the Cellular Jail was reached. A few minutes later the door opened creakily. Savarkar entered inside. The various instruments of torture, such as hand-cuffs, fetter, etc. were suspended from the upper middle part of the two iron gates of that dreadful jail. If one lost courage while looking at them, it was pardonable. But Savarkar's mind remained unmoved. He had read biographies of Russian and other foreign revolutionists. He was going through the same experience. He felt an utter satisfaction that he was not intimidated by this fearful spectacle.

While he was lost in these thoughts, he suddenly saw a stout European officer standing in front of him. He was Barrie, the tyrant of the Silver Jail. After both had looked at each other, Barrie said to the sergeants, "Leave him; he is not a tiger." Then a conversation took place between them. In that a reference was made to the attempt to escape at Marseilles. Then Barrie said that he was an Irishman, that he had participated in the struggle for Ireland's independence; but since then his views had undergone a change. When Savarkar queried: "Is it not the age rather than wisdom which has made him change his views?" Barrie replied, "Murders are murders." Then Savarkar asked him why this wisdom was not taught to the members of Sinn Fein society in Ireland. Barrie finally said that Savarkar should not break the rules, otherwise he would be compelled to punish him; and he further told Savarkar not to make an attempt to escape from here. To this Savarkar replied that he was aware that Port Blair was not Marseilles.

Savarkar came to the Andaman jail in 1911 and was sent back to an Indian jail in 1921. That means he was in this jail for 10 years. It is a long stretch of time. During this time he conducted many activities. Also, a few events occurred in his life here. This story could be narrated in two ways: one, according to time sequence; the other subject-wise. The account of Savarkar's life in London has been narrated subject-wise. The same method is adopted here. Savarkar's life can be classified subject-wise as follows. 1. His jail life. 2. His studies. 3. The activities he conducted and the organizations he created. 4. His literary output.

Savarkar was first locked up in the seventh barrack. Before he was taken there, he was told to take a bath. For purposes of bathing and work, he was given a loin-cloth. As he had not taken a shower for four or five days, Savarkar looked upon this permission as godsend. But soon he was disillusioned. He received three bowls of water and it was salty. His eyes smarted. His body became sticky. His hair became rough. When his bathing was over, he was taken to the third floor of the barrack and was locked up. The barrack was completely vacated in order to keep Savarkar in solitary confinement. Only three Pathan warders were posted as guards.

Savarkar was kept in this confinement for 14 days. Then one day he was brought down and given the work of threshing coconut husks. First he was given one pound of husk. But Savarkar's hands got blistered while pounding the husks. As he had to continue doing this work, his hands began to bleed. So Savarkar showed his hands and requested that he should be given another type of work or should be released from this work for sometime. But the superintendent replied, "All people experience the same trouble. You must thank the government that you were not given two pounds of husks."

For about a month Savarkar did this work of pounding the husks. Then one day the superintendent met Savarkar and said, "Now you will have to go to the oil-press." Barrie smilingly said, "Savarkar has been promoted to the upper class." On the same day in the evening Barrie sent for Savarkar and told him that he had to give him work in the oil-press under the orders of his superiors. But looking to Savarkar's status he had arranged that Savarkar would work for 14 days in the oil-press. He would not burden him like other prisoners with this heavy work from time to time; so Savarkar should not refuse this work. He would try to help him but Savarkar should avoid actions which will result in punishment.

Next morning Savarkar was taken to barrack number 6 where the oil-press was located. On reaching the place he found a Burmese convict working. He was there to help Savarkar. But this concession was in the oil-press work. To one not used to hard labor, the work itself was back-breaking. And the intention of the officialdom in giving this hard work to political prisoners was to break their resistance. Draping himself with a loin-cloth, Savarkar had to go round and round pressing the hand oil-press. This continuous circumambulation made Savarkar giddy. His body would ache at night. Also, the day's quota would remain unfulfilled as he was not used to this work. A week later Barrie came and said, "The next-door prisoner gives thirty pounds of oil by 2 p.m. and you work till evening and yet your quota is short by two pounds. You should be ashamed of this." These remarks would have stung anyone. Savarkar replied with acerbity, "If I were a coolie, I would have felt ashamed. You ask that convict to compose a sonnet in an hour and see how far he fulfills his task! I will knock it off in half an hour. He should not be ashamed for his inability to compose a sonnet, because that is not his job. Those officers who put educated men to work in an oil-press and appoint illiterate persons to clerkship should be ashamed of their method of work."

While working in the oil-press, his body would sweat profusely and the chaff and flour and the filth would stick to it. Savarkar loathed his naked, dirty body. One day while working in intense heat, Savarkar felt giddy and he sat down. He had cramps in his stomach and he held it tightly. In this condition he fell in a stupor just for a few minutes. Then consciousness returned. But the surrounding made no impression on his mind. This was a tranquil, blank and impassive condition. This blankness was akin to death. That night Savarkar felt an unbounded temptation to commit suicide. But his reason overcame emotion.

In this hapless, pitiable, and distressing condition of life, a few cheering things occurred sometimes. The convicts used to express their love, respect, and devotion to him in various ways. One or two convicts would help him secretly in the oil-press work. Some political prisoners would wash his clothes and dishes. The warders harassed them for doing such work. Some times Savarkar would wash the clothes of other prisoners. When they learnt about it, they felt distressed. So Savarkar decided to allow them to do his work.

In the first six months of his incarceration, Savarkar was kept in strict solitary confinement. Other prisoners were sent out of the jail after six months. The only concession that was given to Savarkar was that he could sit alone outside his cell during the day. After 14 days in the oil-press, Savarkar was shifted from there and was given the work of rope making. This considerably reduced his physical hardships. He started this work by sitting outside his cell.

Savarkar got the same food that was given to other prisoners. It consisted of gruel, a bowl of rice, two chapattis - flattened wheat cakes - and a vegetable. Once or twice a week a mug of yogurt was served. But these items of food did not always reach the hands of the prisoners. The chapattis and yogurt had to be given as offerings to wardens and petty officers. Sometimes there was little rock-oil in the gruel. Often chapattis were half baked and the rice was half-cooked. Once in a while the vegetables would contain small reptiles and centipedes. Savarkar protested against such things. But Barrie would imploringly tell him: "You don't worry about these rascals." But repeated complaints had the desired effect and at the end of five or six years there was some improvement in the quality of food.

Having been tired of this hard and humiliating life, the political prisoners had once gone on strike before Savarkar's arrival. Now the number of political prisoners had increased considerably. The political prisoners, who had gone out of the jail, had to undergo greater hardships in the settlement areas and had come back to the jail. One of them was Indubhushan Roy. He was one of the accused in the Maniktola Conspiracy Case. Later because of the hardships and humiliation, he committed suicide. For offenses of writing letters, Savarkar once had to undergo punishment of one month's solitary confinement and at another time he had to suffer a sentence of a week's standing hand-cuffs. Ultimately it was decided to go on strike. As the political prisoners refused to work, their daily food was reduced. Some got little food, while others got only gruel. There was some beating. This caused a riot. Savarkar told Barrie that the enraged young men would not hesitate to hit back. Then the dispute was settled. And those who were sent out of jail were given lighter work.

In 1913 Reginauld Craddock, Home Secretary visited the Andamans. When he met Savarkar, he said to him, "How have you ruined yourself by your own hands! If your knowledge and ability were properly utilized, you would have got any top position in the government." Later there was a discussion about revolutionaries, namely, about the Gaddar movement and Hardayal. Afterwards Craddock asked him, "What are your grievances?" Savarkar listed them. Then Craddock said, "If there were Hindu kings, there would have been more cruelty. They used to kill rebels under the feet of an elephant." Savarkar's riposte was: "In the olden times rebels were killed under the foot of an elephant; but when rebels triumphed, they used to chop the head of the king like that of Charles." After some further talk Craddock promised that the government would send a reply.

But no reply from the government came. Then political prisoners went on strike for the third time. Savarkar joined this strike. He was sentenced to have his feet fettered for 15 days. Nani Gopal was a political prisoner. He went on hunger strike. To persuade him to break his hunger strike, Savarkar himself went on hunger strike. There was a flutter. A case was instituted against Savarkar. But instead of punishment, he was cajoled to take his food. But when Savarkar told them that he had fasted for Nani's sake, he was permitted to meet the latter. Nani agreed to take food when he heard that Savarkar had gone on fast for his sake. In India, the government announced certain concessions to political prisoners. In one form or the other all the political prisoners, except Savarkar, got some relief. He was, as before, kept in solitary confinement in one of the barracks.

Savarkar was arrested in London in 1910 and since then he remained confined in jail. As he was a gymnast in his young days, his body could stand the rigors of life in the Andamans up to 1915. Afterwards his health suffered a breakdown. In 1917 Savarkar's weight was 119 pounds. In a year's time it became reduced to 98 pounds. The malady of dysentery became aggravated. Yet he was not exempted from physical labor. He began to get food from the hospital. Finally the malady became acute. He began to suffer from fever which would go up to 100 degrees. He was then removed to hospital. His body had really become debilitated. He found it hard to read or to speak because of physical and mental exhaustion. His temperature would rise if he made a slight effort to read or speak. For a while he was living under the shadow of death. After his health improved a little, he was again confined to the solitary cell. Sometime after this, Savarkar's wife, his brother and his wife came to the Andamans to meet both Savarkar and his elder brother whose wife had died a few weeks earlier.

Later the jail Commission visited the Andamans. The Commission met Savarkar. During the conversation Savarkar said, "Political prisoners should be released on condition that they will shun politics. They will do social work or enter literary field. You have released Irish rebels ten times. They break conditions. But you release them the eleventh time when they give fresh undertaking! Then at least give one opportunity to Indian political prisoners." The Commission returned to India. In due course an amnesty was announced. Hundreds of political prisoners were covered by it. However Savarkar was excluded from it. But in that little world of the Andamans, Savarkar now had become somebody. He was appointed foreman of the oil godown on a monthly salary of one rupee. Savarkar had always been a front rank leader. It was, therefore, befitting that he should get the post of a foremen.

Since his childhood Savarkar had developed a habit of studying a variety of subjects. His thirst for knowledge remained as acute as before though he was kept in a solitary cell. In spite of his physical and mental sufferings, he continued his studies with the same vigor. When one observes the names of the books or authors he read during this period, one realizes what a vast store of knowledge Savarkar had accumulated. Books by Spencer, Mill, Darwin, Huxley, Haeckel,

Emerson; history books of Carlyle, Macaulay, Gibbon; complete works of Shakespeare, Milton, and Pope; biographies of Napoleon, Bismarck, Garibaldi, Mazzini; standard histories of England, America, India, and other countries; nearly all the works of Dickens, Tolstoy, Kropotkin; essays on political science by Treitschke and Nietzsche, Plato's Republic, Aristotle's Politics, Rousseau's Social Contract; books on theosophy; collected works of Vivekananda and Ramtirtha; works of old Marathi master poets from Jnaneshwar to Moropant; complete translation of the Mahabharat; complete translation of Bramhasutra along with the commentaries on dualism and non-dualism. He first read the Koran in English, then in Bengali, and later in Marathi. But his Muslim friends advised him to read it in the original. So Savarkar studied it in the original, with a pure and devotional mind. He read the Bible twice. He studied all the Upanishads for a year, one for every month. He also read Sanskrit books, like Rigveda, Ramayana, Mahabharat, Bramhasutra, Sankhyasutra, Ishwarchandra's Karikas, and Yogasutra.

In addition to these books, he read magazines and newspapers, such as, Modern Review, Indian Review, Bharatmitra, Pratap, Kesari, Sandesh, Chitramayajagat, Saraswati, Arya Gazette, Bengali and Prabhat. When the revolution broke out in Russia, he was in the Andamans. But he managed to read the history of that revolution as soon as it became available to him. At his instance, a library was established containing these books. Not every one agreed to keep his books in this library. But Savarkar and others donated their books to this library, and thus about 2,000 volumes were collected therein. We can estimate the intellectual attainments of those people who must have read all those books.

While Savarkar was studying these books, it was natural that he felt the need to make notes of important points or topics. But it was difficult to procure a pencil and paper. Savarkar, however, found a way out. He secured an iron nail and used it for writing on the wall. He used this writing method up to the time of his release from jail. Spencer's agnosticism, various definitions from the book of economics by Mill, Kamala - a long Marathi poem, and other such literature were written on the walls of the cell. Alexander Dumas has portrayed the character of 'L'Abbe Faria' in his novel 'The Count of Monte Cristo.' Feria was also in jail. He had collected a vast variety of knowledge in his cell. While reading Savarkar's 'My Transportation', one who has read this novel, is reminded of Feria.

Savarkar by temperament was a propagandist and organizer. He could not have remained passive in the Andamans. When the opportune moment came, he began to take interest in trying to educate the convicts. Of course this task was tedious. But Savarkar abhorred needless worry, yearning and fruitless discussion. Hundreds of learned revolutionaries were then working to spread education in the villages of Russia. The missionaries also worked with the same devotion for the spread of education. Savarkar felt that we should follow their example. That was why he taught the alphabet to a Gujarati prisoner. Also, he conducted class, like college classes, to teach books, such as 'state', to political prisoners and to broaden their intellectual horizon, he made them write essays. Later the number of political prisoners increased, and there were many strikes and protests. So the authorities were reduced to helplessness and they began to tell the prisoners, "You sit together, read, talk, do what you like, but work and do not harass us." So Sunday meetings started and Savarkar began to speak in them.

If there was an opposition from the officials to the reading of books, there was also apathy about it amongst the political prisoners. Their argument was: What was the use of studying? One should work, one must sacrifice. Savarkar countered this argument by saying, "Knowledge alone is lame, while action alone is blind." It was his opinion that without the knowledge of history, of economics, of administration, no solid constructive work was possible. After the revolution in Iran, there was dearth of trained administrators and they had to be brought from America. After the revolution in China, a republic was established. But trained administrative personnel were not available and so had to be obtained from abroad. The study of the French revolution showed that destructive tendencies had to be curbed. After narrating these examples Savarkar used to say that revolutionary party must have in its ranks men of the caliber of liberal leaders, like Gokhale, Dutt, and Sir T. Madhavrao. Savarkar had a very high regard for Honorable Gokhale. When Barrie told him about Gokhale's demise, Savarkar was moved to tears and said that if every Hindu could become as patriotic as Gokhale, much could be achieved. When Barrie heard Savarkar's reaction to Gokhale's death he noted in his diary: "Though apparently they might belong to opposite camps, still, at heart, they are one."

The second movement that he undertook was that of re-conversion. The European officers had given up long ago the effort of converting convicts to the Christian faith. They had learnt a lesson from the eruption of 1857. But the Muslims carried on the work of proselytizing in jail as well as outside. Savarkar found that in a month or a fortnight at least one Hindu left his dining rank and joined the Muslim one. This made him restless. So he tried to make Hindu convicts conscious of this. But his efforts bore no fruit. Every one would say, 'How does it concern me?'

But Savarkar did not belong to this class of people who said, 'How does it concern me?' He girded up his loins to face the problem of conversion. He decided that no Hindu should go over to the non-Hindu fold even if he be a thief, a cheat, or an ignoramus, and that if he had gone over, then he should be brought back to the Hindu fold by re-conversion. Savarkar's contention was that even though a thief, a Hindu thief was less harmful to the Hindu culture than a Muslim thief. Accordingly, Savarkar began his movement of re-conversion. Later in 1913, while the conversion of a Hindu to Muslim faith was in progress, he had the place raided by officials and forced them to prosecute the Muslims involved. Slowly the movement gathered momentum, and the prisoners, both political and non-political, began to take part in it with enthusiasm. Savarkar conducted this movement as long as he was in the Andamans.

The propagation of Hindi was the third movement he started. From 1906, Savarkar was making efforts to give Hindi the status of national language. The vow, that every member of Abhinav Bharat used to take every day in England, included the following sentence: 'Hindi was to be made the national language and Nagari the national script'. When Savarkar began to propagate the necessity of the study of Hindi, a dispute arose whether Hindi had a status as a language. The people from South India, including Maharashtra, thought that Hindi language was a new word. They used to describe it as a Muslim language. Savarkar removed all objections and convinced all that, because of its literature, grammar, dignity, future prospects, competence, and most importantly, its numerical superiority, Hindi deserved to be the national language. He argued that Hindi had been the national language since olden times. The mendicant or trader of Rameshwar used to speak Hindi when he traveled to Haradwar even before the empire of Prithviraj.

Savarkar's advice was that every political prisoner should learn the languages of other provinces. Savarkar taught Hindi and Marathi to Bengalis, Hindi and Bengali to Maharashtrians, and Hindi to Gujaratis. Also, he organized a well stocked Hindi library. Officers stationed in the colony occasionally gave small amounts of money to Savarkar. The latter would tell them that they should utilize these amounts to buy and donate Hindi books to this library. He, however, could not organize a class for teaching Dravidian languages nor could he learn one. This remained a permanent regret to him.

Whoever met him, whether a convict or a free man, Savarkar impressed on him, "You are a Hindu. Hindi is not only your national language but in the Andamans, it has become your sacred language. You must teach the Hindi language and Nagari script to your children. If you all people send an application to the government, Hindi and the Nagari script will be taught in schools. But so long as this does not happen, you must teach Hindi privately at home." Hindi had spread a little amongst the free people. Savarkar arranged to distribute free copies of the Mahabharat in Hindi, some text books and Shivaji's' biography to the children of these people. Before Savarkar's arrival in the Andamans nearly 90% of the outgoing mail was in Urdu. The same was the case with government correspondence and writing. The marriage invitation cards of the Hindus were printed in Urdu. But Savarkar's teaching changed the situation and all correspondence began in Hindi.

Savarkar thought that if the heat and dust raised by the controversies of the earlier times were ignored, Dayanand's 'Satyartha Prakash', was a great book which imprinted on the mind the eternal truths of Hindu culture and which expressed well the national aspect of the Hindu religion. So, he used to make political prisoners read this book repeatedly.

It should be borne in mind that Savarkar's propagation of Hindi was not born out of his hatred of Urdu. He learnt Urdu and read it. His contention was that a Hindu should learn Urdu as he learned German. But we should not champion the cause of Urdu by abandoning our national language or Hindu languages which were derived from Sanskrit and which our ancestors spoke.

Savarkar also introduced a new practice of greeting. Once a Maharashtrian warder greeted Jamadar Mirza Khan with the words 'Ram Ram'. The latter abused the former and in threatening words told him to cease saying 'Ram Ram' in his presence. So Savarkar decided never to say Salaam to any Muslim.

Not only that, he ended the custom of saying Salaam amongst the Hindu convicts. Dassera, Diwali, and Holi were celebrated with enthusiasm in the Andamans. He utilized these festivals for creating public awareness, fostering national feeling and for inter-caste dining. To what extent the people were affected by these various movements led by Savarkar was seen on the occasion of Tilak's death. When Savarkar learnt about Tilak's death, he became restless. But how to give expression to it? Savarkar decided that on that day all people should fast, and the next day meetings should be held to mourn Tilak's death. This message of Savarkar went with lightening speed, and at lunch time from the cellular jail to far away Ras Island and other places, hundreds of people refused to take food.

When Savarkar reached the Andamans, Pathani warders had a whip hand. Savarkar's agitation created a new awareness in the Hindus. Old Pathans began to say that 'Now there is a Hindu Raj'. But this was a real secular state. For, when Hindus got the upper hand, they did not persecute the Muslims. On the contrary, Savarkar taught the non-fanatical Muslims; he wrote their applications, and also interceded for them. When Savarkar became the foreman of the oil depot, Muslims tried hard to grease his palms. But Savarkar said, "Leave the fear that you will be harassed by me because you are Muslims; it is enough if you do not harass Hindus. Make good efforts to do your work properly... But if you conspire to work less because I am a Hindu or harass the Hindus or try to extort money from them, then you beware."[1] During the time Savarkar was supervising the work of the oil-press, no prisoner suffered punishment of fetters, nor did anyone receive corporeal punishment, nor had any prisoner to give one paisa bribe to Savarkar. After narrating this, Savarkar states that the output of oil did not decrease.[2] This is an object lesson of how government can run efficiently if the administrator is competent and uncorrupt.

While he was undergoing the sentence of life imprisonment, Savarkar, along with other activities, also produced some literary works. He was a born poet. So his mind always turned to writing verse. About the many difficulties he had to face in the initial stage he has written, "If a book on prosody was available, the problem could have been solved in an hour. Because of paucity of material, I had to bear hardships in jail for producing my literature. For a particular date or a word

---

[1] V. D. Savarkar : Samagra Savarkar Wangamaya Vol I - p.646
[2] V. D. Savarkar : Samagra Savarkar Wangamaya Vol I - p.646

I had to wait weeks on end. Howsoever attractive the idea may look; it had to be given up. For very many years I had to draw on my memory only."[1] Still Savarkar overcame all those difficulties and wrote long and short poems. What was their total number? Let us see it in his words. He writes, "Once I made a calculation and found that if in the morning I start reciting poems I composed in the jail, then I could continue reciting them the whole day and the whole night barring the period of meals."[2] According to the late Prof. S. G. Malshe, Savarkar had composed about 13,500 lines.[3]

The great Marathi litterateur N. C. Kelkar has rated the literacy value of Savarkar's verse in the following words: "Reading of Kamala reminds one of Canto of Raghuvansha of Kalidas. 'Saptarshi' is very good; full of sentiment. The poem 'Jagannathacha Rathosava' is par excellence. An article will have to be written to explain the metaphors in the poem. A snapshot covers a wide field, the same is the case of these poems. One sees both poetry and learning walking hand in hand."[4]

Savarkar wrote a little prose and that too when he was brought back to Indian jails. In the early part of 1921, the Government of India informed the administration of the Andamans to send back Savarkar brothers to India. Then Savarkar was told to pack up his belongings. Savarkar donated a large number of his books to the local library and a few he distributed amongst the residents. On the last day a large number of outside people on one pretext or another, came to the jail to bid him good-bye. Savarkar's mind shuddered when a thought crossed his mind as to what would happen to them if the authorities arrested a few of the visitors. But the prisoners had turned their backs on fear and the authorities had turned a blind eye at these proceedings. All those who came, as also those who could not come, sent fruits, flowers, sweets, biscuits, soda water, as gifts. A large number of these gifts, Savarkar distributed on the spot. Some of these things he kept with him because a few of the callers insisted that he should. One of the inmates had become one with Savarkar's ideology. He made him take the following pledge: "One God, one country, one aspiration, one community, one life, one language."

At last Savarkar stepped out of the jail. By the grace of God, Savarkar's fear that his bones only will leave the jail precincts proved groundless. Savarkar walked a little distance surrounded by the guards. Suddenly one convict, who was working as a Jamadar, rushed forward, garlanded Savarkar, bowed at his feet, hailed his name loudly, and, before the police could step in, disappeared. It was a real homage paid to Savarkar for his various services rendered in the Andamans.

---

[1] V. D. Savarkar : Samagra Savarkar Wangamaya Vol I - p.337

[2] V. D. Savarkar : Samagra Savarkar Wangamaya Vol I - p.602

[3] P.L. Gawade : V. D. Savarkar - Ek Chikitsak Abhyas - p.315

[4] V. D. Savarkar : Samagra Savarkar Wangamaya Vol VII - p.12

A little while later, Savarkar was taken on board the ship 'Maharaja' and was kept in the same cage in which he was earlier brought to the Andamans. The only difference was that the returning crowd of convicts was mainly composed of lunatics. Because of this crowd, Savarkar became a little restless. So he was taken on the deck for half an hour each day. At night his elder brother, Babarao, narrated to him how he was tortured. On the fourth day while the brothers were enjoying the sea breeze, on the deck, someone drew Savarkar's attention to the shore - the shore of India. Savarkar brothers with devotional thrill stood up and folding their hands they greeted the motherland by uttering the words, 'Hail to liberty' and 'Vande Mataram.'

After disembarking, Savarkar was taken to the Alipore jail. This was in May 1921. Eight days later, he was shifted from this jail. People used to throw fruits and newspapers in the compartment of the train. From that Savarkar guessed that the news of his return had spread in the country. One passenger was sitting on the other side of the bench. He held a Marathi paper in such a way that Savarkar could read it. In addition, he would read news loudly and would give small help to Savarkar behind the back of police officials. In fact, he had undertaken the journey solely for this purpose. Later the train steamed at Nasik station. When Savarkar heard that name, the picture of his past life swiftly passed through his mind. The train reached Bombay. From there Savarkar was quickly taken aboard a ship which reached Ratnagiri. There he was again locked up in prison.

He found the first two weeks in this prison very unbearable. In the Andamans he was given tolerable food and milk. In addition he was given good clothes; he was freed from hard labor and was appointed to a clerical post. He also got pen and paper for his literary activities, and was free to move within the precincts of the prison and meet whomsoever he liked. These facilities were withdrawn in Ratnagiri jail. First he was given the work of cotton-spinning. Being unused to this work, he could not complete the quota. This put an unbearable strain on his nervous system and he felt an irresistible urge to commit suicide. But again he recovered his mental balance. Then he decided to write a book. He began to visualize in his mind the story of his life from the day he was arrested in London to the day he was brought to the Ratnagiri jail. In order that he should not forget the events that had occurred, he wrote on the walls of his cell with pieces of red brick. In a span of three months the work was ready. Later in 1926, it was published under the title, 'My Transportation'. The other book that he wrote was 'Hindutva'. This book has now become the foundation of Savarkar's political ideology. It contains the definition of a Hindu which is really incomparable. The book was published while Savarkar was still in jail. It was, therefore, published under nom de plume 'Maratha'. When Swami Shraddhananda read this definition he said, "It must have been one of those Vedic dawns indeed which inspired our seers with new truths that revealed to the author of 'Hindutva' this 'Mantra'... this definition of 'Hindutva'."

In the Ratnagiri jail, Savarkar also carried on with the movement of 'Shuddhi'. This created disputes and sparked a riot. But Savarkar faced up to these situations quite well. In fact he set up a lesson as to how communal aggression could be met. In addition to this, he also undertook the education of convicts. For that he procured books by making an application to the government. He established a library and, by instituting prizes with his money, created an interest in reading amongst the convicts.

Savarkar was taken from Ratnagiri to the Yerwada prison in 1923. Here too he continued his movements of Shuddhi, education of convicts, and of setting up a library. The superintendent who had worked in the Andamans was transferred to the Yerwada prison. He ordered Savarkar's removal from the cell and appointed him chief of the quinine shop. This officer would often question Savarkar as to what he would do after his release. To this question Savarkar had a stock reply: "If I am released without any condition, I will participate in constitutional politics; and if I am barred from entering the political arena, I will involve myself in social activities."

Later the Governor of Bombay came to see Savarkar. In this meeting the conditions were discussed. The Governor expressed his satisfaction with this discussion. Afterwards the conditions of release were again discussed with the superintendent by Savarkar. Then the superintendent produced a draft of conditions. Savarkar wrote down his reactions to them. The superintendent revised Savarkar's statement and sent all papers to the government. At last the order of release came. The order said that Savarkar should stay as an internee in Ratnagiri district and should not take part in political activities for five years.

When Savarkar heard about this order, he told the superintendent to send Mr. Dhare, who was working in the jail, to the Kesari office to inform Mr. N. C. Kelkar about his release. Accordingly Dhare went into town and met Kelkar who immediately took further action. Mr. Shankerrao Deo, having heard about Savarkar's release, got handbills printed and distributed them. A copy of the release order of Savarkar had been sent by the government to Dr. V. M. Bhat. So Dr. Bhat and Dr. Phatak drove to Yerwada jail. Since Savarkar had no civilian clothes to wear when he stepped out of jail, he sent Dr. Bhat to Dhare's residence. When Dr. Bhat was making inquiries about Dhare's residence, he met one Mr. Mhatre. The latter asked Dr. Bhat, what he wanted Dhare for? Bhat said that Savarkar was in need of clothes. Then Mhatre said, "Why do you need Dhare for that? I will give you the clothes." Saying this he gave a dhoti, a shirt, a jacket, a cap and chappals. Wearing these, Savarkar came to the house of Dr. Bhat. Already about 150 people had gathered there. Amongst them were N. C. Kelkar and S. M. Paranjape, editor of Kal. Savarkar had tea and spoke with them. Then he went to Bombay and from there went to Ratnagiri by ship. Savarkar was released on January 6, 1924 and he reached Ratnagiri two days later. Here again one is reminded of words 'Recalled to life' from Dickens' 'A Tale of Two Cities'.

Figure 1: The three brothers; Veer Savarkar, Dr. N. D. Savarkar, and eldest brother Babarao Savarkar

Figure 2: (From left to right) Bhai Parmananda, Dr. B. S. Moonje, and Veer Savarkar

Figure 3: Veer Savarkar and Subhashchandra Bose, chief of the Indian National Army

Figure 4: Veer Savarkar and behind him in dark glasses the author

Figure 5: Second from left the author, N. C. Kelkar, Veer Savarkar, Dr. B. S. Moonje, and B. G. Khaparde

Figure 6 : Veer Savarkar and Sir Stafford Cripps

Reform Movement in Ratnagiri

"The philosophers have only interpreted the world differently; the point is, however, to change it." - Karl Marx[1]

In his 'Autobiography - Early life', writing about Ranade, Savarkar has said, "For example, it has been observed earlier that Justice Ranade, after doing his routine office work, used to spend his remaining time in the service of his country. This is true; but at the same time, it has to be remembered that the uncommon national service he rendered during his free time, was so monumental that to do it seven lives would not have been enough for an ordinary mortal."[2] When one observes the various activities Savarkar did during his interment in Ratnagiri, one also likes to say that, if anyone were to undertake even one activity, it would have kept him occupied for a life-time.

Savarkar undertook these activities one after another. But in the course of time, these activities overlapped one another. Therefore it is advisable, as was done in the earlier chapter, to follow the course of his life according to these activities rather than chronologically. There were two restrictions on Savarkar's freedom: he had to shun political activities for five years; and he could not leave the Ratnagiri district without prior government permission. Savarkar had stayed in Ratnagiri from January 8, 1924 to June 17, 1937. During this period he was permitted to leave the district on two occasions. The first occasion was when the plague epidemic struck Ratnagiri. So he stayed in Nasik from July 1 to November 13, 1924. The second occasion was in October 1926 when he stayed with his brother Dr. Savarkar at Bandra for 14 days.

When the government interned him in Ratnagiri, it did not assume the responsibility for his maintenance. Nor was he permitted to practice law. So, when the first five-year period ended, and the government extended it by two more years, Savarkar submitted a written protest. Therein he said that he had to suffer compulsory unemployment as he had been forbidden to practice his legal profession. He had somehow managed to make two ends meet during the past five years. Hence forward he should be paid Rs. 100 per month like the political internees in Bengal. In response to this submission, the government began to give him an allowance of Rs. 60. However when Savarkar was released from jail, he was without a penny. Kesari realized his predicament and it started a fund to give financial help to Savarkar brothers. Some rancorous elements, like the Induprakash, a newspaper, opposed this fund. But this opposition proved hollow, and about Rs. 13,000 was collected.

---

[1] S. Radhakrishna : Recovery of Faith - p.55

[2] V. D. Savarkar : Samagra Savarkar Wangmaya Vol I - p.78

As stated above, the government had granted permission to Savarkar to leave Ratnagiri and to stay at Nasik for three months. So he left for Nasik on July 1, 1924. On the way, he was garlanded at Kolhapur, Miraj, Pune, Kalyan, and Devlali. But at Nasik, he was accorded a grand reception. Now he was entering Nasik as a hero which he had once left in fetters. He was taken out in procession from the town gate. It was a mile-long mammoth procession. The streets were thronged on both sides by milling crowds of men and women. The citizens showered love upon the worthy son of their city. At many places women tossed flowers on him. Savarkar was touched by this reception. When he rose to thank the people, he was speechless for a few minutes. But, after all, he was a born orator. So, once he began to speak, the audience sat spell bound by his oration. At the end of his speech, he said, "I am hors de combat. Still there are some fields open to me where I can work unhampered, such as, organizing Hindus, the writing of scientific and literary works, etc. But even if I can not work in such fields, still I will massage the feet of young men exhausted in the service of the motherland." He also paid short visits to Yevale, Bhagur where he was accorded receptions.

The biggest and most resounding reception given to him was held in Nasik on August 28. On that day he was presented with a public purse. Dr. Moonje presided over this function and N. C. Kelkar read the address. In it, among other things, it was said, "The people of Maharashtra hold you in great esteem for your intense patriotism and for undergoing great hardships for the country. ...To come back alive after undergoing the sentence of life transportation is considered, at least in this country, a rebirth. After suffering this long ordeal of jail life, you have still retained your enthusiasm for public affairs without flinching. For this the whole of Maharashtra admires you with a glad heart." After reading the address, Kelkar said, "Every word in it is true. Savarkar's patriotism is not merely emotional. It is translated into action. The purse is being presented to him as a protest against the barriers erected around him by the government." Later Dr. Moonje made a short speech and garlanded Savarkar. Then Savarkar was presented with a shawl sent by Shankaracharya, Dr. Kurtakoti, the address which was earlier read by Kelkar, a silver casket containing Rs. 11,160, and a copy of Gitarahasya. Returning his thanks, Savarkar said, "When I was in jail, I never dreamt that I would see this day, that fetters would become flowers. ... The youth should not merely sing my praises, but they should try to excel me in valor. I am accepting this purse not as a reward for the earlier service rendered without your consent, but as an advance gift by way of encouragement for further national service."

But Savarkar's time in Nasik was not spent only in attending receptions in his honor. Here he also began one of his social activities. During the Ganesh festival he delivered a number of lectures. On the fist day, a small function was held before the Ganapati idol installed by untouchables. Speaking on this occasion, he narrated how untouchables were being converted to the Islamic faith and stressed the need for the abolition of untouchability. He concluded by saying that my bier should be carried on the shoulders of Brahmins, Vanis, as well as untouchables like Dheds, Doms, and others, and that my soul would rest in peace only when they would light my funeral pyre. The overall effect of Savarkar's speeches at various places was wholesome. Every year there used to be disputes as to which community's idol should be at the head of the procession and it would end only in many processions being taken out. But this year, Savarkar put an end to this dispute. The Mahar community's idol was in the forefront of the procession, followed by the idol of scavengers, then that of the shepherds. After the immersion of idols, Savarkar delivered a spirited speech before the audience gathered on the bank of the river.

Savarkar was given permission to stay in Nasik for only three months. But when he drew the attention of the government to the recrudescence of plague epidemic in Ratnagiri, the period was extended. But on November 7, he was informed that he should return to Ratnagiri within a week and that on his way back he should see the Home Secretary. On November 14, Savarkar left Nasik and came to Bombay. Next day Dr. Velkar arranged an 'At Home'. Here, in his short, speech Savarkar said, "When I think that people have forgotten gallant men like Tanaji, I feel embarrassed in accepting honors for my insignificant valor."

In the evening, a public reception was held in his honor at Dadar. The local Congress Committee also participated in it. In his speech at the function, he made an important point. He said, "Muslims participate in the Khilafat movement and Ulema conferences, even while remaining in the Congress; Hindus don't blame them. Similarly Hindus belonging to the Congress have a right to participate in Hindu unification movements."

Two days later, that is, on November 17, Savarkar spoke before the students of the National Medical College. In this speech he made another important point. He said that the progress made in the world was due to men of genius who made discoveries and who did great deeds. In political, social, scientific, and other fields this had also been the case. Unless great men were born in India, the country would not come out of its present degenerate state. The situation is no different today. No great man has emerged yet.

On November 19, he met the Home Secretary and requested him that he be permitted to reside either in Satara or in Ahmednagar district. This request was turned down. Savarkar returned to Ratnagiri where plague epidemic had not abated. He, therefore, shifted to Shirgaon temporarily.

Savarkar first turned his attention, on propaganda level, to two movements, namely, re-conversion of non-Hindus and abolition of untouchability. Four months after his arrival, that is, on April 17, 1924 he spoke for the first time on these subjects and thus started his social reform movement. In the following year he spoke on these subjects at many places in the Ratnagiri district.

But in about a year, he matched his action to his belief in Shirgaon. One Gurav, Mahadeo Laxman, from that place took into his head to install an idol in the Hanuman temple. He invited Savarkar for this function. Savarkar impressed on the mind of Mahadeo the importance of the abolition of untouchability. Later, on April 9, 1925 a function was held and the people carrying the palanquin, in which the idol was kept, circumambulated the temple and in the procession Mahars, Chambhars, Brahmins, and Marathas irrespective of caste, had intermingled. For this occasion, Savarkar composed a song, 'We all Hindus are brothers of one another.'

During this year Savarkar and his colleagues visited the various localities inhabited by Mahars, Chambharas, and Bhangis on Dassera for exchanging traditional greetings. Next year on Sankranti day a social gathering (Haldi Kunku) of Hindu women of all castes was held at Savarkar's instance. There he gave a discourse. Afterwards higher caste women, such as, Brahmin, Kshatriya, and Vaishya, put vermilion mark of the foreheads of all Hindu women without caste distinction and gave them pieces of sugarcane. Sometime later, he and his associates visited the Mahar community neighborhood on Hanuman Jayanti day. Here he spoke on the importance of personal and social hygiene, and distributed 'Ramvijaya', 'Bhaktivijaya', and 'Mala Kaya Tyache' (What do I care) books amongst the residents.

The first public function of re-conversion to the Hindu religion of those who had abjured it took place at the beginning of May 1925. In this ceremony one Mr. Jadhav belonging to the Mahar community, who had become a Christian, was brought back to the Hindu fold. Afterwards on May 25, 1925 a Brahmin family named Dhakras, consisting of eight members, was reconverted from Christianity to Hinduism. After the ceremony an inter-caste dinner was held in which this family partook. Next year the youngest daughter of Dhakras was married to one Mr. Gochade. On this occasion Savarkar gave away the daughter and bore the marriage expenditure himself. Later the eldest daughter was married to one Mr. Puntambekar, who had returned from Africa. The expenses for this marriage were partly borne by Savarkar and partly by Mr. Puntambekar. In 1928, Savarkar, at his own expense, celebrated the thread ceremony of Dhakras' children. All this shows that Savarkar's social activities were not conducted at public expense only.

The band that played at the marriage ceremonies in Ratnagiri belonged to the Muslims. In the procession of village deities as well as during the Holi festival, the Mahars played the big drum. So Savarkar suggested to the young Mahar boys to start their own band. When they accepted this suggestion, Savarkar borrowed Rs. 300 from a bank and bought musical instruments for this band.

Savarkar made a concerted effort to enable the untouchable boys to sit along with other boys in local schools. If such boys were discriminated against, then Savarkar wrote petitions to end it. He used to distribute slates, books, clothes, and candy to small children. He also made the untouchable children participating in the Hindu Mela to commit to memory the Gita, Ramraksha, and Gayatri Mantra and to recite them in public meetings. That was not all. He also got a school built by Seth Bhagoji Keer on the slope of Bhageshwar fort for these boys.

In 1929 he attended a conference of scheduled castes held in Malwan. On the second day of the conference a function was held to distribute sacred threads to the members of the Mahar and Chambhar communities. Speaking on this occasion, Savarkar said, "'For the past seven generations, we have conducted a futile dispute about the right of recitation of the Vedas. Now take these Vedas and sacred threads. Are you satisfied! The Vedas which are read by the non-Hindus are not to be read by the Hindu Mahars! This is absurd. These disputes amongst us are meaningless. Let us end them and do penance and unite as Hindus under the flag of our ancestors." After this speech, there was a tea party in the Chambhar colony.

In 1930 the orthodox group decided to check the growing movement for the abolition of untouchability. They organized themselves and passed a resolution that the untouchables would not be permitted entry into the Vithal temple during the Ganesh festival. Savarkar, therefore, decided to install a separate idol of Ganpati for all Hindus. He gathered together his sympathizers and, despite the short time, celebrated the occasion on a grand scale. On this occasion, the worship of Ganpati idol was performed by Shivu Bhangi. Before the ceremony of worship he had taken a bath with the water from the well which was in the precincts of the temple. In this celebration Nanivdekar recited ballads and gave exhibition of sword-play. Masurkar Maharaj gave religious discourse. Also, there were Melas of young boys and girls of all castes, and a gathering of women for Haldi Kunku. The most important event was that an untouchable boy won the prize for correctly reciting the Gayatri Mantra. Five thousand people participated in this celebration. On the closing day, Savarkar publicly announced his resolve to start a movement for the abolition of caste by birth.

At the all-Hindu Ganpati festival in 1932, Madhavrao Bagal was the main speaker. He said that he was overwhelmed to see the progress made here. It was difficult to get even five or ten women for inter-caste dining in Bombay or Poona. In Kolhapur it had been impossible to arrange it so far. Here hundreds of women were partaking in inter-caste dinners, the credit for which, of course, went to Savarkar. If we were to get such a powerful leader in Western Maharashtra, we would have carried him on our shoulders and danced with joy.[1] Years later, Savarkar did visit Western Maharashtra. But nothing seems to have happened as visualized by Bagal.

Next year the great social reformer Karmavir Vithal Ramaji Shinde visited Ratnagiri, and personally observed the work done in connection with the removal of untouchability under Savarkar's leadership. In his concluding speech he said, "The social revolution that is taking place here is unprecedented. I see that

---

[1] S. S. Savarkar: Hindusamaj Samrakshaka Swa. Veer Savarkar - p.270

people are sitting, eating, and worshipping along with untouchables and others, who are our religious brothers. ... I am so pleased with the success achieved in the social transformation effected by Savarkar, that I pray to God that He should give the remaining years of my life to him."[1]

The Patitpavan Mandir may be called the coping stone of Savarkar's movement for the eradication of untouchability. He had decided to build a temple which would be open for worship to all Hindus irrespective of caste. The Board of Trustees was to consist of one Brahmin, one Kshatriya, one Viashya, one untouchable, and one nominee of Sheth Bhagoji Keer. The foundation stone of this temple was laid by Sankaracharya Dr. Kurtakoti on March 10, 1929. Two years later its construction was completed. Seth Bhagoji Keer belonged to the Bhandari caste. Savarkar had decided that Keer would install the idol with complete Vedic rites. He maintained that whether a man was a Mahar or a Maharaja, he had every right to perform religious ceremonies according to Vedic rites. He argued vigorously about it with learned men and orthodox priests. But he found that these men were not amenable to reason. So with the help of Ganeshshastri Modak, a disciple of Masurkar Maharaj, and other learned Brahmins, Savarkar arranged that the idol was installed by Keer with full Vedic rites on February 22, 1931. In this celebration, Rajbhoj, the leader of the Chambhar community, ceremoniously washed the feet of Sankaracharya. Never before could an untouchable wash the feet of Sankaracharya. Thus an end was put to this custom in this function. But Sankaracharya and others objected to inter-caste dining. So separate meals were served to them, while others dined together.

Savarkar also held the view that every man had a right to follow any calling of his choice and that he had no need to feel embarrassed while pursuing it. But to back up his views with action, he himself did some odd jobs. He took a handcart around selling Indian goods. Also, in order that people should take to mattress-making, he did that work for some time. Not only that, he ran an 'All Hindu Restaurant'. Here a Mahar boy was employed to make tea. The late Mr. Kelkar, the renowned leader of Maharashtra, had taken tea in this restaurant.

For revolutionary activities, Savarkar had to spend ten years in the Andaman jail. But this did not make him lose his faith in revolutionary or terrorist activity. While he was interned in Ratnagiri and was openly carrying on his social activities, he maintained clandestine contacts both with revolutionary organizations and young terrorists. Bhagatsingh and Rajguru had met him secretly. Vaishampayan, Moghe, Prithvisingh, who were accused in the Lamington Road shooting case, were known to him. Prithvisingh was a political prisoner in the Andaman jail with Savarkar. Gogate shot Hotson in the Fergusson College in Poona. Before this shooting incident, Gogate had seen Savarkar in Ratnagiri. To take revenge for 'Bhagatsingh and Chittagong affair', some young men had burst a bomb in the 'Empire' theater. Amongst the arrested young men were some who

---

[1] S. S. Savarkar: Hindusamaj Samrakshaka Swa. Veer Savarkar - p.289

had come into contact with Savarkar in Ratnagiri. Later, on April 23, 1934, Wamanrao Chavan, a follower of Savarkar, shot an Englishman in Dhobi Talao area in Bombay. After his arrest, Chavan declared that none had any connection with his action, and that he had taken recourse to shooting in order to avenge the hanging of Bhagatsingh.

The above mentioned terrorists who had met Savarkar did not have a long contact with him. But the case of Wamanrao Chavan was different. He was in the forefront of many of Savarkar's activities. Savarkar had composed a song about Bhagatsingh on the day he was hanged. Next morning, Chavan and other young boys took out a procession and sang this song. So, when such a person fired a revolver, the effect of that action was bound to affect Savarkar. First his house was searched. Then on May 1, he was arrested. Afterwards Savarkar wrote to the government disclaiming any connection with the action of Chavan. The Government also did not find any evidence connecting him with Chavans's action. So he was released from custody on May 21, 1934.

Savarkar conducted two more campaigns in addition to the campaigns of abolition of untouchability and of re-conversion. The first was in connection with the elimination of foreign words from Marathi. His first article on this subject appeared in the Kesari on April 21, 1925 and the fourth and last appeared on May 13, 1925. Savarkar's writings on the elimination of foreign words from Marathi have been collected in his book 'Language Purification'.

There was much opposition to this movement in the early stage. Amongst the opponents were Hudlikar from Indore, and Tambeshastri. Their rank was joined by eminent writers like B. G. Khaparde and Chintamanrao Vaidya. Later Dr. Patwardhan, Kolhatkar, and Prof. Kshirsagar weighed in. Dr. Patwardhans's opposition ended early. The editor of Vividjnanvistar commissioned Dr. Patwardhan to refute the philosophy of language purification. So, Dr. Patwardhan closely examined this subject. Then, he realized the need for the movement, but for different reasons. Explaining that his approach is different from that of Savarkar he said, "Savarkar considers purification of language as one aspect of the Hindu unification movement. I do not hold with it."[1]

Here, Dr. Patwardhan has laid his finger on a fundamental point. Savarkar's objective was to bring about a renaissance in the Hindu society. The backbone of Hindu society had been broken by the incessant religious, political, and cultural attacks by the non-Hindus for at least a thousand years and that had bred in that society what Churchill had called 'The diseases of defeat.' Savarkar conducted various campaigns to cure the Hindu society of all these diseases. Marathi and Hindi languages had withered away under the onslaught of Arabic and Persian languages during the Muslim rule. Then came the assault of the English language. Savarkar wanted to rouse the national pride of the Hindus. Pride

---

[1]P. L. Gawade : Savarkar, Eka Chikitsak Abhyas - p.545

in one's mother-tongue is an essential factor in the making of a nation. Only nation-builders, like Richelieu, Shivaji, Bismarck, and Kamal Ataturk, are conscious of this. This may be beyond the comprehension of literary men. Belonging as he did to the ranks of nation-builders, Savarkar insisted on the elimination of foreign words from the Marathi language.

In the same way he insisted on the reformation of the Devanagari script. In an earlier chapter a reference has been made to the fact that members of Abhinav Bharat in London used to take a pledge that they would make Hindi the national language and Nagari the national script. Savarkar felt that Nagari must become an all India script. He therefore turned his attention to the problem of how it could be reformed. Since the establishment of the printing press in India, a number of experts had looked into this problem. One of them was Lokamanya Tilak. Now Savarkar also made a few suggestions for script reform. Then he started a vigorous propaganda for popularizing this reformed script. When giving a message to young people, he often used to write 'Adopt a new script for writing.' Savarkar not only suggested some reforms in the script, but also insisted that his writings should be printed in this new script. His articles on the reformation of the script have been collected in the book 'Script Reformation'.

During his internment, a number of leaders came to meet him in Ratnagiri. The foremost amongst them was V. V. S. Aiyar. In London he was considered the right-hand man of Savarkar. Their last meeting had taken place in the Brixton jail in London in 1910. Now after fifteen years they had met in Ratnagiri. Unfortunately Aiyar died in an accident two months later. Savarkar wrote a very moving memoir in the Maratha Weekly. In it he said, "... I met Shriyut Aiyar a couple of months ago... We forgot for a while the bitterness and the keen pangs of the afflicted and tortured past and lightly gossiped as boys fresh from schools meeting again after a long holiday. He took my leave. I watched him disappear and said to myself, now I can call him again any time I like." But that was not to be.

Gandhiji visited Ratnagiri on March 1, 1927. The local municipality presented him with an address. While thanking the municipality for it, Gandhiji spoke about Savarkar's social activities highly, and added that he would like to meet him. Savarkar heard about it. He sent a note to Gandhiji by the hand of Vishnupant Damale and invited him to his residence. Accordingly, Gandhiji came. They talked for about an hour and a half. They discussed topics like Shuddhi (re-conversion), removal of untouchability, and swadeshi. About Shuddhi both leaders disagreed. Gandhiji did not believe that a man falls away from his religion. To this Savarkar's rejoinder was "as long as the notion prevails in society that a person does fall away from religion, till then Shuddhi remains the only remedy." But both of them agreed on the importance of removal of untouchability and swadeshi. Before bidding good-bye, Gandhiji expressed a desire to meet Savarkar's wife Yamunabai. So she came out. Then Gandhiji turned to his wife Kasturba and said, "Let us bow to this saintly woman who showed immense courage in facing all tribulations when her husband was sentenced to 50 years' imprisonment."[1] Savarkar and Gandhiji had met before in London. This meeting in Ratnagiri was their last.

Bhai Parmananda was a great revolutionary from Punjab. He was first awarded the death penalty which was later commuted to life in exile, and was sent to the Andamans. Bhaiji and Savarkar had known each other in London. In 1929 Bhaiji came to Ratnagiri. He was given a rousing reception on the Ratnagiri pier. On landing, Bhaiji first embraced Savarkar. Then he was taken out in procession in an open car in which Savarkar sat next to him. Bhaiji was a guest of Savarkar and stayed with him for two days. One evening Bhaiji spoke on the subject of 'Independence.' During this speech, Savarkar stayed away from the meeting as it was a political one. However, he heard the speech from a distance.

Dr. Moonje came to Ratnagiri during the Ganesh festival in 1935. During the last fifteen years, Dr. Moonje had toiled ceaselessly to protect Hindu interests. He had to suffer opposition from the Congress in his work and had become isolated in Indian politics. But he did not forsake the self-appointed task of protecting the Hindu interests. Such an eminent man was visiting Ratnagiri. Savarkar, therefore, exerted himself hard to ensure that a fitting reception was given to him. He wrote the address to be given to Dr. Moonje and secured signatures of prominent local men. On the next day, after the presentation of the address, a program of inter-caste dining was arranged in Dr. Moonje's honor.

In addition to these prominent men, others like Senapati Bapat, Socialist leader Yusuf Meharali, Savarkar's London colleagues, Gyanchand Varma, his co-prisoners in the Andamans, Sachindranath Sanyal and Nani Gopal, as also Dr. Ambedkar, N. C. Kelkar, Dr. Madhavrao Patwardhan, Marathi encyclopediast Ketkar, and Dr. Hedgewar visited Ratnagiri to meet Savarkar.

On his way from Nasik to Ratnagiri, Savarkar stayed in Bombay for a few days to meet the Secretary, Home Department of the government of Bombay. Reference to this meeting has already been made earlier. At this time, he also met Shaukat Ali. A detailed report about his meeting was carried in the special issue of the Marathi newspaper 'Lokamanya' and in the English Weekly 'Maratha'. This report is printed in the third volume of Savarkars' literature.[2] In their talk Shaukat Ali suggested to Savarkar that the latter should stop his campaign for uniting the Hindus. To this Savarkar replied that Shaukat Ali should withdraw from the activities of Khilafat and All India Ulema Organization. However, Shaukat Ali argued that Khilafat movement was being led by a Hindu. Savarkar countered this argument by saying that the campaign of uniting the Hindus was also being led by a Hindu.

---

[1] A. G. Salvi : Swatantryaveer Savarkaranchya Sahawasat, Part 1 - p.5

[2] V. D. Savarkar : Samagra Savarkar Wangamaya Vol III - p.758-765

Then the question of Shuddhi cropped up. Shaukat Ali maintained that Muslims have been converting Hindus since the beginning. Savarkar replied that since Muslims took an undue advantage of Hindu tolerance, the campaign of re-conversion had become inevitable. Further, Christians, Parsis, and Jews were also organizing themselves. They did not complain about the movement of organizing the Hindus. Then why did only Muslims make an issue of it? Shaukat Ali replied that they would not give up organizing the Muslims. Naturally Savarkar said neither would the Hindus cease from organizing themselves. At last Sahukat Ali stated that there were many countries to which Muslims could go, and if circumstances forced them, then, they would emigrate. To this Savarkar's rejoinder was: "With pleasure they could go. Frontier Mail leaves for the northern borders every day."[1] Before taking his leave of Savarkar, Shaukat Ali, said in a jest, "I am a giant and you are a dwarf. I can easily floor you." Savarkar, in the same vein said, "Try. But remember the story of Afzalkhan and Shivaji. The world knows the historic event as to how the dwarf knocked down the giant."

During his stay in Ratnagiri, Savarkar wrote a lot of essays and poems. He wrote twenty-two poems. And while reading them, the reader realizes that these poems were written to champion certain causes. Savarkar used to say that by temperament he was a poet and an artist. Because of certain circumstances, he had to enter politics. But having become a politician, one finds that quite often Savarkar used his poems for the propagation of social and political aims. But some of those poems were very expressive. One could refer to the poems 'Akhil Hindu Vijay Dhvaja Ha' or 'Tumhi Amhi Sakal Hindu Bandhu Bandhu' as illustration.

However, during this period Savarkar wrote more prose than verse. The first book he wrote was 'Hindupadapadshai'. He began to write it when he was staying at Trimbakeshwar. But he completed it on February 15, 1925 at Shirgaon. From the preface it appears that Savarkar had begun to write a small book on the Maratha history in 1910 after he had completed writing the book on the Sikh history. But having been caught in the tempest of revolutionary activities, the project fell through. Now having regained freedom, he took it up again.

Justice Ranade had written his 'Rise of the Maratha Power' to explain the true springs of Maratha history. The work is in English and hence the non-Marathi people could have a true glimpse of Maratha history. But Justice Ranade had ended his narration at the point of Rajaram's death and Shahu's return to Maharashtra. Since then the Marathi scholars had published voluminous papers about the Maratha history. Savarkar felt that it was necessary to show the aim and glory of the Hindu empire of the Marathas by using this new material and that the work should be in English for the benefit of non-Marathi readers. So he wrote 'Hindupadapadshai.' As Ranade's incomparable volume was available, Savarkar chose to write briefly up to the point of Rajaram's death and then at length about the subsequent period. Ranade's work has been described as 'A Jewel' by Dr. B.

---

[1]Dhananjay Keer : Veer Savarkar - p.169

V. Keskar. Ranade has described the 'Maratha Power' as 'Hindu Nationality' in his preface. If one reads Ranade's 'Rise of the Maratha Power' along with Savarkar's Hindupadapadshai, one fully understands the idea of what Hindu nationality is.

Savarkar wrote a novel: 'What do I care?' ('The Revolt of the Moplahs') in 1926. It graphically describes the atrocities committed against the Hindus, the defilement of Hindu women, burning of towns, and the massacre of devout Hindus by the Moplahs. To open the eyes of the Hindu society was the main reason why Savarkar wrote this novel. It has been a long time since the novel was first published. During this time what lessons the Hindus have learnt from the revolt of the Moplahs and the novel based on it, is for the reader to come to his own conclusion.

After the murder of Swami Shraddhananda, Savarkar brothers started a weekly called 'Shraddhananda' on January 10, 1927 from Bombay. The first issue carried Savarkar's article captioned 'Murder of Shraddhananda and Gandhiji's impartial partisanship'. This weekly continued to be published for about three years. During this period Savarkar contributed about four or five columns every week. These were published under a pen-name or without any name at all. Later these appeared in book form, namely, 'Garma Garam Chivada', 'Gandhi Gondhal', etc. The first half of the book 'My Transportation' was published in Kesari in 1925. The latter half was published in 'Shraddhananda'.

Savarkar wrote three plays. 'Sangeet Ushap' was published in 1927, 'Sangeet Sanyastha Khadga' was published in 1931, and 'Sangeet Uttar Kriya' was published in 1933. Ushap dealt with the problem of untouchability. The government banned this play and seized its copies. The second play attempted to show that the philosophy of non-violence was harmful to society. The last one shows how the defeat at Panipat was avenged.

To popularize his ideology, drama was one of the media that Savarkar used. Amongst his three plays 'Sanyastha Khadga' ranks first. It was once staged in Nagpur. While watching it, the late Dr. N. B. Khare, who was for sometime the Congress Chief Minister in the late thirties of the Central Provinces and Berar, could not control his emotions. He stood up and shouted, "A great man who can speak this language is wanted today in Indian politics."

After the announcement of his decision to launch a crusade for the abolition of caste divisions, he wrote articles in Kesari from November 29, 1930 to May 5, 1931 expounding the reasons for it. Later, Savarkar developed contact with the editor of 'Kirloskar' magazine, who accepted Savarkar's condition that his articles would be published in the new alphabet. So, his first article, 'Break the shackle of ban on inter-dining' was published in the March issue of 1934. Afterwards, Savarkar's articles also appeared in the sister magazines 'Stri' and 'Manohar' published by the Kirloskars. These articles were published in book form as 'Savarkar Literature' by the Kirloskar Press. This literature is thought-provoking. Those who wish to break the caste barriers for creating a homogenous and egalitarian community should study Savarkar's writings on abolition of castes. These give lessons on how social reforms should be brought about by action, how rationalism should be the basis of this action, how caste-bitterness should be avoided, and how an organization should be built for such action. His articles advocating the importance of science are also worth reading. Since 1920, Indians have developed a habit of looking at all problems emotionally. So the solution to them often springs from their emotions. This outlook must change. Savarkar's articles on science are a guide as to how social problems should be viewed rationally and pragmatically.

From 1925 to 1937 Savarkar wrote the following books: 'Hindupadapadshai', 'My Transportation', 'Language Purification', 'Script Reformation', 'The Revolt of the Moplahs', 'Kalepani', 'Essays on Abolition of Castes', etc. He also wrote for Kesari, Kirloskar, Stri, Manohar, Shraddhananda, Nirbhid, and other periodicals. All this written material runs to 2,225 pages. It would take a lifetime for anyone to produce so much literature. In addition to his literary activity, Savarkar also conducted various social campaigns of which we have taken a brief survey earlier.

Savarkar's internment in Ratnagiri began on January 8, 1924. The order for his release had said that he was not to take part in politics for five years. This period ended in 1929. So, the Bombay Government extended this period for another two years. This extension order was reissued at an interval of two years in 1931, 1933, 1935, and 1937. But in February 1937, elections were held to Provincial Legislative Assemblies under the new Government of India Act, 1935. Barrister Jamnadas Mehta was elected to the Bombay Provincial Legislative Assembly. He was one of the prominent men of the Democratic Swarajya Party. However, the Congress had won a majority of seats. Naturally the responsibility was cast on it to form the ministry. But, it did not form the ministry because of disagreement about the Governor's prerogatives. The Governor, therefore, called upon the leaders of the opposition parties to form the ministry. Jamnadas Mehta made Savarkar's unconditional release as a pre-condition to his joining this ministry. After some discussion and haggling, this condition was accepted. Them the Cooper-Mehta ministry was formed. On May 10, 1937 the government informed Savarkar that he had unconditionally been released. The eagle's legs were unfettered and it spread its wings for a take-off.

Declaration of Hindu Nationalism

"Every new opinion, at its starting, is precisely in a minority of one" - Thomas Carlyle[1]

When news of Savarkar's release from internment spread, it was inevitable that people should discuss what political stand he was likely to take. Of course, the Congress was the only party having an All India character. Smaller parties, like, the Socialists, the Communists, the Democratic Swaraj Party, etc. were included in its fold. The Marathi speaking world was fully aware of the progressive views of Savarkar from his writings in 'Kirloskar'. It was natural that the Socialist leaders felt that, if such an active social reformer was to join their party, its ranks would swell faster. Achyutrao Patwardhan and S. M. Joshi, the socialist leaders, therefore came to Ratnagiri and pleaded with him to join their party.[2] Savarkar told them that their party was doing commendable work in getting the Congress out of the Gandhian cobwebs; but he would not join it.

In fact, during his stay in Ratnagiri, it had become obvious that Savarkar was opposed to the Congress ideology of Indian nationalism. His dissertation on 'Hindutva' expounds who constitute a nation in India. But it did not bear his name. So it could be said that no notice was taken of it. To some extent, this too could be said about his articles in 'Shraddhananda', as these too did not appear in his name. However, a little discerning reader would easily have understood that these were Savarkar's views. One gets a preview in them of Savarkar's political ideas expressed after 1937. In his article 'Organization is necessary for Independence', he wrote, "No, no, we not only do not want on these terms the Kingdom of Hindusthan but even the Kingdom of Indra (God). We want to become free as Hindus; and we want to preserve our Hindutva; what ensures our Hindu individuality is freedom."[3] In another article, 'Numbers also count', he stated, "Neither in quantity nor in quality will we permit our Hindu nation to suffer."[4] In an article, 'Which Religion is peace loving?' he said, "The fact is that most of the Muslims do not consider Hindusthan as their fatherland and they find the inhabitation of Hindus in this country as a thorn in their side. This feeling is at the bottom of all conflicts. Barring a section of sensible Muslims, the rest of them deeply desire that, like Turkey, Iran, and Afghanistan, Hindusthan should become completely Islamic, and when it becomes so, they would love it as their fatherland".[5] At the end of the article 'Organization is necessary for independence'

---

[1] Thomas Carlyle : On Heros, Hero-worship and the Heroic in History - p.80

[2] S. S. Savarkar : Hindusamaj Samrakshak Swa. Veer Savarkar - p.393

[3] V. D. Savarkar : Samagra Savarkar Wangamaya Vol III - p.53

[4] V. D. Savarkar : Samagra Savarkar Wangamaya Vol III - p.39

[5] V. D. Savarkar : Samagra Savarkar Wangamaya Vol III - p.100

he wrote bluntly, "Hence we say that, in case of need, Hindus alone will fight and regain their independence."

The above thoughts, expressed in the articles in 'Shraddhananda' and the thoughts he expressed in his addresses as the President of the Hindu Mahasabha or in his other public speeches, were in the same vein. But as said earlier, these articles did not bear Savarkar's' name. This could not, however, be said about articles on the removal of untouchability. In the first article which appeared in November 1930 in the 'Kesari', Savarkar had used the words 'Hindu Rashtra' at the very outset. The Socialists or progressive people should have read these articles on social reforms carefully. For, that would have helped them to know, before Savarkar was released from internment, to which political school he belonged. But it appears that either no notice was taken of his new ideas about nationality or their true meaning was lost on them.

Freed from internment, it was obvious that Savarkar would leave Ratnagiri and go to Bombay or Poona for permanent residence. So the people of Ratnagiri gave a public farewell to him. In thanking them he said, "Though they are in a minority, Muslims want to lord over the Hindus which I do not like. Before I join the Congress, I will ascertain whether the Muslims domination in that organization has been eliminated or not. However, whatsoever party I join, I will never forsake the Hindu cause. I am not merely a friend of the Hindus, I am the son of the Hindus and I will live as a Hindu."[1] Indeed this was a brief manifesto of Savarkar's future political life.

On June 18, Savarkar left Ratnagiri for Bombay via Kolhapur. Accepting a number of receptions on the way, Savarkar reached Kolhapur. His visit to Kolhapur is important for the following two things. Here he went to see the studio of 'Hans Pictures.' There he found all the nameplates in English. Savarkar suggested to Baburao Pendharkar to replace them by Marathi nameplates. Baburao said that Savarkar should give him their Marathi translations which his company would use and also persuade others to use them. Later, Savarkar supplied the necessary translations to the proprietors of Hans Pictures who, as promised, used them and appealed to the film industry to use them.[2] Digdarshak - Director, Chitrapat - Film, Chayachitran - Cinematography, Dhwanilekhan - Sound recording, Kalamandir - Studio, Bolpat - Talkie, Nepathya - Costume, and other words, which are now very common in Hindi and Marathi films, were coined by Savarkar. This needs mention again in order that Savarkar should get his due credit.

The second thing concerned the Indian States. In this connection, Savarkar's stand was dramatically opposed to that of the Congress leaders. It was here that Savarkar gave expression to it. He said in a public speech that the

---

[1] S. S. Savarkar : Swa Veer Savarkar Part 1 - p.3

[2] V. D. Savarkar : Bhashashuddhi - p.8

Congress position, which considered Indian states as blots and hence these should be abolished, was not correct. The present day Indian states were really the sacred relics of our former independence. They were also the centers of power. If they are not being useful, then the fault rested with the administration. To persuade one prince to join our camp is as important as persuading fifty thousand people. Many agitations were conducted to make Hindi the state language. By one royal edict, the Baroda ruler made Hindi the state language. The Kolhapur ruler made strenuous efforts to end untouchability in his state. So, at present, every Hindu must guard the interests of the Hindu states. For removal of untouchability, for starting the cooperatives, for industrial progress, and for such other reasons, the Indian states must be kept intact. They should not be merged in British India. His deep knowledge of the process of history told him that once India achieved independence, Hindu states would merge or would have to merge in the Indian Union. And he explicitly stated this later in his statement 'Hindu Sabha and the Hindu States!'[1]

Later a public welcome was accorded to Savarkar at Miraj. In his speech at this function, he stressed the need to check the aggressive designs of the Muslims, and to illustrate the Congress attitude about it he referred to an instance that had occurred in the Central Assembly. Hindu girls were abducted by the Fakir of Epi in the North-West Frontier Province. Bhai Parmananda had asked a question about it when Dr. Khansaheb suggested that these four girls should be given away to the rowdies of that province. Savarkar observed that the behavior of those Congressmen who laughed after Khansaheb's remarks was befitting eunuchs only. This observation displeased the Congress camp and it boycotted all functions of welcome arranged in honor of Savarkar. It could be said that this incident was the flash-point of Savarkar-Congress conflict. Receptions were also given to him at Pandharpur and Sangli from where he went to Poona. The City Congress issued a directive that the function welcoming Savarkar should be boycotted. Still a huge procession was taken out from Shaniwarwada. But, before it started, some people said that the saffron flag should not be flown during the procession. However, Savarkar said that, if the saffron flag was not flown, he would not participate in the procession. In the meanwhile Dr. Shinde and others from Ratnagiri, who had brought with them saffron flags displaying Kripan-Kundalini, hoisted one on the hood of the car and procession meandered through the city successfully. The flag incident gave a glimpse to the people that Savarkar's political stand would remain a distinct entity.

From the various public and private meetings he addressed, it became obvious to those who were present that Savarkar's outlook was entirely different from that of the Congress. A gathering was held to give welcome to Savarkar on behalf of the editorial section of the city newspapers. About 75 representatives were present. A discussion took place. Answering a question from the late Mr. R. K. Khadilkar, Savarkar said, "I think it is better to remain separate from the

---

[1]A. S. Bhide : Veer Savarkar's Whirlwind Propaganda - p.81

Congress if one feels that one cannot reach the goal of independence by holding to the Congress creed. I insist that our people should occupy every important post in the administration run by the civil service." Replying to P. V. Gadgil's question on communism Savarkar said, "Communist ideology has brought some vividness to the Congress program." Regarding the question of religion, Savarkar gave a telling explanation. He said, "I will not insist on the Hindu religion, provided there was no religion left in the world. But so long as this does not happen, I prefer my own religion." On the same day, late in the evening, he was accorded a reception in Vithal Mandir by the Mithganja branch of the Democratic Swaraj Party. While expressing his gratitude for the reception, he made his position clear regarding Hindu-Muslim Unity. He said, "Twenty-five crores of Hindus are unable to win freedom on their own. I therefore do not hold with the view that if the less qualified seven crores join them, that would help to win freedom."

Savarkar came to Bombay from Poona. His younger brother was residing in Bombay. Here also he was given a reception in which the Bombay Congress Committee joined. The reception committee had requested Indian leaders to send messages for this occasion. Accordingly Pandit Nehru, M. N. Roy, Subhaschandra Bose, Rajaji, and Aney sent their messages. Gandhiji did not send any. Probably he had no time. Before the reception, Savarkar was taken out in a huge procession. Later there was a reception. In this meeting Nariman, Lalji Pendse, Tersi, and Roy spoke. Roy suggested that Savarkar should join the Congress. A few years later Roy had to quit the Congress. The same suggestion was made by Subhaschandra Bose and he was forced out of the Congress. As Savarkar had stayed away from the Congress, he was spared this ignominy.

On August 1, 1937 at a public meeting in Poona, Savarkar, after analyzing the Indian political situation, announced that he was joining the Democratic Swaraj Party. His speech on this occasion held the audience spellbound.

As he did not join the Congress, its leaders began anti-Savarkar propaganda. Savarkar replied to it pointedly in his speeches he delivered on his various tours. The Indian intellectuals, however, did not take notice of his replies even for their information. A provincial Hindu Conference of the then Central Provinces and Berar was held at Akola. In his presidential speech, Savarkar answered his critics. He said, "The earlier movement for Swaraj - Independence - was merely for the word. Its aim was to establish our right to demand independence and to create an intense desire for it in the public mind. But now independence is within sight. Hence we must have a clear concept of what constitutes independence. In my recent speeches, as there are no repeated references to the words Swaraj - Independence -, people think that the liberty worshipper Savarkar has disappeared and a communal minded Savarkar has taken his place. But this is not correct. Today people are sufficiently awakened and a little power has been transferred to them. So the limit of academic discussion of

Swaraj - Independence - has passed away and the time for practical politics has come."[1]

He further added, "With the emergence of practical politics, the struggle for power became inevitable." The Congress and other parties were involved in this struggle. But there was also the Muslim League - a party which had acquired a habit of repeatedly increasing its demands. Savarkar referred to the French Revolution to illustrate what happens when power struggle begins. He said, "During the French Revolution, there were constitutional, progressive, and revolutionary parties - a mixed bag of liberals and radicals. Their fury was directed towards the King. So, the parties forgetting the differences amongst them, rose as if they were moved by one aim. As long as the King was there, this facade of unity endured. But once the King was eliminated by their fury, the same people who all had rushed at the King with daggers now flew at one another's throats with the same daggers."[2]

Now who was to inherit the power that was slipping by stages from the hands of the British? That was the practical question: What is a nation? Whose freedom? Dealing with these questions, Savarkar said, "... A minority has been clamoring for changing the name of Hindusthan - after independence the name of Hindusthan was changed to India i.e. Bharat - and they have already settled on the name of Pakistan by detaching a part of Hindusthan where they are in a majority. When all other communities are wide awake about their future, how can we afford to go to sleep? What do you mean by a country's independence? Do you mean thereby the independence of stones, rocks, dust, rivers, and mountains of Hindusthan?"[3] Savarkar never thought of independence in these terms. He had written in 'Shraddhananda', "We want to become free as Hindus."

From 1920 Gandhiji had continuously repeated the slogan "There will be no Swaraj without Hindu-Muslim unity."[4] And for this unity he was prepared to accept the ever increasing demands of the Muslims. Finally he had said, "The Congress will have no objection to the British Government transferring all the power it today exercises to the Muslim League."[5] According to him, "It would be still Indian rule."[6] Gandhiji had gone to this extent and he was the dictator of the Congress. How could Savarkar look upon this Congress kindly?

Further, from 1920, the Congress slowly came under the sway of Gandhiji's followers and in every province there was a lieutenant like, Nehru,

[1] V. D. Savarkar : Samagra Savarkar Wangamaya Vol IV - p.326

[2] V. D. Savarkar : Samagra Savarkar Wangamaya Vol IV - p.326

[3] V. D. Savarkar : Samagra Savarkar Wangamaya Vol IV - p.327

[4] D. G. Tendulkar : Mahatma, Vol 2 - p.10

[5] Pyarelal : Mahatma Gandhi, The Last Phase Vol 1 - p.69

[6] Dhananjay Keer : Veer Savarkar - p.384

Patel, Pattabhi, Rajaji, Pant, Azad, and Deo, to carry out his directives. No astrologer is needed to tell with whom they would have sided in Gandhi-Savarkar conflict. The Nariman, Khare, and Bose episodes are sufficient eye openers. Being keenly alive to this, Savarkar said, "It would not be a sign of manliness if I were only to nod before the Congress leaders to get some high post in that organization... Also, I do not wish to be treated like Nariman, for expressing my candid views."[1] Because of this outlook, Savarkar chose a new party and a new way for the propagation of his independent political ideology.

Savarkar's name was twice suggested for the presidentship of the Hindu Mahasabha during his internment. First, it was suggested in 1924, when the Hindu Mahasabha session was held at Calcutta. The second time was in 1933, when the session was held at Ajmer. But on both those occasions, the order of internment came in the way of the final election. Now in 1937 that hurdle had disappeared. So Savarkar was elected President for the Karnavati-Ahmedabad-session of the Hindu Mahasabha. This news reached him when he was on a whirlwind tour of the then Central Provinces.

He did this tour in two stages. The first stage began on November 26. In it, he covered Akola, Murtijapur, Karanja, Washim, Pusad, Digras, Dharva, Yevatmal, Amaravati, Ellichpur, and Telhara. It lasted for nine days. The second stage began on December 11. In it, Savarkar first went to Nagpur. There was a big crowd that had assembled to garland him. Dr. Moonje, being the leading personality of Nagpur, had the honor to garland Savarkar first. As he raised his hands, Savarkar held them and put the garland around the neck of Dr. Moonje.

Savarkar was elected president of Marathi literary conference of the Central Provinces. He had come to Nagpur to preside over it. In his presidential speech Savarkar stressed that they were first Hindus and then Maharashtrians and that Hindi was the national language and Devanagri was the national script. Savarkar also attended, in addition to this conference, a number of public and private meetings. Later in his propaganda tour he visited towns like Aravi, Devali, Wardha, Chanda, Varoda, Bhatana, Mulgaon, Rajuri, Navargaon, Talodi, Bramhapuri, Mowni, Bhandara, Raipur, and Vilaspur and delivered about 30 to 40 speeches.

He came back from this tour and then he began to work on the presidential speech to be delivered at the Karnavati session of the Hindu Mahasabha. This proved to be an epochal speech. For in it he enunciated the fundamentals of the political ideology of Hindu nationalism. In this session, an announcement was made that the Hindu Mahasabha was entering the political field and that its aim was complete political independence.

---

[1] V. D. Savarkar : Samagra Savarkar Wangamaya Vol IV - p. 351

At the beginning of his speech, Savarkar paid homage to His Majesty the King of Nepal. Then he lauded the work done by the Hindus in various parts of the world and sent a message of sympathy to those Hindus who were living in French and Portuguese India. Then he categorically stated that "The Hindusthan of tomorrow must be one and indivisible" After making a declaration of a united India, he proceeded to define the word Hindu and to give its origin and then explained how Hindus constitute a nation. To the opponents, who called the concept of Hindu nationalism as parochial, he asked an ironical question: "But is not the concept of an Indian nation itself a parochial conception in relation to Human State?"

Since the establishment of the Congress, the words Swarajya, etc. have been slowly gaining currency. But no one had as yet posed the fundamental question which Savarkar had raised: What does India's Independence or Swarajya really mean? He said, "The time has come when these expressions should be fully analyzed and understood." While answering the question, "What is a nation?" he said that a country or a geographical unit did not in itself constitute a nation. Our country was dear to us because it had been the abode of our race. The independence of India meant, therefore, the independence of our race, our nation, and which would enable the Hindus to grow to their full height. The real meaning of Swarajya was not merely the geographical independence of the bit of earth called India, but of the Hindus who inhabited it. After having said this, he went on to add that Hindus had been in the forefront in the struggle for Indian independence. He further said that the Hindus were in majority and that they had fought for independence single-handed and though fully alive that other communities, especially the Muslims, were not in the forefront of this fight, still Hindus were willing to form a common united Indian nation and did not advance any special claims, privileges or rights.

Then he drew an outline of the Indian state in the following words: "Let the Indian state be purely Indian. Let it not recognize any invidious distinctions whatsoever as regards the franchise, public services, offices, taxation on the grounds of religion and race. Let no cognizance be taken whatsoever of man's being Hindu or Mohammedan, Christian or Jew. Let all citizens of that Indian state be treated according to their individual worth irrespective of their religious or racial percentage in the general population. Let that language and script be the national language and the script of that Indian state which are understood by the overwhelming majority of the people as happens in every other state in the world... Let 'one man, one vote' be the general rule irrespective of caste or creed, race or religion. If such an Indian state is kept in view, the Hindu sanghatanists will, in the interests of Hindu sanghatan itself, be the first to offer their whole-hearted loyalty to it."

After having drawn the above outline of the future Indian State, Savarkar asked Muslims the following questions: "Are the Mohammedans ready to join such a truly national Indian state without asking any special privilege, protection, or weightage on the fanatical ground that a special merit attaches to them of being Mohammedans and not Hindus?" Savarkar was a deep student of world history including that of India and knew that the Muslim answer would be in the negative. Hence he further added, "Let the Hindus remember that the real cause of this mischief is nothing else but the hankering of the Hindus after the will-o-the-wisp of a Hindu-Muslim unity. The day we gave the Mohammedans to understand that Swaraj could not be won unless and until the Mohammedans obliged the Hindus by making common cause with them, that day we rendered an honorable unity impossible. When an overwhelming majority in a country goes on its knees before a minority so antagonistic as the Mohammedans, imploring them to lend a helping hand and assures it that otherwise the major community is doomed to death, it would be a wonder if that minor community does not sell their assistance to the higher bidder possible..." Giving a permanent answer to the Muslim threat that they would not cooperate unless their demands were met, Savarkar said, "Friends, we wanted and do want only that kind of unity which will go to create an Indian state in which all citizens irrespective of caste and creed, race and religion are treated all alike on the principle of one man one vote... We are not out to fight with England only to find a change of masters but we Hindus aim to be masters in our own house.. If India is not freed from foreign domination, the Indian Muslims cannot but be slaves themselves. If they feel it to be true, if and when they feel they cannot do without the assistance and the good-will of the Hindus, let them come then to ask for unity and that also not to oblige the Hindus but to oblige themselves. A Hindu-Muslim unity which is affected thus is worth having." Having thus elaborately spoken on Hindu-Muslim unity, he finally said that we would observe the following formula in respect of Hindu-Muslim unity: "If you come, with you; if you don't without you; and if you oppose, in spite of you the Hindus will continue to fight for their national freedom as best as they can."

Being aware of the historic mentality of the majority of the Muslims, Savarkar knew well that they would never extend their hand for unity. Hence he gave a permanent warning in these words, "... the Mohammedans are likely to prove dangerous to our Hindu nation and the existence of a common Indian state even if and when England goes out." The Indian intellectuals who read Marx, Engels, Lenin, Mao, Stalin, Ling Yutang, Edgar Snow, Sydney and Beatrice Webb, G. D. H. Cole, Twaney, and carried on profound discussions, did not take notice of this speech which had realistically analyzed the real state of affairs in India.

In January 1938, Savarkar went to Baroda. He had been elected president of the Marathi Literary Society of Baroda. In his presidential speech at this conference, he dealt on the necessity of purification of the language. A few months later, on April 15, the 22nd session of the Maharashtra Literary society was held in Bombay. Savarkar was elected president for this session. His speech at this conference is considered very important. In it, he dealt with various important issues. As usual he stressed the importance of the purification of the Marathi language and of the importance of Nagari script. Then he invited the attention of the literary writers to the paucity of verbs in the Marathi language and showed the way in which this deficiency could be overcome. After that he emphasized the need for translating Marathi books into English and suggested that a Board of translation should be established. In speaking about the aim of literature, he first divided it into scientific and imaginative types and discussed both of them at length. Talking about the modern and progressive literature, he said that it could not be assumed that the literature was realistic or would reveal truth merely because it was progressive. A bullet that overshot the target could not be called progressive merely because it goes in the forward direction. In the end he strongly advised the writers to forsake the pen and lift the rifle. For he said "A nation that is protected by arms is a nation where various subjects can be discussed."

During this year, Savarkar went on many tours for propagating the Hindu Mahasabha ideology. In the first fortnight of April, he journeyed through Uttar Pradesh and spoke in Kanpur, Faizabad, Barabanki, Lucknow, and Agra. In May, he went to Punjab and visited Lahore, Amritsar, Hoshiyarpur, and Ajmer. In September, he went to Sindh and visited Hyderabad, Kothari, Karachi, Sukkur and Shikarpur. In addition to these far-off places, he visited and spoke in Panvel, Chalisgaon, Nagar, Kopargaon, Belapur, Sholapur, Nasik, Igatpuri, Pimpalgaon, Chandwad, Malegaon, Nandgaon, Thane, Gwalior, and Jodhpur. He paid a number of visits to Poona and Delhi. His tour itinerary shows to what extent Savarkar was carrying on his own shoulders the burden of party propaganda.

The Hindu Mahasabha session for the year 1938 was held in Nagpur. This year too he was elected president. Savarkar went to Nagpur on December 28, to attend this session. Dr. Moonje, Dr. Khare, Dr. Kedar, and Dr. Hedgewar received him on the station. Outside the station, the R.S.S. volunteers gave him the guard of honor. Then, he was taken out in a grand procession which reached the conference venue after five hours. The address he delivered at this conference was, like his address at Karnavati, of historic importance and contains a deep analysis of various aspects of nationality in India.

In the beginning, he traced the 5,000 years history of India and showed how united the country was. Then he said the Hindu nation was an organic growth and no papier-mâché make-shift. After this, he traced the origin and growth of the idea of an Indian nation as propounded by the Congress. In this, he referred to the advantages and disadvantages of English education. He further stated that, because of English education, the first two generations got cut off from Hindu traditions and they conceived a notion that it was in the nation's interest to imitate the European nations. Amongst the things they wanted to imitate was in respect of the concept of a nation. They found that in Europe a national unit was a geographical unit. People living on the French soil were French, those living on German soil were Germans, and on Spanish soil were Spaniards, and on English soil were English. From this they drew the following conclusion. Hindus, Muslims, Christians, Parsis, and others were inhabiting the land called India for hundreds of years. Hence they all constituted a nation. Therefore all of them must henceforth forget that they were Hindus, Muslims, Christians, and Parsis and must become Indians.

For the Hindus it was easy to become Indians. Their western education had taught them that Hinduism was a bundle of superstitions. As western education had spread faster and wider amongst the Hindus, the number of supporters of Indian nationalism grew apace. The territorial patriots wanted that politically people should cease to call themselves Hindus. Some of them even gloried in not being Hindus. They were Indians and that they thought Muslims would follow their example and would forget their communal individuality and merge themselves into the territorial Indian nation. But the Muslims remained Muslims from first to last. They never became Indians.

In further elucidation he said that common land could not become the only criterion of nationality. To support his contention, he narrated the earlier history of the differences between Catholics and Protestants and how that had affected England, France, and Holland. But he did not stop there. He referred to the contemporary examples of Germans from Sudetanland and Englishmen from Ulster. And then finally he asked the following question: "Have the Indian Muslims, then, that will: to be one with the Hindus?"

Savarkar had analyzed very critically the question of nationality in India. But those who considered themselves as trustees of knowledge did not bother to take notice of Savarkar's ideas in order to understand them at least on an intellectual plane. Who can say that in the conditions obtaining today, after a lapse of 67 years, the analysis made by Savarkar and the questions posed by him are not relevant?

One more important event took place at Nagpur. Hindus were politically persecuted in the then Hyderabad state. In this session, it was decided to start a campaign of civil resistance in the state to highlight this persecution. Later the Working Committee meeting of the Hindu Mahasabha was held on February 4, 1939 in Delhi in which Savarkar was appointed the sole leader of the civil resistance movement in the Hyderabad state.

Like last year, this year too, that is in 1939, Savarkar traveled extensively in India. In February, he toured Bengal. In March, he visited Bihar. In April, he traveled through Berar. In June, he journeyed through Mahakoshal. And in September, he visited Hubli and Dharvad. In addition, he paid flying visits to Delhi and Meerut. Also, as the civil resistance movement had begun, he had to visit Poona and Sholapur quite often.

It was only in March that the civil resistance movement assumed a bigger form. About 200 civil resisters entered the Nizam state. Slowly the movement gathered momentum. The participants were both old and young, like Senapati Bapat, L. B. Bhopatkar, Chandrakiran Sarada, Mamarao Date, V. G. Deshpande,

Balashastri Hardas, Bhaiyaji Dani, and Madhavrao Mule, the last two later became the General Secretaries of the R.S.S. The Arya Samaj took part in this movement more vigorously. While the Hindu Mahasabha sent 5,000 civil resisters, the Arya Samaj sent 10,000. At last, on July 19, the Nizam government announced some political reforms. The Hindu Mahasabha and the Arya Samaj then withdrew the civil resistance movement. In this new dispensation, 50% seats were reserved for the Muslims. And yet the Hindu Mahasabha accepted these concessions. So now, as well as later, the arm-chair intellectuals criticized this policy of the Hindu Mahasabha. It is true that these were partial reforms. But considering the earlier position this surely was a step forward. Savarkar therefore with a sense of triumph, said, "Where there was not a single seat, we have secured 50% seats and thus have humbled the Nizam. The civil resistance movement has greatly shaken the colossal inequity of the Nizam government. Sir Akbar Hydari and the Nizam who refused to meet the leaders of the Hindu Mahasabha or Arya Samaj have now climbed down before the Hindu Mahasabha."[1]

The civil resistance movement had another important aspect. From 1920, a conviction had grown that Gandhiji alone was able to build and launch a mass movement. To some extent that was true. For, in the previous eighteen years all the movements had been conducted under the leadership of Gandhiji. The other leaders were merely his followers. This persuaded Gandhiji that he alone could start a mass movement. After the civil resistance movement began, Gandhiji sent for Dr. Moonje and told him, "You see, Doctor, Satyagraha is a technique and I am its originator. Others may fumble in handling it." To this Dr. Moonje rejoined, "Mahatmaji, the Hyderabad movement is not a satyagraha. This is a civil resistance movement. Its founder is not an ordinary man. It is a technique pioneered by Lord Krishna, Shri. Chatrapati Shivaji Maharaj."[2] Gandhiji realized that Savarkar did not belong to the type of leaders like Nehru, Rajendra Prasad, Pattabhi, and Vallabhai. Like Gandhiji, Savarkar had his own will power to create his own world.

Having failed in his guile to stop the civil resistance movement in Hyderabad, Gandhiji resorted to another trick. The Prime Minister of Hyderabad Sir Akbar Hydari suggested to the Viceroy that in order to close the camps and movement in the British territories, 'Princes Protection Act' should be brought into operation with reference to Hyderabad. The Viceroy replied that the Act would also have to be made applicable to other states. Then Gandhiji assured him that he would stop the Satyagraha movements in other states. According to this assurance, satyagrahas in various states were stopped. But Hyderabad struggle was led by Savarkar. He said, "So far we have fought against the Nizam, tomorrow we shall also fight the British."[3]

[1] S. S. Savarkar : Swa. Veer Savarkar, (Hindumahasabha Parva), Part 1 - p.241

[2] V. D. Savarkar : Samagra Savarkar Wangamaya Vol IV - p.390

[3] V. D. Savarkar : Samagra Savarkar Wangamaya Vol IV - p.389

How the Congress policy was double-faced could be seen from its stand about Kashmir and Hyderabad states. The Kashmir ruler was a Hindu and the majority of his subjects were Muslims. So, the demands of the Kashmir leaders were that the ruler's powers should be curtailed and that he should be pensioned off and that Urdu should become the state language. Nehru supported these demands. The Hyderabad ruler was a Muslim and the majority of his subjects were Hindus. Did the democratic principle, as broadcast in Kashmir, applicable in Hyderabad? The answer was 'No'. According to the policy of the Gandhian Congress, this demand was communal.[1] Be that as it may. If the Hyderabad struggle succeeded, despite opposition from the Congress, the credit goes to the civil resisters and their leader Savarkar. This will be the judgment of history.

The 1939 session of the Hindu Mahasabha was to be held in Calcutta. Savarkar was again elected president for this session. But the various tours, public and private meetings had told on Savarkar's health and he fell ill. He, therefore, felt that he should not shoulder the responsibility of presiding over this session. When Barrister Nirmalchand Chatterji came to know of Savarkar's feelings, he implored him to accept the presidentship and Savarkar submitted to this importunity. Savarkar's address in the Calcutta session, like his previous two addresses, is of historic importance.

In it, he first dealt with the history and the ideological background of the civil resistance movement in Hyderabad and also of Satyagraha at Shiva Mandir in Delhi. Then he dilated upon the basic principles of Hindu Sanghatan movement. He spoke at length on the points he had referred to in the earlier sessions.

In his Nagpur address, Savarkar had discussed the attitude of the Indian minorities. He had then said that minorities like Parsis, Christians, and Jews were not troublesome like the Muslims. Now in his Calcutta address, he spoke about the rights of the minorities. He said that the anti-national and aggressive designs of the Muslim minority constituted a danger to all non-Muslim Indians in India and not only to the Hindus alone. It was the anti-national attitude of the Muslim minority alone which was giving a handle to the British government to obstruct the further political and constitutional progress in India. The League posed itself as the champion of all non-Hindu minorities. But the fact was that the relations of Christians, Jews, and above all our Parsi brothers had been for centuries most cordial with the Hindus and these non-Muslim minorities had never advanced any anti-national or unreasonable claims and had never indulged in political hooliganism or fanatical riots as a silly means to impress their political importance... If the Christians, the Jews, the Parsis, and all non-Muslim minorities and the Hindus presented a common understanding and a common front at any would-be Round Table Conference or Constitutional Assembly, the Muslims would find themselves singularly isolated and would be forced to cease to speak 'in the name of minority problem.'

---

[1] V. D. Savarkar : Samagra Savarkar Wangamaya Vol IV - p.389

In this Calcutta session, Savarkar first enunciated the basic principles of his economic policy. He began by saying, "Besides hunger, the problem of bread, man has other appetites as fundamental as those like sensual, intellectual, sentimental, some natural, some acquired, some personal, and some social and his being is a complex one; so also is his history. Man has a stomach, but the stomach is not man. Therefore, the solution that is sometimes suggested to the effect that the economical community of interest provides the only and the best solvent of all religious, racial, national, and other antipathies that divide mankind in the world is as superficial as it is simple. The fact that in Europe the very races and nations wherein the prophets of this school arose and preached and where giant efforts were made to revolutionize all human institutions and recast them into economic mold alone, religious, racial, and national differences have been assuming formidable proportions and have been persisting to assert themselves in Germany, Italy, France, Poland, England, Spain, etc. in spite of centuries of the most intense propaganda to insist on economic community of interest..." He further said that leaving aside the doctrinaire solutions, we as practical politicians should restrict our immediate economic program to the economic advance of the Hindu nation alone. Having made this important point, Savarkar went on to state his principles of economic policy, as under: 1. Welcome the machine 2. Support the handicraft industry but national production to be done by machine 3. The peasantry and working class, being the chief sources of national wealth, special effort should be made to reinvigorate them 4. The interests of both capital and labor to be subordinated to national interests 5. If possible, all key industries to be nationalized 6. In some cases government should take over the land for state cultivation in order to educate peasants in the use of machine tools 7. Strikes or lock-outs which are harmful to national production are referred to state arbitration, and in serious cases to be quelled, etc.

Savarkar mentioned 'National coordination of class interests' as a formula which summed up his economic policy. After India became free the 'First Five Year Plan' was formulated. There are very few differences between the ideas mentioned in this plan and those of Savarkar's. In the report of the 'First Five Year Plan' the following principle has been stated as the fundamental one: 'Constant reconciliation of the interests of all section.'[1] Now what is the big difference between this principle and Savarkar's 'National coordination of Class interests'?

---

[1]First Five-Year Plan - p.572

Militarization of Hindudom

"The revolutionary army is needed because great historical questions can be solved only by force and in the modern struggle organized force means military organization." - Lenin[1]

During the First World War of 1914-1918, Savarkar was in jail in the Andamans. According to the plan of revolution of Abhinav Bharat, when the British Empire was entangled in an Armageddon, that opportunity was to be seized to gain India's freedom. Savarkar has described in his book 'My Transportation' how miserable he felt in finding himself in an helpless condition when that golden opportunity, which occurs once or twice in a century, had come.[2] That opportunity came and went. Prisoner Savarkar could do nothing.

Twenty years later war clouds began to gather in Europe. In 1933, Hitler came to power, and soon he began his aggressive policies. In 1936 Hitler and Mussolini formed an axis. In March 1938, Germany annexed Austria, and in October, it occupied Sudetanland, a province of the then Czechoslovakia. It began to appear that Hitler's politics of aggression was likely to spark a war in Europe and that its flames were likely to engulf other continents. So the guardians of world peace and the supporters of non-violence began their peace efforts. During this period Savarkar spoke in Poona on 'India and Czechoslovakia'. From that speech one gets a glimpse of how Savarkar was looking at the prospects of world war.

Savarkar said, "Very recently, it was felt that the Second World War would break out. Some of our people were shaken and began to say that there should be no war. But I am of the opinion that from the point of view of Indian interest the Second World War must occur. In the last war England did not worry much about the defense of Indian Empire. But the situation has changed. England's main sea-lane to India is through the Mediterranean. Italy which was a weak state in the First World War has now become powerful and there is a fear that it may block England's sea lanes through the Mediterranean. If this should happen, then England would be strangulated and it would find it difficult to maintain its communication with India and its hold on this country."

"This is the scenario of Europe. What about the East? In this part Japan has become a powerful country. If it should decide, then its airplanes could reach Calcutta within two hours. Of course, if war were to begin at this juncture, England would not necessarily be defeated. But its empire in India is certainly in jeopardy. Our first enemy is Britain. Others are neither our friends nor foes. We

---

[1]David Shub : Lennin - a biography - p.49

[2]V. D. Savarkar : Samagra Savarkar Wangamaya Vol I - p.521

need not incur their enmity on account of Czechoslovakia. We must look to these events strictly from the viewpoint of our interest."[1]

This speech was delivered on October 11, 1938, and the Second World War began on September 3, 1939. An opportunity for the deliverance of one's country which comes once or twice in a century had come for the second time. And Savarkar was free. So he began to guide the people as to how India could use that opportunity. When his writings on this subject are read today what comes to one's mind is that, from the beginning to the end, there is a consistency in his thinking and aim. There is no fickleness or confusion like Gandhiji.

Seventeen days after the war began, Savarkar issued a statement mainly addressed to all the Indian legislators, capitalists, and the working class. Its purpose was to tell them that the opportunity created by this war should be utilized for expanding Indian trade. The important part of this statement was: "What twenty years of 'Swadeshi' preaching or efforts to have prohibitive duties on foreign articles could not have done in uprooting the foreign formidable competition, which used to kill our infant industries, could be achieved in a couple of years if but our legislatures, capital, and labor coordinate their efforts in a spirit of patriotic and mutually just accommodation and both by working up the existing and by starting new industries and manufactures at full speed, replace these foreign articles by Swadeshi ones and capture the market for them while it is uncompleted by foreign supply."[2] Also, he prepared brief drafts of resolutions which he wanted the Hindu Mahasabha to adopt. In one such draft it was stated: "That the Government of India should take immediate steps to encourage the Indian manufacturing firms to start manufacture of Aero Engines and Motor Engines and implements of modern warfare so that India may be made self-sufficient and not dependent helplessly on foreign countries for the supply of implements of modern mechanization for the Indian Army."[3] When many of the leaders in the British Empire during this period had not yet grasped the importance of the mechanization of the army, Savarkar was laying emphasis on the manufacture of mechanical things for modern warfare.[4] It was but natural that the people busy in Khadi and Village industries and peaceful agitation should find these ideas absolutely alien.

Soon after the war started, the Viceroy began to meet with Indian leaders of various political parties. The purpose of these meetings was to find out what help Indian leaders would give to the British war effort. Savarkar met the Viceroy on October 9, 1939. This meeting lasted for about an hour. The discussion that took place in this meeting was, of course, confidential and it was a convention that subjects discussed were not to be divulged. But some of the anti-Hindu Mahasabha

[1]S. S. Savarkar : Swa. Veer Savarkar ,(Hindumahasabha Parva) Part 1 - p.146-147

[2]A. S. Bhide : Veer Savarkar's Whirlwind Propaganda - p.134

[3]A. S. Bhide : Veer Savarkar's Whirlwind Propaganda - p.155-156

[4]Correlli Barnett : The Desert Generals - p.85

newspapers carried stories giving false accounts of this meeting. To refute this misrepresentation, Savarkar issued a statement stating the points which he had emphasized in this meeting. In brief it stated:

"The Hindu Mahasabha feels that none of the belligerent powers in Europe, including Poland and above all Russia, was or is actuated by any moral or human principle as 'Democracy', or 'The liberties of the down-trodden', or 'Political Justice and equity' beyond what suited to the self-interest of the respective Nations and States. So Hindu Mahasabha looks at this war from the point of view of protecting interests of the Hindu nation. Therefore it makes the following suggestions: 1. The British Government should grant India the status of self-governing dominion so that the Hindus may feel that in fighting this war they are serving the cause of their national freedom. 2. Any such constitution to be immediately introduced ought to be based on the principle of 'one man one vote'. The Depressed Classes alone may be given a weightage. 3. All citizens should be granted full freedom to follow their faith, culture, and language so far as it does not infringe on the equal rights of others. 4. The doors of the army should be thrown open to all and the distinction of the enlisted and non-enlisted classes should be removed. Every step should be taken to modernize the Indian Army, Navy, and Air Force. 5. Indian forces should not be used in any theater of war outside India which has no direct connection with the defense of India."

After having met nearly all leading personalities in the Indian public life, the Viceroy issued a statement. He said that Britain was fighting to resist aggression whether directed against it or others. He quoted the British Prime Minister who had said, "We are seeking no material advantage for ourselves. We are not aiming only at victory, but looking beyond it to laying a foundation of a better international system which will mean that war is not the inevitable lot of every succeeding generation." As regards India's future he said, "As matters stand today, the constitutional position of India and the policy of His Majesty's Government are governed by the provisions of the Government of India Act 1935... The natural issue of India's progress as there contemplated is the attainment of Dominion Status." He further added, "And I am authorized now by His Majesty's Government to say that at the end of the war they will be very willing to enter into consultation with representatives of the several communities, parties, and interests, in India, and with the Indian Princes, with a view to securing their aid and cooperation in the framing of such modifications as may be seen desirable."

Savarkar's rejoinder to this statement was a little caustic, but it also contained constructive suggestions. In short, it stated, "Viceroy's statement is disappointing to a degree. The four or five columns of the verbose statement could have well been compressed into four or five sentences so far as substance is concerned. The Viceroy should realize that India is sick of running after this wordy mirage. A dominion status must be conceded by the British to India just at the end of this war at the latest. The British government must bear in mind that

India can never extend a willing cooperation unless she feels that the cause of her own freedom is likely to be served in a substantive measure by offering responsive cooperation to Britain. The Advisory Board contemplated in the statement is welcome. But then it has not its functions and powers defined. If it is going to be a mere appendage to serve as a camouflage to conceal autocratic high-handiness, then it can only mean an insult added to injury. But if it is made to serve as a tentative measure with powers more or less equal to a Federal Board of Ministers and if its advice is carried into effect as that of a responsible Council of Ministers, it may prove a step in advance on the line of political progress. But much will depend on its composition. The Hindu Mahasabha must secure such a representation on it as is in keeping with proportion to the population of the Hindus."[1]

In his 1939 presidential address to the Hindu Mahasabha session held at Calcutta, Savarkar had briefly touched on the subject of war. This was quite natural. Because only four months had elapsed since the war had begun. Germany had conquered Poland, and except for the Russian attack on Finland and the naval actions at sea, the battlefield was quiet. Hence this period was humorously described as a 'Phony War'

In 1940, Savarkar also toured some parts of the country for rousing public opinion. He first traveled in Maharashtra. He went to Kalyan, Chalisgaon, Songir, Shirpur, Sindkhed, Shahade, Talode, Nandurbar, and Nizampur. In March, he visited Madras. In May, he toured the state of Travancore. He went to Poona three times and in every visit he had to fulfill a tight schedule of public and private meetings. He also went to Delhi and Simla. His visit to Simla took place in July and it was mainly for the purpose of meeting the Viceroy. However, in his two days' stay there, he fulfilled a crowded program of public engagements. On his return journey from Simla, at Kalka Station, the then Chief Minister of Punjab, Sir Sikandar Hayat Khan, walked into his compartment. For a few seconds, Savarkar could not place him. But soon he recognized him.[2] It has already been mentioned that Sir Sikandar had brought revolvers and copies of 1857 with him from London. After sometime Sir Sikandar took Savarkar to his special compartment where both discussed some Indian problems for half an hour.

During August of this year, Savarkar began to suffer from attacks of sciatica. So his private and public engagements as well as tours were canceled. Finally, he had to be removed to a private hospital for undergoing surgical treatment. During his sickness he appointed Dr. Moonje as working President.

Four months later, the annual session of the Hindu Mahasabha was held at Madura. Savarkar was again elected president for this session. His Presidential address at Madura, like his earlier addresses, is of historic importance. The first

[1]A. S. Bhide : Veer Savarkar's Whirlwind Propaganda - p.157-159

[2]A. S. Bhide : Veer Savarkar's Whirlwind Propaganda - p.627

part of his address was devoted to explain as to how the Hindu Mahasabha was defending the interests of the Hindus. Then he mentioned the following important point which is as true today as it was then. "It is not want of resources, oh Hindus, which forces you to be so helpless and hopeless, but it is the want of practical insight in political realities to know your resources; and the tact to use them. You have lost the political eye altogether."

Savarkar then turned his attention to the war situation. Sixteen months had passed since the war began. There had been considerable changes in the war scene. Savarkar, therefore, explained in detail his approach to the war and what program the Hindu Mahasabha should adopt in connection with it.

Savarkar contended that countries involved in the war, such as, England, Germany, Poland, France, Russia, and others were not actuated by altruistic motives. Under the circumstances the demand of the Congress leaders, like Pandit Nehru, that Great Britain should state its war aims was an idle exercise. The same could be said about 'isms'. Nothing could cover up the armed dominion of various peoples because their conquest could pass under the name of Bolshevism, Nazism, Fascism, or Republicanism. It would be suicidal folly to allow ourselves to be charmed by the slogans of these 'isms'. Under the present circumstances we should befriend those who serve our interests without bothering as to what 'ism' they champion and should continue to be friends with them till it suits our purpose.

Savarkar categorically stated that there was no possibility of England being defeated so disastrously that it would be compelled to hand over its empire to Germany. If such a possibility arose, England would not only grant dominion status to India, but would hand over some of her possessions to us as she had done in the case of United States. So we must chalk out our program as to how best we could use this war opportunity to safeguard and promote Hindu interests. And while doing this we must not ignore our weakness as well as strength.

Savarkar then raised the most vital question: Was an armed revolt possible in the country? He said that the first and the only course open to a subject people, while its rulers were involved in a life and death struggle with a powerful foe was to raise the standard of armed revolt. But as our society was disarmed, disorganized, and disunited, it was not possible to stage an armed revolt. Then what was the alternative? Savarkar's answer was that the Hindus must participate in all war activities which should be helpful to the militarization and industrialization of India. Such an opportunity did not come our way in the last 50 years, and, despite our empty protests and demands, would not come our way in the next 50 years.

Savarkar bluntly stated that Britain was raising the military forces and accelerating the process of industrialization in India not for the good of Indians but to help its own war efforts. We, on our part, were participating for our own good in this war effort. This had to be said publicly and plainly. For Indians had developed a habit of thinking that as the interests of India and Britain are antagonistic, to join hands with Britain was an anti-national act. Savarkar was of the view that, in practical politics, there could be an alliance between two parties on a point of common interest even though there could be a conflict as regards other interests. Those who were always afraid of being duped by others must be simpletons deserving to be duped. Stating that the Hindu Sanghatanists were so conscious of their political wisdom and were so self-confident that they could take good care of themselves against being duped by the crafty statesmanship of Great Britain. He further said that the Hindu Sanghatanists felt no hesitation in participating in war efforts.

In the wartime, the numerical strength of the Hindus in the army was increasing. Earlier the Muslims proportion in the army was about 75%. Now about a hundred thousand people had enlisted and out of them 60,000 were Hindus and 30,000 were Muslims. The Air Force was also expanding and Hindus were joining in large numbers. The representation of the Hindu Mahasabha to the government that more Hindus should be recruited in the navy was favorably received. The land forces had increased from two hundred thousand to a million. So the earlier system to have Indian officers only in special Indianised units was scrapped and all units were opened to Indian officers. So Savarkar said a little derisively that the British government used to trot out an excuse that it would still take 50 years to train up the Indian officers. But suddenly the Government had discovered that, as in Europe, so also in India an officer could be trained in a few months.

Savarkar described how the circumstances were sucking an Indian in the technical world. He said that the manufacture of war materials on an enormous scale had already afforded an opportunity to thousands of our artisans, craftsmen, workers, and technicians to specialize themselves in producing rifles, tanks, and ammunition. Not only that, they were being trained in building factories which produced these weapons. The government had permitted, rather reluctantly, Seth Walchand Hirachand to build a shipyard at Bezwada and a factory for the manufacture of airplanes at Bangalore with Indian capital. In addition, other manufacturing industries had also received a fillip.

Why had these things happened? Savarkar explained them as follows: "But not that military exigencies have forced England to raise India to a self-sufficient economic and military unit - a center commanding the defenses of the whole Eastern part of their empire from Egypt to Australia, they are compelled to see that key industries and even industries in general are started and flourish in this country to such a wide extent that if ever the connection of the Eastern part of their empire is at least temporarily cut off from the Western empire, they may be able to depend for all the sinews of war chiefly on India which abounds in the resources of men and materials."

After analyzing the situation thus, Savarkar asked: "Whether you could have ever been able to take such rapid strides in militarization and industrialization within a year with our own resources? Could the Hindu Mahasabha or the Congress or any party have ever been able to raise half a million up-to-date army personnel on its own resources?" Then he said, "We could not have conducted even lathi clubs on such a large scale. War had given an opportunity to thousands of Hindus to enlist themselves in the army, the navy, and the air force. This would enable them to become up-to-date soldiers and officers. They would get training in building shipyard, and aircraft factory, an ammunition factory, etc. Also, thousands of mechanics would be trained to become specialists in production of modern weapons. Should we turn our backs on this golden opportunity because some fools would call it cooperation with the British Government or somebody would describe it as an act of violence?" Having said this, he added that, a million of our people were going to be employed in the army and armament factories. So at least five million of our people belonging to the class which faced perennial unemployment would get food and clothing. This would ease the burden on our agriculture class.

Savarkar drew a very fine picture of how the military importance of India had increased. He said that in earlier European wars, England was not relying nor did it wish to rely on India. But now the longish shadow of the dwarfish Japan had of late fallen on the Bay of Bengal. So changes in the British military policy had become inevitable. A war with Japan, whose declared objective was to free Asia from European domination, had become unavoidable. If Japan was to be fought, then a huge army would have to be raised in India. So England had perforce to depend on India.

Explaining why Hindus should under any circumstances take part in the militarization and industrialization and why it was in their interest, Savarkar said, if the Hindus did not enlist in the army, the navy, and the air force or serve in the armament factories, the Muslims would enter all these fields. Thus, the British would not be militarily weakened. Instead you would see that you had helped to increase the strength of the second enemy who wished to enslave the Hindus.

How many Congress leaders both at the national and state level could be seen analyzing the problems confronting the country so rationally, pragmatically and in plain language? Intense solicitude about the future of India and about the regeneration of the Hindu society is manifest in the above Savarkarian analysis. How many people took notice of this Madura speech?

In the Madura session, a resolution was passed to start a direct action movement against the British Government. The resolution was opposed by Dr. Nimkar of Madras. The points he stressed during the discussion showed that very few people like him had really understood the essence of Savarkar's policy. Dr. Nimkar argued that when we had not enough strength, it was unwise to take on both the English and the Muslims. Instead we should concentrate on militarization and industrialization. It could only be said that this 'direct action' resolution was merely a reflection of the mentality created by the Congress philosophy is those days in India.

Savarkar had to meet a tight schedule of tours, public meetings and personal interviews, in 1941. In January, he toured Nasik. In April, he went to Nagpur. On this occasion, the editor of 'Savadhan', Mr. Mavkar had come to the station to greet Savarkar. On the platform he slipped his foot and came under wheels of the train and died. Savarkar toured Bengal in June. He visited Poona three times. On the first occasion, he came for the election campaign of Jamnadas Metha who was later elected. On the second occasion, he did the naming ceremony of a gymnasium at the Maharashtra Mandal. On the last occasion, he attended the Sapru conference. In addition, he also toured Sangli, Miraj, and Kolhapur. In his public speeches he generally dealt with the subject of militarization, and with various illustrations and arguments, he brilliantly expounded the importance of this subject.

In a speech before the students of the Scottish College at Calcutta he said, "Since the days of our First War of Independence in 1857, it has been the policy of the British Government to keep the army out of politics. Our policy should be to carry politics into the Indian army by all possible means and once we succeed in this, the battle for freedom will be won."[1] In another speech he said, "You know your enemies. I ask you to join the army to learn to wield the guns and turn them to the cause of freedom. I tell you this as plainly as I told the Viceroy himself about it. Do not worry about the bonds and agreements. The reverse of those scraps is blank. You can write new bonds and new agreements on it when the time comes."[2]

In an earlier chapter mention has been made of how Savarkar tried to carry politics into the Indian army during his London days. Lala Hardayal and others had attempted the same thing during the First World War. It was during the Gandhi era, that is, from 1920 to 1940, that the movement of taking politics into the Indian army ceased because of the creed of non-violence.

During this year Savarkar issued a number of statements on various subjects. The statements on two subjects were important not only at the time they were issued but they are also important today from the point of view of the future of the Hindus.

The first subject was Census. Savarkar issued five statements. The first was issued at the end of 1940 under the caption, 'The Census and the Hindu Sabhas'. Then came the statement 'The Census Week', followed by 'An appeal to the Aryasamajists Brethren regarding the Census question', 'The Census and the Pan-Hindu fold', and 'Hindus! Wake up! The hour of the Census strikes'. These

---

[1]Dhananjay Keer : Veer Savarkar - p.257

[2]Dhananjay Keer : Veer Savarkar - p.257

four statements were issued by him during January and February 1941. By these statements, he drew the attention of the Hindus to the importance of the census, to the necessity of all castes to register themselves as Hindus, and also to the definition of the word Hindu and appealed to them to act accordingly.

Incidentally, he gave the following piece of advice about the census: "When National duty commands to conduct sensational campaigns of fighting in the field or facing imprisonment with beating of drums and flourishing of trumpets, it is indeed heroic to join these ranks. But it should not be forgotten that, it is no less heroic to address oneself to a plodding, tiresome, lonely, and constructive work of nation-building when national interests demand that."[1] It must be borne in mind that the General Secretary of the Congress, Acharya Kripalani, had then issued a statement saying that the Congress refused to have anything to do with the census as it was a communal question.[2] After independence came, it does not appear that Acaharya Kripalani during the Congress rule got the census work abolished as it was a communal question.

The second subject was Assam. Savarkar issued a statement under the caption 'Hindu Assam in danger' on July 8, 1941. In it he said that a deep laid design to increase the Muslim population in Assam by colonizing it by Muslim immigrants from Bengal and other provinces was put into operation years ago and was being systematically and very effectively carried out. The Congress ministry had not put a stop to these inroads... Advising the Assamese Hindus as to what steps they should take, Savarkar said that the Assamese Hindus must free themselves from the mental slavery to the Congressite creed and organization. The Congress could not, because of its fundamental creed and because of the Gandhian grip on that organization, fight in defense of the rights of Hindus as Hindus. In the end he said that Hindus must remember that weeping and wailing over grievances inflicted upon them by others could not by itself save them. It was by adopting the technique of their adversaries that the Hindus could defeat them.[3] It does not appear that this statement made any impact on the minds of the Assamese. They espoused the Congress creed. The result is that India has to face the problem of Assam today. Who is responsible for this? And what is the alternative even today to the solution suggested by Savarkar?

Later in November, Savarkar toured Assam. He repeatedly told the Assamese Hindus that the danger they were facing could be averted only by voting for Hindu Sanghatanist candidates. In one of the discussions, a participant narrated the following exchange: Nehru was told that if the open land was permitted to be occupied by the Muslims and if their population increased, this land would go to Pakistan. Nehru replied that nature abhorred vacuum. To this Savarkar rejoined that Nehru was oblivious to the fact that nature also abhorred poisonous gas. Be

---

[1] A. S. Bhide : Veer Savarkar's Whirlwind Propaganda - p.283
[2] A. S. Bhide : Veer Savarkar's Whirlwind Propaganda - p.322
[3] A. S. Bhide : Veer Savarkar's Whirlwind Propaganda - p.443-451

that as it may. Nehru's above remark reminds one of his famous statements in regards to the Chinese incursion in Ladakh that, "not even a blade of grass grows there."[1]

It was decided to hold the 1941 session of the Hindu Mahasabha at Bhagalpur. But the government put a ban on this session. So Savarkar directed that December 14 should be observed as 'Bhagalpur Day' and a demand should be made to lift the ban. But the government stood firm. Then to assert his legitimate right, Savarkar decided to hold the session in Bhagalpur, and bands of volunteers were sent to Bhagalpur to defy the ban. Savarkar was arrested at Gaya. About two thousand civil resisters, including Dr. Moonje, Bhai Paramananda, and Dr. Shyama Prasad Mukerjee, were arrested and kept in Bhagalpur jail. They were released soon after the period fixed for the session was over. This civil resistance struggle again conclusively showed that for such struggle the leadership of the Congress or Gandhiji was not necessary.

After returning from the Bhagalpur struggle, Savarkar spoke at a public meeting where he said, "It was Hindu Mahasabha that came forward to fight for the Hindu cause. The honorable Hindu members from the Liberal party supported us and passed resolutions accordingly. But the Congress Working Committee which deliberates for seven days and which boasts that it fights for the civil rights, did not take cognizance of this struggle. Pandit Nehru, who has founded the Association for the Civil Rights, is a member of the Committee. These people wail for the distant China and Russia. Is it not a matter of shame for an organization which calls itself national and which says that it fights for the civil rights? Or is it likely, that as the British people are fighting for the freedom of all countries except India, so also these Congressmen, the supporters of the civil rights, are fighting for the rights of all except the Hindus?"[2] What more light could be thrown on the hypocrisy of the Congress?

Savarkar's political speech at Bhagalpur, like his earlier speeches, is also very important. First he dealt with the question as to why the ban on this session was being broken. Then he traced the progress of the Hindu Mahasabha and afterwards turned his attention to the present situation. He said that all countries were following the policy of self-interest. India must follow the same course. Our first objective must be militarization and industrialization.

Finally he said. "The Great War today has dwarfed all other issues and no one can say with certainty who will emerge successful out of this world chaos. But one thing can still be said as the most probable to happen that but if the Hindus stick to this immediate program and take advantage to the fullest extent possible of the War situation with the Hindu Sanghatanist ideal in full view, pressing on the movement for militarization of the Hindu race, then our Hindu nation is bound to

---

[1] Jawaharlal. Nehru : India's Foreign Policty - p.334

[2] V. D. Savarkar : Samagra Savarkar Wangamaya Vol IV - p.551

emerge far more powerful, consolidated, and situated in an incomparably more advantageous position to face issues after the war - whether it be an internal anti-Hindu civil war or a constitutional crisis, or an armed revolution."

Look back at the history of those times and try to find out how many leaders, whether belonging to the Congress or to the other parties, were thinking about the problems India would face after the war. There was one who went by the title of modern Chanakya and some others who were attempting to resolve the constitutional impasse created by their own actions. How would Satyagraha movement end but in constitutional negotiations?

On December 7, 1941, Japan attacked Pearl Harbor, and Asia was engulfed in the flames of war. Soon Philippines, Malaya, and Java were overrun by the Japanese and by May 20, Burma fell in their hands. Seventeen months earlier, Savarkar had said in his Madura speech that the longish shadow of the dwarfish Japan was falling on the Bay of Bengal. Now it was no longer a shadow. By conquering the Andaman Islands, a fully armed Japan, was riding the Bay of Bengal and England became conscious of the danger confronting her. Savarkar had made reference to this danger in his Madura speech.

In a statement issued after the fall of Singapore on February 17, Savarkar said, "I urge the British government not to underrate the blunt truth that if Japan is allowed to forestall the British government in this case and to proclaim, as soon as and if her invading forces reach the borders of India, that their immediate objective is to free and guarantee the independence of India, such a proclamation on their part cannot but capture the popular imagination of the Indian people by storm and usher in incalculable political complications. The sooner the British forestall the invaders in making India feel that fighting in alliance with Britain is fighting for Indian political freedom, the better for all of us concerned."[1]

Now the British government also became concerned about the seriousness of the situation. In addition, the Chinese and American leaders keenly felt that the British government should seek the active cooperation of the Congress. So the British government formulated a plan to break the political deadlock and sent Sir Stafford Cripps to India to discuss the plan with the leaders of diverse political parties. Cripps reached India on March 22, 1942 and soon started meeting these leaders.

Before leaving for Delhi to meet Cripps, Savarkar addressed a meeting on the platform of the Bombay Central station. He said, "India's freedom is no longer in the gift of anyone. It is a certain event destined to happen."[2] On March 28, Savarkar, along with Dr. Mukherjee, Dr. Moonje, Sir Jwalaprasad Shriwastava, and Ganpat Rai met Cripps. There was a passage of arms between Savarkar and

---

[1] V. D. Savarkar : Historic Statements - p.36
[2] S. S. Savarkar : Swa. Veer Savarkar : Akhand Hindusthancha Ladha Parva - p.76

Cripps about the principle of self-determination. Cripps argued that the constitution of the Commonwealth countries, like South Africa, Canada, contained that principle. To this Savarkar rejoined that earlier there were states in Canada and in other countries and while bringing them together this principle was introduced into their constitution. But India had been an integrated nation from time immemorial. When people in England were in a primitive state, pitchers of water from Varanasi were taken to Rameshwar and vice versa. This could not have been possible unless India was a united country. We could not consider a plan which destroyed the unity of India. However, as the Cripps plan was to be accepted or rejected in toto, the Hindu Mahasabha rejected it. Later the Muslim League and the Congress followed suit. Thus the Cripps plan fell through.

Then Gandhiji took an aggressive posture. He began to say that the British should entrust India to God and quit it. Slowly Congress propaganda warmed up and Gandhiji began to think in terms of having the resolution of 'Quit India' passed by the Congress. Gandhiji had conducted some movements against the British. He was aware of the British methods. But in 1942, Britain was not alone as she was in 1940. On the battlefield she was marching arm in arm with Russia and America. Also, Britain was led by Churchill who could rudely say that he had not become the King's First Minister in order to preside over the liquidation of the British Empire. Churchill and Gandhiji had one common quality. Both had the mental strength to stand alone against the world. In 1940, Churchill had stood out against the victorious Hitler. Now in 1942, Churchill's position had considerably improved. So one wonders why Gandhiji decided to cross swords with a man like Churchill. Gandhiji always failed to fathom the plans of the British and the Muslims. This happened because he ignored the course of history. Sometimes it is said that Gandhiji was creating history. It may be so. But one wonders whether Gandhiji really felt elated about the event that occurred from the time of 'Quit India' movement up to the partition of India?

Like Savarkar, Sardar Patel[1] and Pandit Nehru[2] felt that India would become independent at the end of the war. Gandhiji was aware of their views. And yet he began to harp on his Quit India slogan. Maulana Azad gives the following reason for it: "Gandhiji's idea seemed to be that since the war was on the Indian frontier, the British would come to terms with the Congress as soon as the movement was launched. Even if this did not take place, he believed that the British would hesitate to take any drastic steps with the Japanese knocking at India's doors. He thought that this would give the Congress the time and the opportunity to organize an effective movement."[3]

Savarkar thought that the Congress should not start any movement at all. He was of the firm view that no struggle should be precipitated only for the sake of

[1] Sardar Patel's Correspondence, 1945-50 (Editor) Durga Das Vol 1 - p.26
[2] D. G. Tendulkar : Mahatma, Vol 6 - p.65
[3] Maulana Abul Kalam Azad : India Wins Freedom - p.89

demonstration and excitement at the risk of courting an inevitable failure.[1] He felt the country would derive no benefit from this movement and therefore we should concentrate more on militarization and industrialization.[2] Gandhiji was not in a mood to listen to what Savarkar was saying. He launched the movement. In a few days' time the momentum of the movement died out. On November 20, 1942 Savarkar made the following forecast: "The 'Quit India' movement will end in the split India movement."[3] It is unfortunate that this forecast came true.

During this year the only long propaganda tour he undertook was to Kashmir. It was a 10 day tour. While proceeding to Kashmir, he said on the Delhi station platform that he had toured all over India and the Kashmir tour was the last long journey he was undertaking. In this tour he gave 40 speeches. In addition, there were discussions and private meetings. During this tour the President of Jammu and the Kashmir Conference published an open letter to Savarkar. First, he complimented Savarkar by saying that the latter's views were clear-cut and well-defined unlike those of the nationalist leaders of the Congress and then requested him to back the principle of 'representation according to population' in Kashmir. After the tour ended, Savarkar issued a long statement answering the points made in the open letter. The most important part of the statement was as follows: "Moslems in Kashmir and outside may rest assured that as soon as the democratic principles on which Hindu Mahasabha takes its stand are applied on a uniform basis in Hyderabad, Bhopal and throughout India, the Mahasabha shall never fail to apply it in case of the Kashmir Moslems too."[4]

In the month of June of this year, Louis Fischer, the American Journalist, who later wrote Gandhiji's biography, met Savarkar. During their talks the question of self-determination came up. Fischer asked Savarkar, "Why don't you concede Pakistan?" Savarkar asked a counter question, "Why don't you concede Negrostan in America?" Fischer replied, "It will be an anti-national act." Savarkar retorted "Here also, conceding Pakistan is an anti-national act."

The 'Quit India' movement launched by the Congress had disquieted a section of the people in Britain. Churchill assured the members of Parliament that there was nothing serious about the Indian situation to cause any worry and said that there were now more British troops in India than there had ever been. Savarkar gave a scathing reply to Churchill. He said: "We do not want to disturb them by reminding that just a week before the fall of Singapore they were similarly assured and liked to be assured that Singapore was as impregnable a fortress-guarding the far-eastern gate of the British Empire as ever, and was sure to withstand foursquare all the storms that blew." Then he added, "Even in his speech

---

[1] V. D. Savarkar : Samagra Savarkar Wangamaya Vol VI - p.385

[2] S. S. Savarkar : Swa. Veer Savarkar, Akhand Hindustancha Ladha Parva - p.98

[3] S. S. Savarkar : Swa. Veer Savarkar, Akhand Hindustancha Ladha Parva - p.101

[4] V. D. Savarkar : Historic Statements - p.73

which Gandhiji delivered just on the eve of his arrest he spoke confidently of the moral obligations which were bound to compel England to set India free. Mr. Churchill's speech has served a smart reminder to all concerned that moral obligations have no place in stern and realistic politics where steel alone counts... Nevertheless it should be remembered that it was not only Mr. Churchill, the Prime Minister of the mighty British Empire, who forwarded this argument to fortify his own courage. For, let it be remembered that thus spake Nebuchadnezzar - the mighty King of Babylon also when he stood-on the precipice of his pride. With what consequences we know!"[1] It was Savarkar's knock out blow to Churchill. Subsequently events happened just as Savarkar had indicated.

The Hindu Mahasabha session for this year was to be held in Kanpur. His propaganda tours for five years and the bouts of illness he suffered, from time to time, had impaired Savarkar's health. So on July 31, he resigned his presidency of the Hindu Mahasabha. But in November it appeared that Munshi, Rajaji, and some other Congress leaders very much wanted Dr. Samaprasad Mukherjee to become the President of the Hindu Mahasabha and moves were being made to that effect. These leaders were trying that, under Mukherjee's leadership, the Hindu Mahasabha should concede the principle of self-determination and follow the Congress lead in other matters. In order to thwart these attempts, Savarkar reluctantly fought the election to the Presidency of the Hindu Mahasabha and won it. Thus Savarkar was elected President of the Hindu Mahasabha for the sixth consecutive time.

Savarkar's presidential speech at Kanpur is again of historic importance. He surveyed the important events that had occurred during this year. In order to show to what extent the leaders affected by the illusion of Hindu-Muslim unity were going for India's freedom, Savarkar quoted the following paragraph from the letter Gandhiji wrote to Jinnah: "... the Congress will have no objection to the British Government transferring all the powers it today exercises to the Muslim League on behalf of the whole of India including the so-called Indian India. The Congress will not only not obstruct any Government which the Muslim League may form on behalf of the people, but will even join the government." Criticizing this letter Savarkar said, "The betrayal of Hindu rights or genuine Nationality could have gone no further." He furthermore said that some years ago it was the Muslims only who were fighting for Pakistan and we were disputing with them. But since the Cripps Mission and since the Congress had come round to concede the demand of Pakistan, a preposterous position had arisen. As regards the Congress stand that there should be a united demand for independence, Savarkar's emphatic view was that even if the Congress, the Hindu Mahasabha, and the Muslim League made a common demand signed by millions of Indians, Britain would not give independence as demanded.

---

[1] V. D. Savarkar : Historic Statements - p.80-81

Observing that the Hindu Mahasabha was the only organization that had warned the Muslims of grave consequences if India's unity was broken, Savarkar said, "Oh Hindus! Assert boldly that just as America, Germany, China, and every other country, not excluding Russia, so also in Hindusthan, the Hindus by the fact that they form an overwhelming majority were a nation and Muslims were but a community."

Then he turned his attention to the war situation. He contended that as no group - the Allies or the Axis - had secured a decisive result on the battlefield, it was desirable for the Hindus to remain neutral and in the meanwhile, to continue the work of militarization more intensely. He said that every officer and soldier who served in the Indian army was as patriotic as those who went to jail in Bhagalpur.

At the end of his presidential speech he said, "The dice of destiny are loaded already and recklessly thrown on a world battlefield. All nations are thrown in the crucible! The very seas are on flames. ... No nation after this world war can emerge just as it was. Many of those who were at the pinnacle of their power will be reduced to the dust. Many who were trampled down in the dust may all of a sudden find themselves in a position to rise and come into their own. The face of the earth is bound to get revolutionized in any case and in that revolutionary upheaval which at present lies in the lap of the War Gods, one thing only could be said with some certainty so far as India is concerned that she also cannot but be one of the factors whose future is bound to get revolutionized though we cannot and may not point out definitely the course and the aspects of it."

He concluded the speech with a message, "Hinduise all politics and militarize Hindudom."

Cast your eyes back to those times today and see how many leaders were able to foresee the future events with such revolutionary insight.

Lone Fight for United India

"Thus it comes about that all armed prophets have conquered and unarmed ones failed." - Machiavelli[1]

In 1940, the Muslim League passed the resolution about 'Pakistan'. There was nothing surprising in it to anyone except those who had obstinately closed their eyes. It was the final outcome of the philosophy of Sir Syed Ahmad. In 1885, the Congress was established. Three years later Sir Syed Ahmad wrote a letter to Badruddin Tyabji in which he said, "Is it supposed that the different castes and creeds living in India belong to one nation, or can become nation, and their aims and aspirations be one and the same? I think it is quite impossible... I object to every Congress in any shape or form whatever - which regards India as one nation..."[2] In the same year in his speech at Meerut, he said, "Now suppose that all the English were to leave India, then who would be rulers of India? Is it possible that under these circumstances two nations, the Muhammadan and the Hindu, could sit on the same throne and remain equal in power? Most certainly not. It is necessary that one of them should conquer the other and thrust it down. To hope that both could remain equal is to desire the impossible and the inconceivable."[3] This will show that the Muslim League's Pakistan resolution is the political culmination of the stand of Sir Syed Ahmad.

The Congress leaders had and have persuaded themselves that Muslim separatism is the creation of the British. This is a mistaken view. The imperialist British took advantage of the Muslim tendency to remain separate. The worlds over the Muslims have always treated themselves as a separate community from those with whom they may be living. But the Congress leadership never took notice of it. Also, the Congress leaders were wedded to constitutional agitation, and, therefore, in their armory there was only one weapon, namely, conferences and agreements. In these circumstances, what else could happen except that the demand for Pakistan would be made and that it would be conceded?

The Congress always surrendered its position to Muslim aggression. Savarkar had correctly read the mind of the Congress leaders. And hence he could, as early as April 14, 1940, say in a public statement, "And here I sound a grave warning to all Hindus, whether Congressite or not; that a number of Congress leaders of eminence are very likely to go a long way in acquiescing even in this nefarious demand of the Moslems to break up the unity and integrity of India and

---

[1]Machiavelli : The Prince - p.32

[2]Source material for a history of the Freedom Movement in India, (collected from Bombay Government Records) Vol II, - p.71

[3]Dr. R. C. Majumdar : British Paramountcy and Indian Reniassance, II - p.309

the Indian state, if the Hindus do not repudiate in time the claim of the Congress to speak on behalf of Hindudom as a whole."[1]

The ordinary Congressmen and the Hindu voters could not, in their wildest dream imagine that India would be partitioned. This happened because the reaction of the top Congress leaders to such schemes was always severe. After the Pakistan resolution was adopted Pandit Nehru in a public speech said, "The League is not interested in the Indian nation but in something else, and hence there can be no common meeting ground between the Congress and the League. On the other hand, it has become the clear duty of the Congress to fight out the League and its scheme of denationalizing India."[2]

The speech was delivered on April 13, 1940. The words of Pandit Nehru that the Congress must fight the scheme of 'denationalizing of India' are, of course, brave. But was he really serious about translating them into actions? The following excerpt of December 31, 1943 clarifies the position: "Instinctively I think that it is better to have Pakistan or almost anything if only to keep Jinnah far away and not allow his muddled and arrogant head from interfering continually in India's progress."[3]

Pandit Nehru thought that the demand for Pakistan was Jinnah's demand, and not that of the Muslim community. After Independence and after Jinnah's death Mallapuram district containing predominantly Muslim community was created in 1969. The Majlis-E-Ittehadul Muslimeen in Andhra Pradesh demanded in 1968 that a separate state should be carved out on the eastern seaboard between Vishakapatnam and Madras for the Muslims.[4] These facts could never teach anything to the Congress leadership.

Gandhiji had said, "Vivisect me before vivisecting India." This is often quoted to show how Gandhiji was opposed to Pakistan. But it was merely rhetoric. For in 1940 Gandhiji had said, "The Muslims must have the same right of self-determination that the rest of India has. We are, at present, a joint family. Any member may claim a division."[5] In 1942 he said, "Those Hindus who, like Dr. Moonje and Mr. Savarkar, believe in the doctrine of the sword, may seek to keep the Musalmans under Hindu domination. I do not represent that section. I represent the Congress."[6] Who can say that there is no conceding of Pakistan in these remarks? And then what could stop the creation of Pakistan?

---

[1] A. S. Bhide : Veer Savarkar's Whirlwind Propaganda - p.186

[2] Jawaharlal Nehru : Selected Works, Vol II - p.17

[3] Jawaharlal Nehru : Selected Works, Vol XIII - p.324

[4] Political Identity in South Asia: Editor David Taylor and Malcolm Yapp- p.125

[5] D. G. Tendulkar : Mahatma, Vol 5 p.334

[6] D. G. Tendulkar : Mahatma, Vol 6 -.196

On the political battlefield there was the Congress on one wing, the Muslim League on the other wing, in front were the English and on the rear was the listless Hindu community habituated to voting for the Congress. Thus encompassed Savarkar, in the tradition of Bhausaheb Peshwa, decided to fight single-handed for united India. He was of the view that such a fight was absolutely essential. In Kanpur speech he had said, "Oh! Hindu Sabhait and Hindu Sanghatanists you form the last citadel in which the Hindu Hope and Hindu Future have come to seek refuge. .. You form the last faithful army... If you at any rate, oh! Hindu Sanghatanists, do not betray yourselves and that tradition of Chitor, then rest assured you will in near future be able to rally out or by your falling in the struggle as indomitable and uncompromising warriors enable your race to rally out of the Chitor of martyrdom to the Raigad of Victory."

In 1943 the only long tour Savarkar undertook was to Haradwar. The 37th yearly convocation of 'Rhushikul University' was being held there and Savarkar was elected as President for this function. For presiding over that function he went there in April. The journey was through the most beautiful scenic land. Despite his indifferent health, he enjoyed fully the natural scenery of the land and this gave him immense mental peace.

One of the pleasing events for him personally, during the year, was the celebration of his 61st birthday. The celebrations began in May and lasted till October. The first function was held on May 25 in Bombay. The next one was held in Poona. This was the biggest and the most imposing function. On this occasion, he was presented with a purse of Rs. 2,50,000.00. In his speech, expressing his thanks to the public, he said: "Some thoughts are so delicate that they cannot bear the touch of words... I have observed so far the vow of fighting for freedom. So long as Lokamanya Tilak was alive, the unadulterated nationalism prevailed. But Gandhiji loaded on our heads the dangerous Khilafat movement. It was because of that philosophy that Gandhiji before his arrest showed his willingness to hand the Government of India to Jinnah. And, according to Rajaji, partition is the right thing to do. I have been continuously fighting hard this suicidal philosophy of the Congress. My first task is to fight for freedom and my second task is to keep the motherland united. Let me, therefore, tell you that India's freedom or bondage, its unity or division, is not in the hands of other people, but is entirely in the hands of the Hindus who are the custodians of India's future. If 28 crores of Hindus unite and arm themselves, they will be able to stand up to the English-Muslim alliance."[1]

On June 6, in Bombay a big function was held at the Gowalia Tank ground. In his speech on this occasion, he said that only when people voted for the Hindu Sanghatanist candidates who stood for freedom and unity of the country, was it then possible to put an end to the demand for Pakistan. The third function was held on August 1 at Amaravti. Dr. Moonje presided over this function. In his

[1] S. S. Savarkar : Swa. Veer Savarkar, Akhand Hindusthan Ladha Parva (1941- 1947) - p.205

speech, thanking the public for the reception, he said, "The question of Pakistan did not assume such dimensions during Lokamanya's time. Now it has become very acute. And hence I have to propound more emphatically than him, the philosophy of Hindu nationalism. I am carrying forward the work of Lokamanya through the Hindu Mahasabha by adding something to his message as dictated by the circumstances. In honoring me you are honoring the inspiration of Tilak." Fifteen days later, Savarkar was given a reception at Nagpur. Dr. V. Naidu presided over this function. A day before this function, Nagpur University conferred on him the degree of D. Litt. The last two receptions were held at Baroda and Navsari respectively. Savarkar had to travel extensively to attend these receptions held in his honor and in all these functions the main theme of his speeches was that the demand for Pakistan must be opposed.

Another important event of this year was his election as President of the Marathi drama Centenary Celebrations. He was a playwright. He had written three plays. Also, in his young days, he had studied Sanskrit, Marathi, and English plays. But now as he was involved in the stupendous campaign of popularizing the idea of Hindu nationalism, he had scarcely any time to see or read plays. So Savarkar playfully suggested to Babasaheb Khaparde, a connoisseur and master of letters, to write a speech for him.[1] But finally, Savarkar took time out to read old and new plays before preparing his speech. He read it on November 5 in the centenary festival at Sangli.

Because of incessant work of the past few years, Savarkar was not keeping good health. Now it broke down. So on September 30 he resigned and handed over the charge of the Presidency to Dr. Mukherjee. Yet he was elected as President of the Hindu Mahasabha session to be held at the end of the year at Amritsar. Due to his ill health and on the advice of the doctors, Savarkar canceled his visit to Amritsar. So Dr. Shmaprasad Mukherjee officiated in his place. On December 25, a procession was taken out by the Hindu Mahasabha. The police resorted to lathi-charge to disperse it. A Committee, comprising of Bakshi Tekchand, retired High Court Judge, Ganga Ram Soni, retired District and Sessions Judge, and Badri Das, an advocate of the Punjab High Court, was appointed to inquire whether the lathi-charge was justified. This Committee examined some of the leaders of the Hindu Mahasabha as well as those who had received lathi blows. After examining all the evidence before it the Committee came to the conclusion that the lathi-charge was not called for. The Report of the Inquiry Committee was published by the late Mr. V. G. Deshpande who was then the Secretary of the Hindu Mahasabha.

Championing Indian nationalism, adopting non-violent methods and declaring that Hindu-Muslim unity was essential for winning Swaraj limited Gandhiji's field for political maneuvers. He was, therefore, left with no alternative but to seek audiences with Jinnah. In 1940 Gandhiji had said, "Unless the rest of

---

[1]S. S. Savarkar : Swa. Veer Savarkar, Akhand Hindusthan Ladhaparva (1941-1947) - p.244

India wishes to engage in internal fratricide, the others will have to submit to Muslim dictation if the Muslims will resort to it. I know no non-violent method of compelling the obedience of 8 crores Muslims to the will of rest of India."[1]

Did Gandhiji ask himself or did any one ask him this question: If the unarmed Muslims could not be persuaded by non-violent methods how was it possible to persuade the armed English?

But Savarkar was not cramped in his tactics. For, he had not shackled himself to the non-violent methods, nor did he believe in the slogan 'no Swaraj without Hindu-Muslim unity.' And he was ready for civil war. Gandhiji had written an article in 'Harijan' under the caption 'Hyderabad'. Savarkar had given a rejoinder to it. The important paragraphs from it run as under: "If such an anarchy as Gandhiji takes for granted in his article, does ever set in, leaving Hindus and Muslims face to face in India, there cannot now be even a ghost of a chance for the Nizam to make his way to the Indian Imperial throne, even if all the Frontier tribes are expected to come down to Hyderabad en masse to support him."

"They (Hindu Princes) cannot long remain unconcerned, if the Muslim princes threaten a nation-wide civil war. The foremost of the Hindu princes have realized that if Hindudom falls, the Hindu States must fall with it. As defenders of Hindu faith and Hindu honor they form the reserved forces of Hindudom, organized centers of Hindu strength which even today will outweigh by far the utmost which a Hyderabad here or a Bhopal there can do to spite the Hindu cause."

"From Udaipur, Jodhpur, Jaipur, Gwalior, Indore, Dhar, Dewas, Baroda to Kolhapur, it is almost an unbroken chain of Hindu military camps of organized Hindu governments which animated by the new Hindu spirit cannot but come forward in their own interest as well as those of Hindudom as a whole to defend the Hindu cause.... Pressed by these overwhelming Hindu forces from the north and those of Mysore, Travancore, and Cochin in the south, the poor Nizam will simply be sandwiched between them."

"So far as the Frontier tribes are concerned, they will have to first settle their account with our heroic Sikh brotherhood before they cross to Ravi!"

"And when all is said and done there still remains the most deciding factor which of all other factors is most likely to settle the future destiny of India in case such anarchy as we are discussing sets in. It is the independent Hindu Kingdom of Nepal..."[2]

---

[1] D. G. Tendulkar : Mahatma, Vol 5 - p.333

[2] A. S. Bhide : Veer Savarkar's Whirlwind Propaganda - pp.252-255

The foregoing statement gives a complete idea of how Savarkar was ready to face up to a situation either of anarchy or of civil war.

The Muslim League leaders used to utter threats in their public meetings that, if Pakistan was not conceded, there would be a civil war in India. Savarkar was not frightened by these threats. On the contrary, the warrior in him was roused by them. In April 1941 in a public statement he replied to these threats. In brief, he said: "We hope the chivalrous knights in the camp of the Moslem League will not hesitate to enlighten us on these few points if indeed they themselves are sufficiently enlightened on them."

"For example, where is the standing army on which the Moslems depend to give this battle in near future? Does it only constitute of the Moslem goondas and loafers who keep prowling about the towns and cities in India and are responsible to cause the riot-waves now and then to pass over the land disturbing for a while public peace and security here and there? If so, it is a pity that our Moslem friends should have so completely lost all sense of proportion as to fail to realize that such riots are bound to recoil on their perpetrators before long.. Such Moslem riots might have cowed down the Congressite Ministries in the past, but what if the Hindu Sanghatanists come to hold the reigns in almost all provinces in India as they are likely to do before long? ..."

"The Nizam state is about the only trump card in your hand and perhaps the Frontier tribes to boot. But opposed to them, the Hindus are sure to marshal out in that case at least some 50 larger Hindu states which are at any rate as well-equipped, well-armed and powerful as any one of you can boast of. Then again over and above this all, stands there the Independent Hindu Kingdom of Nepal..."

"Under these circumstances 'Absolutely Incorrigible' Hindu Sanghatanists also wish to assure you in return that if ever such an anarchy does set in and the Moslems are found itching for a civil war, then instead of fighting shy of it, the Hindus are sure to welcome it as a life's chance in the history of the Hindu Nation to regain all that they had lost."[1]

Savarkar had assumed a possibility of a civil war to keep India united and, like Abraham Lincoln of the United States, he was ready for it. For such a war, he was mainly dependent on militarization, on Hindu states and on Nepal. How many Congress leaders had such a resolute mind like that of Savarkar? And who was expressing his thoughts in such plain words?

In April 1944, Savarkar went to Shimoga in the Mysore state. The first session of the All India State's Hindu Mahasabha conference was held there. Mr. Babarao Khaparde was its elected President. In inaugurating this conference, Savarkar spelt out his approach to Hindu States in the following words: "It is not

---

[1] A. S. Bhide : Veer Savarkar's Whirlwind Propaganda - pp.366-368

in the Hindu interests at present to indulge in violent struggles for democracy in progressive Hindu States. Presently the whole of India is dominated by the British. The Hindu States, which enjoy a little freedom and which have some power, are the bastions of the Hindu nation. We must make proper use of them. To demand the abolition of Hindu States now is detrimental to Hindu interests. So instead of making such a demand, we must use these states as bastions as far as possible."[1]

From Shimoga Savarkar went to Bangalore. Here he visited the Science Institute where Sir S. V. Raman explained how research on diamonds was carried on. While speaking about this research, he said, "I have examined a number of diamonds, they shine brightly, they emit light. But today I have seen a true and luminous diamond which is giving true light to the Hindu Society, and I feel that my life's purpose has been fulfilled by seeing it."

In July, Savarkar went to Delhi to attend the Working Committee meeting of the Hindu Mahasabha, when a press conference was held. In this conference, a reporter asked him why did he not meet Jinnah. Savarkar replied, "Jinnah has sent me invitation for a meeting through Subhaschandra Bose, Dr. Ambedkar, Dr. Mukherjee, Dr. Wadhwani, and others. (It is pertinent to note that Jinnah never personally invited Savarkar) But I did not go to see him. Because, if I had gone to see him as a matter of courtesy, he would have made political capital out of it. This is his bad habit. I informed him accordingly and told him that as I was unwell, I would appreciate if he came to tea at my house. But he did not come.' The reporter persisted, 'Why can't you bear humiliation for the cause of the country's freedom?"

Savarkar explained his stand thus: "If freedom is going to come by touching the feet of Jinnah or anyone else, I will surely do it. But your assumption is wrong. I am convinced that even if Jinnah, Gandhiji and I, plus the thirty crores of Indians, were to demand independence with one voice, even then it will not be granted. But if five million soldiers aim their bayonets at them, the English will quit. This is the way to freedom and not often visiting Jinnah's house."

In 1940, Jinnah demanded Pakistan and by a sustained campaign for four years he secured the support of the majority of the Muslims to it. Now it was through Rajaji that Gandhiji began to canvas support for it. So Savarkar opened a barrage of propaganda to rouse Hindu public opinion against Pakistan.

In a statement issued on July 14, Savarkar said, "Many prominent leaders have said that they were simply astonished by the recent publication of Jinnah - Rajaji correspondence, which disclosed the fact that Rajaji with the explicit and often repeated consent of Gandhiji himself expressed readiness to accept the principle of provincial self-determination to secede from the central Indian Government, ... It is really unjust to look upon Rajaji alone as the villain of this

---

[1] S. S. Savarkar : Swa. Veer Savarkar, Akhand Hindusthan Ladhaparva (1941-1947) - .269

tragedy. His fault is that he allowed himself to play as a willing tool in the hands of Gandhiji... Let Rajaji remember that he is a 'Raja' in name only and that the Indian provinces are not his nor Gandhiji's private property to make a gift of them to anyone they like...."[1]

Two days later, he issued another statement and directed all the branches of the Hindu Mahasabha to observe the first week of August 1944 as an 'Akhand-Hindustan and Anti-Pakistan Week'. Also, on August 5, he sent a letter to the leaders of various political parties requesting them to participate in the Akhand Hindustan leaders' Conference. This conference was held on October 7 and 8 in Delhi. Dr. Radhakumud Mukherjee presided over this conference and about 300 eminent leaders, including the Shankaracharya of Puri, Master Tara Singh, Sir Jogindra Singh and Dr. Khare, both members of the Viceroy's Executive Council, and Jamnadas Metha, attended it. In his concluding speech, Savarkar said, "It is foolish to say that we Hindus cannot fight the British without the help of the Muslims. This weak attitude will lead to Pakistan. Those who do not consider themselves as sons of India are not our brothers but enemies."

The annual session of the Hindu Mahasabha was to be held in December. Savarkar publicly announced that he was not a candidate for the presidency and requested that his name should not be entered in the list of candidates. Dr. Moonje personally appealed to Savarkar to change his mind. In his view, Savarkar was the only leader capable of facing the coming stormy times. But Savarkar said that his decision was irrevocable. Later Dr. Shyama Prasad Mukherjee was elected President. This year's session was held at Bilaspur.

Savarkar attended this session but he did not have to carry the responsibility of Presidency. Though one responsibility ended still he was burdened with another. In 1945 the All India States Hindu Mahasabha session was held at Baroda from April 19 to 21. Savarkar was elected its President.

His Presidential speech contained very good advice. He said, "Our organization is in its infancy. Do not worry about the dearth of workers. Shivaji Maharaj did not wait for Tanaji or Netaji. Neither did Rana Pratap. You begin your work. People will help you. It is not necessary to wait till the whole country is organized. The freedom fighters in America and Ireland did not wait for the entire community to join them. A determined minority, fighting for independence, can win it. If there is such a determined minority ready, then the Muslims, who are demanding partition, will be happy with what they get and will stay in united India."

For some years past, Shinde, Purandare, Sant brothers, Palkar, Paranjape, Desai, Velankar, Lele, Vinod, Purkar, and other young men were celebrating Shivaji festival with great enthusiasm. This year's festival was held on a grand

---

[1]V. D. Savarkar : Historic Statement - 124

scale. Amongst the speakers for this celebration were the late Mr. V. G. Deshpande, Mr. Bhopatkar, and Dr. Moonje. Savarkar spoke on the last day. This festival, as well as this speech, is an important event in the history of Baroda.

During the first half of this year, two events, one sad and one happy, occurred in Savarkar's family. His elder brother Babarao Savarkar died in Sangli on March 16. His eldest daughter Prabhat was married on May 8. In the second half of the year Savarkar visited Karnavati (Ahmadabad). There, on August 22, under the chairmanship of Dr. Shyama Prasad Mukherjee, Savarkar was presented with a purse of Rs. 11,111.00 at a public function held in his honor. In his reply to the felicitations, Savarkar said, "I am a Maharashtrian while you are Gujaratis. And yet you have given me a purse because both of us are Hindus. I am fighting for the independence of the Hindus. And I assure you that if we make determined efforts our country will achieve freedom.... The present day Congress is giving 50% representation to 25% Muslims. Hence in the coming elections you should not vote for the Congress but elect Hindu Mahasabha candidates."[1]

On June 15, 1945 the Viceroy released all the Congress leaders from jail and a new political situation was created in the country. But the news items published earlier had indicated in which direction the wind was blowing. One of the news items had said that an agreement had been reached between Bhulabhai Desai and Liaquat Ali Khan to the effect that there should be equal representation to the Congress and the League in the Central Government. In this connection Savarkar had issued a statement on March 10. The important portion in it was as follows: "What could not be done then owing to the tactics of the Hindu Sanghatanists is now being surreptitiously attempted through the Liaquat-Bhulabhai pact. This is a long stride towards the realization of Pakistan. The Congressites who were elected by the Hindus to protect their birth-right have betrayed the Hindus. In their pact a minority of about 25% is given an equal representation in the Central Government with the Hindu majority which forms about 75% of the total population. Nothing could be more treacherous, anti-national, and anti-Hindu."[2]

In the month of July 1945, elections were held in Britain, in which the Labor Party was overwhelmingly elected and its ministry was formed with Attlee as Prime Minister. Later in August Japan surrendered. So Attlee decided to bring normalcy in the political life of India. On September 19, he announced that a Constituent Assembly would be set up to frame India's future constitution and that election to the Central and Provincial Legislatures would be held.[3] In connection with these elections Savarkar issued a statement on October 28, 1945 addressed to the Hindus in the Congress under the caption 'choose one: Congress or Conscience.' After narrating the history of the betrayal of Hindu interests by the

[1] S. S. Savarkar : Swa. Veer Savarkar, Akhand Hindusthan Ladha Parva (1941-1947) - p.333

[2] V. D. Savarkar : Historic Statements - p.156

[3] L. K. Punjabi : The Indomitable Sardar - p.114

Congress which was founded and conducted by such illustrious leaders like Justice Ranade, Dadabhai Nowrojee, Banerjee, and other patriots, Savarkar concluded: "Will you kindly, O Hindus in the Congress camp, whose heart is with us, who are blood of our blood and bone of our bone, join us so that we may grow stronger and the victory of our cause is rendered quicker and more certain. But remember, if we few who are fighting for the Hindu cause are defeated, the blame of the defeat can never be attached to us who continued the good fight, but to those millions of Hindus who did not join the fight, but kept on the fence and simply witnessed the Hindu banner sullied, the unity of India cut into pieces, the Hindustan turned into Pakistan."[1]

Later elections to the Central Legislative Assembly were held. The Muslim League won all the Muslim seats and the nationalists Muslims forfeited their deposits in many constituencies. The Congress secured 91.3% of the votes cast in the non-Muslim constituencies, and the Muslim League 86.6 % of the total votes cast in Muslim constituencies. The final tally was: Congress won 57 seats, Muslim League won 30 seats, Independents won 5 seats, Akali Sikhs won 2 seats, and the Europeans won 8 seats.[2] The Hindu Mahasabha leaders like Bhai Parmananda, Bhopatkar who had undergone suffering in the cause of the country were defeated in the elections. Ghatate from Nagpur, Shyama Prasad Mukherjee and others withdrew from elections.

Earlier, in one of his statements Savarkar had asked, "Let us know who is with us and who is not."[3] By voting for the Congress, the Hindu electorate announced that it was not on the side of the Hindu Mahasabha. What could the Hindu Sanghatanists now do for the Hindu society which had turned its back on them? What means had they at their disposal? The most important point was that public opinion and power was on the side of the Congress. The critics who cavil at the Hindu Sanghatanists that they did nothing at the time of partition should take note of this historical situation. When the Hindu society declared through the ballot box that it did not approve of Savarkar's leadership then the subsequent events were inevitable. The terrible wounds inflicted on the body of the Hindu society by the partition were the results of the Hindu electorates' blind faith in the Congress. The Congress leaders who were oblivious of the true history of India and the Hindu electorate that put blind faith in them are responsible for the partition of the country.

The elections held in 1945 were won by the Congress. For seven years, Savarkar had made a tremendous effort to keep India united. But the political climate he hoped for did not come about. Naturally his talks reflected frustration, pain, and anger. On January 1, 1946, he was taken to Walchandnagar to

---

[1]V. D. Savarkar : Historic Statements - p.181

[2]V. P. Menon : The Transfer of Power - p.226

[3]V. D. Savarkar : Historic Statement - p.125

recuperate. Twenty days later he suffered a mild heart attack. He stayed there for about three months. Then he came to Poona for a change and some rest.

In the earlier months of 1946, elections to Provincial Legislatures were held. In one of his campaign speeches, Sardar Patel said, "Granting of Pakistan is not in the hands of the British Government. If Pakistan is to be achieved, Hindus and Muslims will have to fight. There will be a civil war."[1] This was a great rhetoric. Patel had threatened civil war. Such a civil war took place between the Congress and the Hindu Mahasabha through the ballot box. And in this war the Congress triumphed!

In March the Cabinet Mission visited India. It called Savarkar and other Hindu Mahasabha leaders for discussions. Savarkar did not go for the talks due to his ill-health. But Bhopatkar and Dr. Mukherjee met the Mission members. In this meeting, Cripps asked Bhopatkar in a jest tinged with sarcasm: "Whom do you represent?" Bhopatkar replied, "We represent those voters who voted the defeated Hindu Mahasabha candidates in the last elections. You also remember that your party was once defeated... We, Marathas, are not afraid of Jinnah. We have destroyed their established Pakistan 150 years ago."[2]

During the year Savarkar had a personal satisfaction of seeing his proscribed literature freed. On May 24, the Congress Government of Bombay issued the necessary orders. Thus the ban on 'The War of Independence, 1857', 'Mazzini's Biography', 'My Transportation', and 'The ballads of Tanaji and Baji Prabhu Deshpande' was lifted.

Now the Congress decided to join the Viceroy's Executive Council. Accordingly, on September 2, 1946 Pandit Nehru was sworn in as the Vice-president of this Executive Council. Sometime later, talking to the American reporter Marcuse, Pandit Nehru said, "Marcuse, there are three things I want you to remember. One, India will never be a Dominion. Two, there will never be a Pakistan. Three, when the British go, there will be no more communal trouble in India."[3] All the three things proved wrong. Pandit Nehru later admitted this to Marcuse.

Congress won the elections. But the Congress leaders could never visualize the shape of things to come. Also, Pandit Nehru and his band of devotees never cared to find out how Savarkar was able to predict the course of future events. Winning of elections is one thing and the capacity and ability to rule is another thing. The history of the past 40 years is an eloquent proof of this.

---

[1] Dhananjay Keer : Veer Savarkar - p.372

[2] S. S. Savarkar : Swa. Veer Savarkar, Akhand Hindusthan Ladha Parva (1941-9147)- p.348

[3] Sarvepalli Gopal : Jawaharlal Nehru, Vol 2 - p14

But now the government was in the hands of the Congress. It used that power against the Hindu Sanghatanists. They were the first to be arrested when riots broke out. Heavy security deposits were demanded from the editors of Kal, Agrani, the Maratha and other newspapers. There were big riots in Naokhali. There was retaliation in Bihar. Nehru threatened Bihari Hindus with aerial bombardment if the riots continued. But these planes, for shortage of fuel, could not be sent up to Naokhali! Now on October 26, five Muslim League ministers joined the Viceroy's Executive Council of which Pandit Nehru was the Vice-president. Thus Congress accepted 'Parity'. It was in 1896 that Haji Muhammad Ismail Khan had asked the Congress President Rahimtullah Sayani that the Congress grant 'Parity' to the Muslims. Sayed Ahmad, the founder of Aligarh Muslim University, had endorsed this demand. But Sayani had turned it down.[1] That 'Parity' was now accepted by the Congress! The League took the decision to join the Executive Council with one and only one aim and that was 'to sabotage it from within.'[2]

Savarkar had described 'Parity' as 'a long stride towards the realization of Pakistan.' Now Sardar Patel found, while running the administration, that 'almost every Muslim servant in the Government was a Pakistani.'[3] Looking to this state of affairs Savarkar realized that the Congress leaders would finally concede the demand for Pakistan. So he thought that it was possible to cut at least some parts of this proposed Pakistan. On March 8, the Congress passed a resolution demanding the division of the Punjab. As usual, it was a half measure. It was necessary to separate all Hindu majority areas from the Pakistani land. Savarkar therefore issued a statement on April 2, 1947 demanding such a partition. In it he said, "To frustrate the vivisection of our Akhand Hindustan, we must first vivisect their Pakistan. To this end, three immediate steps are imperative. The first, the creation of a Hindu province in West Bengal; the second, the expulsion of Muslim trespassers from Assam at any cost, so as to sandwich and smother the eastern Pakistan between two Hindu provinces; the third, the creation of a Hindu-Sikh province in East Punjab and to rejoin the contiguous Hindu districts in Sindh to the Bombay Presidency. Thus about ten large Hindu provinces will get consolidated into a strongly centralized government of Akhand Hindustan and will enable it all the more effectively to re-annex the revolting Pakistani areas in near future."

"But all this or any other jugglery will fail to help Hindudom if we do not emphatically declare it and manfully act up to the rule that Muslim minority in Hindu provinces shall be given the same treatment as is meted out to the Hindu minority in Muslim provinces."[4]

---

[1] Dr. R. C. Majumdar : British Paramountcy and Indian Renaissance, Part II - p.316

[2] L. K. Punjabi : The Indomitable Sardar - p.121

[3] Dhananjay Keer : Veer Savarkar - p.380

[4] V. D. Savarkar : Historic Statements - pp.193-194

In this statement, there is a reference to the Muslim trespassers in Assam. Savarkar had alerted the Hindus of Assam, when he had toured that province, about the danger posed by these trespassers. Now on April 26, 1947 he sent the following telegram to Gopinath Bardolai, Chief Minister of Assam. "... Moslem trespassers old and new must be ejected to a man and no inch in Assam should be surrendered. It is by yielding inches in the past that the Hindus are challenged today to surrender the whole of Hindustan...."[1] To this wire Mr. Medhi, Minister in charge of Finance and Revenue, Government of Assam, sent the following reply: "We can assure you that we are fully alive to the responsibility to see that the interest of the people of Assam will not, in any way, be jeopardized and it will be always our endeavor to protect the interest of the people of Assam against the aggressors. All effective steps will be taken to repel aggression from any quarter."[2] Now Assam has become a problem state. It shows how alive the Assamese leaders were to their responsibility and how effective their steps were.

The news of the massacre of the Hindus in Calcutta and Naokhali spread in the neighboring province of Bihar. The aggressive attitude of the Muslim League added fuel to the fire. Dr. Rajendra Prasad told Gandhiji, "The Muslim League with its national guards had been preparing for a fight. Arms from Aligarh had been imported into the province in bulk even after the outbreak of disturbances."[3] It was but natural that there should be an angry reaction to all this. Still, as usual, the Hindus were blamed for all that was happening. Gandhiji toured Bihar in March 1947. Savarkar on June 11 issued a statement addressed to the people of Bihar in connection with the news that was coming from that province. He said. "... I am aware of the campaign of vilification and persecution carried against you by the Moslems and the Hindu Quislings all over India. ..I learn that Gandhiji has been exhorting that before the rains fall every Hindu householder in Bihar should shelter some homeless Moslems under his roof and treat them as the members of the family. That gentleman does not seem to think his life mission fulfilled by merely cutting off the parts of our motherland and handing them over to the Moslems to make room for their Pakistan. He wants now to turn every Hindu house into a bit of Pakistan and of Naokhali even before Mr. Jinnah demands it all. I ask you to brush aside these exhortations as the ravings of a monomaniac. If a Hindu has a corner under his roof and a morsel of food to spare let him shelter and feed some Hindu refugees from Bengal or the Punjab before the rains fall. For they are indeed your brothers in faith, in flesh, in blood, and essentially in the will to love and live together as bothers."

"But above all, oppose tooth and nail the sinister attempt to allot separate areas to the Moslems in Bihar to settle down. Beware of the fact that within a few

---

[1] V. D. Savarkar : Historic Statements - p.195

[2] V. D. Savarkar : Historic Statements - p.196

[3] Pyarelal : Mahatma Gandhi, The Last Phase, Vol I - p.620

years these Moslem areas would be claimed as stepping stones in the progress of the Pakistani corridor."[1]

In this statement, Savarkar had advised the Bihari Hindus to oppose tooth and nail the attempts to allot separate areas to the Muslims. But was there really any such attempt? It is better to seek an answer to this question in the words of Pyarelal who was Gandhiji's private Secretary. Pyarelal writes, "The Muslim League continued to obstruct the work of rehabilitation. Having got the refugees under its influence, it sought to create conditions which would make the schism between the two communities permanent, and, if possible, secure nearly half of Bihar for Pakistan."

"The demand for pockets became a vital link in its strategy. It was natural, while the feeling of insecurity prevailed, for the Muslims to want to congregate in villages where they were in large numbers. The League sought to make this into a permanent feature of Bihar's policy. The government tried to meet their demand half-way. But to yield an inch to the League meant always a demand for an ell. From the idea of selected pockets they proceeded to the idea of contiguous pockets, and from contiguous pockets to the division of Bihar itself, to provide an independent homeland for the Muslims, which along with Jharkhand would join Pakistan."[2]

Two more pages in this volume are filled with additional information in this regard. This information is an eye-opener to one who has the desire to see. Such was the League in Bihar. And how did Gandhiji deal with it? It is better to seek again an answer to that question in the words of Pyarelal. He writes, "Later, when the Muslim League's overbearing tactics alienated even the Bihar Muslims and brought it into open conflict with other Muslim parties, he consistently refused to lend any encouragement or support to its opponents or do anything that might undermine its prestige. He advised the government again and again to strive with the League."[3]

When some people taunted Gandhiji that he had sympathy for the Muslims only and that he had undertaken this fast for their sake, Gandhiji replied, "They are right. But all his life, he has stood, as everybody should stand for the minorities or those in need."[4] As Gandhiji always stood by the side of the minorities, his lieutenants and the Congress party had lost the habit of standing up for the interests of the majority. Thus the Hindus were left to fend for themselves. Naturally Savarkar felt that in these critical times there should be some one to defend the Hindus and that destiny had decreed that role for him. So in those

---

[1]V. D. Savarkar : Historic Statements - pp.199-200

[2]Pyarelal : Mahatma Gandhi, The Last Phase Vol I - p.680

[3]Pyarelal : Mahatma Gandhi, The Last Phase Vol I - p.683

[4]D. G. Tendulkar : Mahatma, Vol 8 - p.305

stormy days before the partition, he left no stone unturned to keep India united or to ensure that history would note that at least he had raised his lone voice against the Partition.

On June 3, Attlee announced in Parliament that India would be divided and that the power which the British were holding would be transferred within one year to the two dominions - India and Pakistan. The Congress and the League leaders had already given their consent to the plan. But as a formality, it was put before the All India Congress Committee for its approval. On this occasion, Gandhiji in support of the resolution said, "Those who talked in terms of an immediate revolution or an upheaval in the country would achieve it by throwing out this resolution, but he doubted whether they had the strength to take over the reins of the Congress and the Government. Well, I have not the strength."[1] Later when the resolution was put to vote, 157 voted for it, while 29 voted against it, and 32 remained neutral.

The Congress having given its approval to Pakistan, Savarkar issued a statement calling upon the Hindus to observe July 3, as 'Black Day' and the 'Day of Protest' - against the vivisection of Hindustan. In it he further said, "...It will do good even to the Moslems if they realize the import of this historic truth. The fate which overtook them when they had succeeded in converting the whole of Hindustan into an actual and factual Pakistan led by the might of an Aurangzeb cannot but overwhelm the puny Pakistan of today led by Mr. Jinnah!"[2]

On July 7, Savarkar sent the following telegram to Dr. Ambedkar, Dr. Rajendra Prasad, Sardar Vallabhai Patel and Dr. Khare expressing his view as to how the Flag of free India should be: "The standard of Hindustan must be Bhagwa – Ochre-colored. At any rate, no flag which does not bear at least a stripe of Bhagwa color can be recognized by the Hindus as a standard they can respect. The Charkha too must be replaced by the Chakra-wheel-or any other such symbol signifying progress."[3] But some statements appeared in the press regarding the wheel on the flag which were strictly not correct. So on July 29, Savarkar issued a statement explaining the correct historical position regarding Chakra.[4]

Gandhiji felt unhappy about the removal of the Charkha symbol from the flag. He wrote about his mental anguish in the Harijan. He said that if the interpretation as given was correct, he would refuse to salute the flag. But Pandit Nehru explained the position in the Constituent Assembly. Then Gandhiji's opposition ended.[5]

---

[1]D. G. Tendulkar : Mahatma, Vol 8 - p.19

[2]V. D. Savarkar : Historic Statements - p.201

[3]V. D. Savarkar : Historic Statements - p.204

[4]V. D. Savarkar : Historic Statements - pp.204-205

[5]Pyarelal :Mahatma Gandhi, The Last Phase Vol 2 - p.335

Savarkar was in Poona from August 1 to August 3. He attended Maharashtra Political Conference presided over by Barrister Ramrao Deshmukh. Next day he spoke on the subject of united Maharashtra. The same evening he addressed a mammoth gathering on the grounds of Sir Parshurambhau College. In this speech he said, "I am not going to address my words to anyone, not even to the Congress. I am addressing my words to those who want the Hindu community to survive. I am speaking in order to reinvigorate the nation.... Mistakes are to be pointed out not to rake up quarrels but to ensure that these are not repeated. Without indulging in party politics, I want to point out how this mistake occurred. It was not a deliberate mistake. The terrible mistake occurred because of unawareness of what constitutes a nation and what is meant by treachery. And if this mistake is not rectified even when it has been realized, then the future generations would be lost."

He further said, "See how politics went wrong. The first mistake began with Sindh. (It was separated from the Bombay Presidency) The second was about the communal award. (The Congress neither accepted it nor rejected it) The third was boycotting the census... Why are you ashamed of calling yourself Hindus? It is no use blaming the leaders only for all the mess. Who made them leaders? Have not we elected them? ... If all Hindus unite then even now Pakistan can be incorporated in Akhand Hindustan."[1]

Five days later, after his return from Poona, Savarkar went to Delhi. In its session held here on August 9, the Working Committee of the Hindu Mahasabha resolved that hundreds of thousands of Hindus were stranded in Pakistan, and as there were riots and forced conversions, the Hindu Mahasabha could not participate in the August 15 celebrations. It recommended that on that day the Hindus should hoist the Bhagwa flag on the house-tops. On the same day in the evening the session of the All India Hindu Conference was held. The President - elect was Dr. Khare and the ruler of Alwar was to inaugurate it. But Dr. Khare could not come to Delhi as he had to stay in Alwar to quell the riots of the Mayo Muslims. So Savarkar presided over this conference. In his speech on this occasion he said, "Pandit Nehru says that they accepted Pakistan to avoid bloodshed. But this is wrong. This will not help to avoid bloodshed. On the contrary, they will again use threats of bloodshed in order to press their additional demands. If you do not stop them, there would come about 14 Pakistans. They will demand Mayostan near Alwar; in the south they will demand Moplastan in Kerala (The district of Malayapuram was later created), and in Hyderabad they will demand Nizamistan. Their demands will have to be crushed by the policy of reciprocity. For that purpose, the Hindus, irrespective of political party, must unite and consolidate their strength."

---

[1] S. S. Savarkar : Swa. Veer Savarkar, Akhand Hindusthan Ladhaarva (1941-1947) - pp.403-407

On August 15, India became free. Savarkar hoisted two flags on his house-top, one was the Bhagwa-Ochre-colored and the other was the one approved by the Constituent Assembly. When the Pakistan resolution was passed, Pandit Nehru had spoken of fighting out the League. Sardar Patel had talked of Civil War. In 1926 Gandhiji had said, "This fighting, (Hindu-Muslim riot) however unfortunate it may be, is a sign of growth. It is like the war of Roses. (Civil War in England was called the War of Roses) Out of it will rise a mighty nation."[1] Pandit Nehru and Sardar Patel did not suit action to their words. Gandhiji did not permit the War of Roses.

After reading a report of Dr. Moonje's speech, Pandit Nehru made the following noting in 1941: "But the prize of cowardice, lack of intelligence, and degradation must surely be awarded to some of the leaders of the Hindu Mahasabha. It makes me sick to read their contemptible and disgusting fulminations."[2]

Pandit Nehru's thoughts have been expressed in chaste English. But the question is, after partition, to who do they really apply? It is better to leave that matter to the judgment of history!

---

[1]D. G. Tendulkar : Mahatma, Vol 2 -p.311
[2]Jawaharlal Nehru : Selected Wroks, Vol XI - p.657

The Sheathed Sword

"Treating alike pain and pleasure, gain and loss, victory and defeat, engage yourself in the battle. Thus you will incur no sin." [1]

In the Delhi public meeting held on August 9, Savarkar had observed that Pandit Nehru and other leaders' argument that they accepted Pakistan to avoid bloodshed were wrong. Before Pakistan came into existence, there was bloodshed in Calcutta. So also there were riots in Naokhali and Bihar. But now a still greater horrendous situation developed. Boundary Commissions were appointed under the chairmanship of Sir Cyril Radcliffe, one for the partition of Bengal and the separation of Sylhet from Assam; and the other for the partition of the Punjab. The Radcilffe award was announced on August 17, and a campaign to drive out the Sikhs and Hindus from West Punjab and the North West Frontier Province systematically began. There were serious riots in Sheikhupura, Lahore, Sialkot, and Gujranwala districts. There was a massacre on an unprecedented scale in Sheikhupura in West Punjab. This caused a violent anti-Muslim reaction in Amritsar. Thereafter communal frenzy gripped the people on both sides of the border. This took heavy toll of lives and created an exodus of population between the two dominions, the like of which was never before known in history.[2] After the riots in Bihar, Jinnah, "mooted his favorite idea of exchange of population."[3] But the Congress leaders did not respond to it.

No efforts were made for the protection of the Hindus who were being systematically uprooted in Pakistan. But when there were reactions to these riots in India, the Congress leaders from the Prime Minister down to the chief of a Gram Panchayat (Village assembly) began to parrot that it was unlawful for the people to take the law in their own hands. Gandhiji in a statement said, "I am prepared to understand the anger of the refugees, whom fate has driven from West Punjab (What has fate to do with this? Was not the Congress responsible for rejecting the idea of transfer of population?) But anger is short madness... Retaliation is no remedy. It makes the original disease... worse. I, therefore, ask all those who are engaged in committing senseless murders, arson and loot, to stay their hand."[4]

In these terrible times, only Savarkar understood the anguish of the Hindu refugees. And it was he who stood up to speak on their behalf. In a statement issued on September 25, 1947 he said, "The vital interests of Hindudom demand that some maxims and arguments emphasized in chorus by the Congressite ministers, leaders and the press should be promptly refuted. For example, Pandit

---

[1] The Bhagavad : Gita Chapter 2 – Stanza 38

[2] V. P. Menon : The Transfer of Power - p.418

[3] Pyarelal : Mahatma Gandhi, The Last Phase Vol I, p.641

[4] Pyarelal : Mahatma Gandhi, The Last Phase Vol II, p.434

Nehru has been reiterating of late that the right of retaliation or punishment belongs to the state alone and in no case the people (meaning in this case the Hindu-Sikhs) could be justified in exercising it on their own initiative and responsibility. In laying down this maxim Panditji has happily refused to indulge in the mischievous mumbo jumbo of Gandhistic morals.... So far so good. But he conveniently forgot to touch the most crucial and practical aspect of the question - what were the people to do, when the state proved either so unwilling or so pusillanimous as to fail miserably even to defend its own people - not to speak of retaliating to avenge the wrongs perpetrated on their hearths and homes and honor?"

"Even an individual has a legal right of self-protection and of retaliation in so far at any rate as it forms an inevitable weapon of self-defense against a violent aggressor, - when the Police is nowhere in evidence or is unable or the worst of it all, is unwilling to face the aggressor for fear of displeasing him. Verily a people must have this fundamental right which even a citizen possesses."

"What were the thousands on thousands of Hindus-Sikhs to do when faced by an imminent danger of being massacred in cold blood, looted, burnt alive, forcibly converted...?"

"While the Moslem state was planning in this wise definite campaign of invading Eastern Punjab and capturing Delhi in order to celebrate the inauguration of Pakistan - what was the Government of India doing in its capital at Delhi to counteract these dangerous developments on the part of our enemies? ..."

"The Hindu Sanghatanists kept shouting from house-tops throughout India 'Danger Ahead!' This is no time for rejoicing while you are stranded on the top of a volcano already in eruption!"

"But while that Moslem province was resounding with shrieks of thousands on thousands of Hindu-Sikh women, men, and children being outraged, murdered, thrown into flames alive, and was having a blood-bath in rivers of Hindu-Sikh blood there, here in Delhi the Ministers of the Indian State were literally feasting and fiddling to celebrate their bloodless revolution!"

"Under these circumstances what wonder is there that millions of Hindu-Sikh prompted by the instinct of self-preservation and animated by the spirit of Pan-Hindu consolidation rose in arms in East Punjab, in Bharatpur, in Alwar, in Patiala and in Delhi itself and retaliated to the best of their might and means so furiously and effectively as to checkmate the Moslem hordes from attempting an invasion of East Punjab, threw them on their defensive and saved Delhi itself from being captured by the Moslems concentrated there. If Panditji and his Congressite comrades are still safe and secure in their seats, they owe it to this brave fight which Hindu Sanghatanists and Sikh forces gave in the nick of time. And still it is he who unblushingly comes forward to deliver to them a sermon on the exclusive right of the State to retaliate!"

"... Nevertheless in all sincerity I exhort once more my Hindu brethren in the Congress and the Cabinet to take a lesson, at least now, from past errors, cease to be idealists and join hands with Hindu Sanghatanists to face realities as revealed by the recent happenings."

"If the Congressite Ministers are unwilling to accept this indispensable programme they should at least be patriotic enough to resign and hand over Government to the Hindu Sanghatanists and Sikhs. It is a self-conceited plea that questions the ability of the Hindu Nation to replace the present Congressite Ministers by leaders as able or even by better ones. If the Government is handed over to a Sikh - Hindu Sanghatanists Coalition, a cabinet could be formed within a week which will be not only more efficient but what is chiefly important, shall also be far more willing to accept and carry out undauntedly, the above programme which, as we have proved, is absolutely indispensable to face the stark realities as noted above."[1]

In the All India Congress Committee meeting, held on June 14, Gandhiji had asked whether anyone, excepting the Congress leaders, had the capacities to assume the reins of the Government. Now Savarkar declared that he was ready to take over the reins of the government. It needs tremendous confidence, like Richelieu, Bismarck, Lenin, Kemal, in oneself to make such a bold statement. An illustration from the life of Lenin will elucidate this point. In 1917, the Czarist regime in Russia had collapsed and a provincial government was installed. Later the first All-Russian Congress of the Soviets met in Petrograd. In this Congress, Tseretelli, pleading for a coalition government, challenged the delegates to say whether there was a single party in Russia prepared alone to shoulder responsibility of government, Lenin interrupted from the floor to say that his party was prepared for that. The majority drowned Lenin's words in hilarious laughter.[2]

The descendants of those who laughed in Lenin's face saw a mighty Soviet Government rise and until 1991 was nearly a match to the United States. India became free in 1947. What is the state of affairs in the country? This question need not be asked. One gets the answer on the street of any city or village. Now there is no need to deride the last Peshwa!

It was not Savarkar alone who was opposed to the policies of Gandhiji and Nehru. Sardar Patel and Dr. Rajendra Prasad were also opposed to them. Nehru wanted certain residential areas reserved for Muslims and to employ Muslims to deal with Muslim refugees. Patel opposed this policy. Dr. Rajendra Prasad wrote to Nehru that one-sided action could not bring the desired results but

---

[1] V. D. Savarkar : Historic Statements - p.209
[2] Issac Deutscher : The Prophet Armed - p.267

would, in fact, lead to most undesirable and unexpected consequences. There was no use bringing in the army to protect the Muslim residents of Delhi if the Hindus and Sikhs were being expelled from Pakistan. Nehru's comment on this was: "I quite realize that I am out of tune with this environment..."[1]

If this was the case, then why were not the reins of the government handed over to others as advocated by Savarkar? Chamberlain had stepped down for Churchill when he found that he could not cope with the war situation. This has happened often the world over. At this moment, it was a question of millions of Hindu-Sikhs in Pakistan. Indian nationalism, Secular State, Hindu-Muslim unity may be fine words. But they were of no use in solving the problems of millions of Hindu-Sikh refugees. But Gandhiji and Nehru only uttered shibboleths. Pandit Nehru did not do any introspection as to why his ideology had failed. Instead he began to upbraid the Hindu Sanghatanist parties.

Savarkar's reply to Nehru's upbraiding was pragmatic and scathing. In a statement issued on October 22, he said, "The Gandhist ministers, leaders, and newspapers have recently trotted out a new stunt to cover their dismal and disastrous failure to protect the life, property and honor of our nation and perhaps with a crafty design to capture Moslem votes in the joint electorates to come. Pandit Nehru, their megaphone, has recently been addressing a number of meetings wherein instead of assuring and enlightening the people as to how his government is going to forestall and frustrate the covert machinations and overt challenges of the Moslems to conquer and convert the whole of Hindustan into a Pakistan, he has been indulging into furious denunciations against the demand for a Hindu State! As if the mere demand for a Hindu Raj constitutes a danger to his government so much more imminent, impending, incalculably disastrous, as to call for his immediate attention than the already established Moslem Raj in Pakistan where fanatical atrocities, arson, blood-shed, and butchery have been the order of the day and millions of Moslems keep parading the streets with such war cries as 'Haske liya Pakistan! Marke lenge Hindustan!''

"Pandit Nehru swaggers on that, if the Hindu Sanghatanists persist in their efforts to establish a Hindu Raj, they would meet with the fate of Hitler and Mussolini. He forgets that the Hindu Sanghatanists are led by hundreds of those seasoned veterans who had fought in the vanguard of Indian Revolutionist forces against Britain when Gandhiji, speaking politically, was still in his swaddling clothes and the Pandit was not yet born. ... They cannot be terrorized by the threat of such carpet knights as the Pandit and his clan."

"You contend further on that our country and our state cannot be called Hindustan and a Hindu state as some non-Hindu minorities too are citizens thereof. But how is it that, in spite of the presence of Hindus, Christians, Parsees, and other non-Moslem minorities in its territory, all of you and Gandhiji in

---

[1] Sarvepalli Gopal : Jawaharlal Nehru, Vol 2 - p.16

particular keep salaaming and saluting the newly carved out Moslem Raj as Pakistan which avowedly and literally means a Holy Moslem Land, a Muslim State? Is it not a fact that almost all states and nations are called after the names of what the League of Nations termed 'National Majority' predominating in each? Nor have you yourselves ever felt any qualms of conscience in recognizing Baluchistan, Vaziristan, Afghanistan, Turkiastan or the Turkish state as such in spite of the presence of non-Muslim minorities there? How is it then that the very mention of the name Hindustan or the Hindu state alone takes your breath away as if you were smitten by a snake bite?"

At the end of his statement, Savarkar said, "The choice, therefore, is not between two sets of personalities but between two ideologies, not Indian Raj or Hindu Raj but Moslem Raj or Hindu Raj, Akhand Hindustan or Akhand Pakistan?"

"The Hindu Sanghatanist ideology alone can, therefore, save our nation and re-establish an Akhand Hindustan from the Indus to the seas."[1]

The point that Savarkar made at the end of his statement is most important. Truly it was not and is not Savarkar versus Gandhiji-Nehru dispute. The dispute was and is this: What is the position of the Hindu society in India? In this world which land can the Hindus claim as their own? Who is to protect their culture and their interests? The leaders, who have been always elected to power by the votes of the Hindu community have always turned a blind eye to these questions. The only reason for this has been their allergy to the word 'Hindu' as their minds have been conditioned by Indian nationalism. A good illustration of this is Gandhiji's speech delivered at a prayer meeting on June 12, 1947. He said, "The Muslim majority areas may call themselves Pakistan, but the rest and the largest part of India need not call itself Hindusthan. In contradistinction to Pakistan it will mean the abode of the Hindus. Do the Hindus feel so? Have the Parsis, Christians, and Jews born in India and Anglo-Indians who do not happen to have the white skin, any other home than India? (It may be noted that a large number of Jews have gone to Israel and Anglo-Indians to Australia, Canada, and New Zealand) I will omit the Muslims for the time being. I suppose such is the reason why Panditji refuses to call the non-Pakistan areas as Hindustan..."[2]

Here, as was their wont, Gandhiji and Pandit Nehru have turned their backs on history. They did not wish to take into account that for a thousand years people have always called this country Hindusthan and its native Hindus. After the failure of the 1857 War of Independence, the last Mughal emperor Bahadur Shah wrote a poem wherein he used the words 'Sword of Hindustan'. Dr. Muhammad Iqbal, who later became the advocate of Pakistan, wrote 'Sare Jahanse Acha Hindostan Hamara'. When the late Maharaja of Baroda, Sir Sayajirao Gaikwad,

---

[1]V. D. Savarkar : Historic Statements - p.214

[2]D. G. Tendulkar : Mahatma, Vol 8 - p.14

went to the United States, he found that the Americans call the natives of India Hindus. But all this was ignored. And as desired by Gandhiji and Pandit Nehru, the country's name Hindustan was effaced.

On October 22, the day on which Savarkar's foregoing statement was issued, the Pakistani tribesmen invaded Kashmir. On this occasion, Gandhiji told Nehru, "There could be no peace by submission to evil in Kashmir."[1] (An ordinary man wonders why Kashmir! What about the rest of India?) With the blessings of Gandhiji, it was decided to send the army to Kashmir. Mr. Gopal writes gleefully, "To be fighting side by side with the people of Kashmir against fanatic hordes was a heartening experience which set aside for the moment, memories of communal strife and partition; and the fact that Hindu communal elements in India were opposed to the accession of Kashmir because it had a Muslim majority added to the thrill of adventure."[2]

One wonders where from Gopal got the information that Hindu communal elements did not want Kashmir to accede to India. He might have been thrilled to write these lines. But Lt. Col. Narain Singh, who was defending the Kashmir border with Dogra and Poonchie Muslim battalions, was denied this thrill. On October 22, in the early morning while commanding officer Lt. Col. Narian Singh and other soldiers were asleep, the Poonchie Muslim soldiers rose in rebellion, and killed Narain Singh and Dogra soldiers. Then with the help of Poonchie Muslim soldiers, the tribal raiders dashed into the Kashmir valley.[3] However, later the tribal invasion was defeated by the Indian army.

After the Partition, an agreement between India and Pakistan was arrived at whereby Pakistan was to receive Rs. 550 million. But the Government of India decided to withhold this payment on the ground that the amount would be used to purchase arms for the war in Kashmir. Sardar Patel said not a pie would be paid. Nehru was in total agreement with this decision. When Gandhiji discussed this issue with Mountbatten, the latter described the decision as 'the first dishonorable act by the Indian Union Government.' Gandhiji was probably hurt by the word 'dishonorable'. He felt that the amount should be paid to Pakistan. Nehru and Patel explained to him the Government of India's stand. But Gandhiji remained unconvinced. On January 13, Gandhiji began his fast unto death. So the Cabinet reopened the question. It was decided that its earlier decision was correct. However, in deference to Gandhiji's wishes, it was decided to pay Rs. 550 million to Pakistan. During the fast, some refugees shouted, 'Let Gandhiji die.' Once Pandit Nehru had an angry exchange of words with one refugee group.[4] During this period, Sardar Patel met Gandhiji. Patel said to Maulana Azad, "He (Gandhiji)

---

[1] Sarvepalli Gopal : Jawaharlal Nehru Vol 2 - p.20

[2] Sarveepalli Gopal : Jawaharlal Nehru Vol 2 - p.20

[3] Lt. Gen. P. Sen : Slender was the thread - p.36

[4] Pyarelal : Mahatma Gandhi, The Last Phase, Vol II - p.711

seems determined to blacken the name of the Hindus before the whole world."[1] Gandhiji had said, "My fast, as I have stated in plain language, is undoubtedly on behalf of the Muslim minority in the Union, and therefore it is necessarily against the Hindus and the Sikhs of the Union and the Muslims of Pakistan.[2] Whatever slogans might have been shouted, the fact remained that Gandhiji and the Congress had the support of the Hindus. The fast against the Hindus was bound to make them bend. But Pakistani Muslims were not going to yield; for Gandhiji was never their leader. However, finally leaders of all parties gave a written pledge and Gandhiji broke his fast on the sixth day.

The pledge contained the following conditions 1. The life, property, and faith of the Muslims shall be protected. 2 The annual fair at Khwaja Qutabuddin's mausoleum will be held this year as in the previous years 3. The Muslims will be able to move about in Sabzimandi, Karol Bagh, Paharganj and other localities 4. The mosques which have been left by the Muslims and which are now in possession of Hindus and Sikhs will be returned. The areas which have been set apart for the Muslims will not be forcibly occupied. 5 The Muslims who have migrated from here may return to Delhi.

On January 30, 1948 at about 5:30 p.m. Nathuram Godse shot dead Gandhiji at the prayer ground. This news was like an earthquake. When it spread, there was an angry reaction in Maharashtra and the Brahmin community suffered considerably. In Bombay, the Hindu Mahasabha offices were forced open and the contents there were taken out and set on fire on the road. About 1,500 people came to the house of Savarkar who was on the first floor. He was calm, yet armed. His wife was standing near him while his son was at the door. He had told both of them to seek safety elsewhere. But both refused to do so. The hooligans threw stones at the house. As some of them were trying to find the staircase to go to the first floor, the police arrived. The area around Savarkar Sadan became peaceful. Now the hooligans took their way to Dr. Savarkar's house which was later subjected to stone throwing. In this Dr. Savarkar was severely injured. Then he was removed to the hospital but he never recovered from those injuries.

The police officers who had come to Savarkar Sadan suggested to him that he should go to an unknown place to stay. Savarkar firmly turned down this suggestion. He said that the whereabouts of a well-known man like him would not remain secret for long wherever he might go. If the officers were to keep two policemen outside his house, that would be enough. But if this was not possible for them, that would also be all right with him. He was ready to die for his principles.[3]

However, Savarkar issued two statements condemning the assassination of Gandhiji. The first was issued on January 31. And the second was issued of

---

[1] Maulana Abul Kalam Azad : India Wins Freedom - p.254

[2] Pyarelal : Mahatma Ghandhi, The Last Phase, Vol II - p.717

[3] V. V. Savarkar : Athawani Angaryachya - 1967 April issue of Painjan

February 4. In this latter statement he said, "Let every patriotic citizen set to his heart the stern warning which history utters that a successful national revolution and a newly born national state can have no worse enemy than a fratricidal civil war, especially so when it is encompassed from outside by alien hostility."[1]

During the period from February 1 to February 5, nearly all Hindu Sanghatanists were rounded up by the police. Amongst them were eminent men like Jamnadas Metha, Dharap, Tatnis, Golvalkar and some others. About 25,000 people were arrested all over India. On February 5, the police came to arrest Savarkar. At that point Savarkar said. "I will go to lavatory". The officers became suspicious. So Savarkar smiled away their fears by saying, "I am an old man. So there will be no Marseilles again and there is no need for it."

On March 11 Savarkar was charged with an offense of being a member of the conspiracy to assassinate Gandhiji. Then the late Mr. G. V. Ketkar, who was then the editor of 'Kesari', announced in his paper that Nyayya Sahaya Nidhi-Fund to help get justice-has been started, and the fund began to receive small amounts of one or two rupees. Donations came from far away places like Bengal, Madras, Punjab and Gujarat. In the end, the amount collected came to about a hundred thousand rupees.

On May 25, Savarkar was taken to Delhi by air and was lodged, along with the other accused, at the Red Fort. The trial formally opened on May 27. But the proceedings really started on June 22. At this time in the dock were Nathuram Godse, Apte, Karkare, Madanlal, Kistaya, Gopal Godse, Dr. Parchure, and Savarkar. Bagde had turned approver, while Dandavate, Jadhav and Sharma had absconded. A few days after the trial began, Savarkar was given an easy chair to sit.

During the trial 149, prosecution witnesses were examined. On November 21, Savarkar submitted his statement. All accused were represented by lawyers. Bhopatkar appeared for Savarkar, but Barrister P. R. Das argued for him. His speech was par excellence. Inamdar, who was one of the defense lawyers, has delightfully described the mocking style of address of Barrister Das in the following words, "Now whom Das Babuji is going to show to be a fool? But soon I began to see at whom he was drawing a bead on. ... Dasbabu's statement made my dull mind see a few things in a new light. But more, it was a great delight to see a smile on Judge Atmacharanji's face. It was supreme pleasure to watch Atmacharanji smiling while occupying a judge's chair. While concluding his address, Barrister Das delivered a coup de main which was the height of derision.... Prosecution has examined 149 witnesses from the list of 275 and has left out 126 witnesses. Has not the prosecution under pressure of work left out one or two important witnesses against my client? Then raising his head high he said to

---

[1] The Times of India - February 7, 1948

judge Atmacharanji, 'Sir, let the prosecution even now produce witnesses. I am waiting; and when your Honor summons me, I will be at your service.'"[1]

Barrister Das also argued the charge of conspiracy on behalf of all accused. He said, "Your Honor is bound to ask the question: Was he likely to join a conspiracy of this nature? Did he not know that the shot which killed Gandhiji would also kill the organization which he helped to usher into manhood? It was inconceivable that he would have joined a conspiracy of this nature." And finally he submitted "a mere verdict of not guilty would not satisfy Savarkar. He was entitled to a verdict that he leaves the court without a stain on his character."[2]

In support of Barrister Das's submission that the shot which killed Gandhiji would also kill the organization, an illustration can be quoted. Deutscher writes: "In assassinating Alexander II, the 'Freedom of the people' had itself committed suicide. Its leaders had expected that their deed would become the signal for a nationwide upheaval, but they failed to evoke any response and the nation maintained silence."[3]

Mr. Atmacharan, the special judge, delivered his judgment on February 10, 1949. He sentenced Godse and Apte to death, and Karkare, Gopal Godse, Madanlal, Kistaya and Dr. Parchure to life imprisonment. He declared Savarkar not guilty. After the judgment was delivered, the judge rose to go. At that time all the accused shouted 'Akhand Bharat Amar Rahe.' Twenty years old Madanlal said, "We will conquer Pakistan."[4] When he was told of his father's acquittal by the reporter of The Times of India, his son Vishwas Savarkar said, "He and other members of the family were always confident that Mr. Savarkar would be acquitted as they felt that he was innocent of the charges leveled against him."[5]

Patriotic India heaved a sigh of relief. Savarkar was showered with messages of congratulations. But the moment he was set free an order was served on him not to leave the precincts of the Red Fort. So Savarkar could not be taken out in procession. A little later another order was served on him which prohibited him from entering Delhi for a period of three months. He was sent to Bombay by train. He reached Bombay on February 12. Hundreds of his admirers welcomed him. After staying in Bombay for a month, he went to Bangalore for a vacation.

After coming back to Bombay, he slowly picked up the threads of his political life. On August 5, 1949 he sent the following wire to the President of the Constituent Assembly: "I am voicing the sense and sentiment of millions of our

---

[1] P. B. Inamdar : Lal Killyatil Abhiyogachi Kahani - p.132

[2] The Bombay Chronicle: December 22, 1948

[3] Isaac Deutscher : The Prophet Armed - p.18

[4] The Times of India : February 11, 1949

[5] The Times of India : February 11, 1949

countrymen when I beseech the Constituent Assembly to adopt Bharat as the name of our nation, Hindi as the national language and Nagari as the national script."[1] Whatever may be the reasons, the Constituent Assembly decided to name India as Bharat, and to make Hindi the official language and Nagari the official script.

During this year a sad event occurred in Savarkar's family. His younger bother, Dr. N. D. Savarkar, died on October 19, at the age of sixty-one.

Dr. Khare was elected president of the Hindu Mahasabha session to be held at Calcutta in December 1949. Because of pressing invitation Savarkar went to Calcutta to inaugurate this session. There, he was taken out in a huge procession. In his inaugural speech, heard by a hundred thousand people, he declared, "You may call this country by whatever name you like. Call it Hindustan, call it Bharat, call it India, call it non-Muslim state, and yet it remains a Hindu nation. For Hindus are in a majority and it is the majority that goes to make a nation. Therefore so long as Hindus continue to be in majority, the country will remain a Hindu nation."

On January 26, 1950 India was declared a Sovereign Democratic Republic. For this auspicious day Savarkar gave a message. He said, "... It is thus a hard won national victory that we mean to commemorate on the day of the birth of our Bharatiya republic. There is no cause for any sense of self-diffident frustration. Even the painful consciousness of the 'Partition' which we all so deeply deplore should not be allowed to instill a sense of defeated mentality in us. If, when all was lost, we have succeeded in liberating three fourths part of our country, we can surely recover the rest if we are bent on doing so. True, the Partition today is a 'settled fact'. But had not Alexander himself torn off these very parts from our motherland and dubbed it a settled fact? Yet history tells us Selucus handed back to us all those parts of our natural frontiers right up to Hindu Kush and gave his daughter in marriage to Chandra Gupta Maurya to seal mutual friendship. Verily we have our own ways to resettle settled facts. Let us first consolidate what we have already got and follow courageously the policy of tit for tat to all outsiders concerned and all will go well with us."[2]

A month after the inauguration of the republic, refugees from East Bengal began to migrate to West Bengal. So Pandit Nehru sent a wire to the Prime Minister of Pakistan, Liaquat Ali Khan, suggesting that both the Prime Ministers should together tour the two Bengals. Pandit Nehru was not agreeable to the transfer of population. Also, he did not think it was possible for India to rehabilitate another billion or half a billion refugees. So he felt that there was a necessity to create a sense of security amongst the Hindus of East Pakistan. But Liaquat Ali spurned the idea of a joint tour and the stream of refugees continued.

---

[1] V. D. Savarkar : Historic Statements - p.224

[2] V. D. Savarkar : Historic Statements - pp.228-229

So 'the Government of India redeployed the army in fresh disposition.'[1] This told on Pakistani rulers and Liaquat Ali came to Delhi. For a week, talks went on. And a draft of agreement had to be redone eleven times. Finally it was signed on April 8. In protest, Dr. Shyama Prasad Mukerjee resigned from the cabinet.

The Hindu Mahasabha leaders, as usual, became the victims of the situation created by East Pakistan. On April 4, Savarkar, Bhopatkar, Ketkar, Date, Limaye, Nalawade were put in prison under the Preventive Detention Act. Bhopatkar and others were charged with conspiracy to commit acts of violence against the ministers of the government. Savarkar was lodged in Belgaum jail. On July 12, habeas corpus petition filed by his son came up for hearing in the Bombay High court. He was released on his giving an undertaking that he would not take part in political activity for one year.

In a few days, the Nehru-Liaquat pact became a worthless piece of paper. Liaquat Ali Khan and his wife visited the United States where they made speeches. Sardar Patel complained that the speeches were violating the Delhi agreement. So Nehru sent a wire of protest to Liaquat Ali Khan. But the Indian ambassador, Shrimati Vijayalaxmi Pandit, Nehru's sister, did not deliver it because these speeches were being revised for publication.[2] This was how the government was functioning. What can one say? And what is the use!

The Hindu Mahasabha session was held in Poona in December 1950. Savarkar did not attend it. But his wife, Yamunabai, was given a reception and presented with a purse of Rs. 10,000.00 by the women of Poona. Speaking on this occasion she said, "I am like a flower offered at the feet of God. It is the dedication that has brought merit to it. In my youth, I had taken the oath of Women's wing of Abhinav Bharat. I have, therefore, faced without complaint the difficulties that came my way. So the honor you are bestowing on the flower really belonged to God and not to the flower." Gandhiji, along with his wife Kasturba, had met Yamunabai in Ratnagiri to salute her courage. Her above remarks show how worthy she was of that honor.

A great celebration was held in Poona from May 10 to May 12, 1952 announcing the disbanding of Abhinav Bharat. The idea originated with Savarkar. He had founded this organization to liberate India by armed revolution. As India had become free, the object of the organization was achieved. And hence a celebration was organized for its dissolution. A Krantismriti Nagar was constructed where a column in memory of the martyrs who had laid down their lives for their country from 1857 to 1947 was raised. Homage to these martyrs was paid before this column. The living revolutionists had especially come to attend this function. An exhibition of pictures showing the daring deeds of the

---

[1]Sarvepalli Gopal: Jawaharlal Nehru, Vol II - p.84

[2]Sarvepalli Gopal: Jawaharlal Nehru, Vol II - p.89

revolutionaries and thrilling events in their lives was arranged in Tilak Smarak Mandir.

On May 10, Savarkar declared this exhibition open and made a speech at the time. Then for three consecutive evenings Savarkar spoke at length. On the first day his speech emphasized the point that winning independence had been a collective effort. On the second day, he first talked about the living revolutionists who were honored and then about how Subhaschandra Bose had met him, and how he had suggested to Bose to go abroad to organize the freedom movement and what had been its results. On the last day in this lecture series, he emphasized that however extreme the differences might be, in a free country their solution must be sought through the ballot-box; he also told the audience that Ramrajya - a welfare state - does not arrive on the day freedom dawns.

On May 8, 1953, Savarkar went to Nasik. The local Abhinav Bharat Memorial Committee had raised a monument to that institution. On May 10, he inaugurated it. Deshpande was hanged for the assassination of Jackson. Savarkar met his wife who herself was a member of the women's wing of the Abhinav Bharat Society. He also met members of the families of Datar, Barve, and others. He visited Bhonsala Military School and laid a wreath at the Samadhi of Dr. Moonje. In his speech in Jackson garden, he declared that its name had been changed to Shivaji Garden. Savarkar, however, expressed his anguish that the proposal to name one of the gates after Kanhere was not approved. Next day he went to Bhagur, his birth-place. He visited the house where he had taken the oath. The ownership of this house had changed hands. He spent a few minutes in complete silence. In the evening he was presented with an address in a public meeting. While expressing his gratitude for the honor, he said that being old, he was taking his leave of them. Then he visited the depressed class colony. Here he said that he had struggled hard for their political, religious, and social rights. But if change of faith was going to help ameliorate their conditions, then they should certainly change faith. But if ever they wished to return to their original faith, then the doors of the Hindu society were open to them.

During the British rule, the Christian missionaries were freely conducting their activities of converting Hindus. But in free India, these activities increased. If change of faith was limited to a belief in spiritual life, there could be no objection to it. But in India, change of faith has resulted in change of national outlook. Its proof is the creation of Pakistan. Savarkar genuinely began to fear that the activities of Christian missionaries would create the same problem. In 1931, he had written an article under the caption 'Why Naga Hindus become Christians?' In course of time, the problem of Nagaland cropped up. So Nehru who was sympathetic to the missionaries had to order 'that foreign missionaries in this area be informed that they would have to leave India if their complicity in such activity (anti-national) were established.'[1] In Madhya Pradesh, its government had to

---

[1]Sarvepalli Gopal: Jawaharlal Nehru, Vol II -.209

appoint 'The Christian Missionary Activities Inquiry Committee.' On December 11, 1953 Savarkar spoke in Poona on the subject of 'Change of Religion is a Change of Nationality' to focus public attention on this new danger. How far this maxim is true in India is evident in every day happenings.

The Centenary year of Lokamanya Tilak's birth fell in 1956. The main centenary celebrations were held in Poona. An All Parties Committee was formed for these celebrations. It invited Savarkar to deliver the main address. Savarkar in his speech expressed his regrets that the function was not held in Delhi. The function was presided over by Lokanayak Aney, a devoted lieutenant of Lokamanya Tilak.

Fortunately the centenary celebrations of 1857 were held on a grand scale in Delhi. Savarkar was invited by the Delhi Citizens Centenary Celebrations Committee to be the main speaker on this occasion. On May 10, the Congress held a public meeting at Ramlila ground. Pandit Nehru spoke at this meeting. Two days later, Savarkar spoke at the same place to a bigger audience. In his speech, he reiterated his thesis that '1857 revolt was a war of Independence.' Then he referred to the often-repeated statement that the world was faced with the dilemma 'Yudha Ka Buddha.' He said that India had cherished the doctrine - Mantra - of non-violence from the Vedic times. But 'Mantra' did not prove efficacious for defense and hence one had to have recourse to arms.

For this centenary occasion, Dr. Sen and Dr. Majumdar had written books on 1857. Their views were opposed to that of Savarkar. A controversy began. Its echoes were heard during the press conference held in connection with the centenary celebrations. In it, Savarkar replied logically and pointedly to the arguments as also to the questions raised by the controversy. He said, 'Revolutions are sparked by trifles. In the beginning, there are never lofty ideals. Also, the mass of people is not drawn into it. At the beginning of the French revolution, the people of Paris were only demanding bread. They did not demand freedom, equality, and brotherhood. The noble thoughts came later. In 1917, the Russian people were tired of war. They wanted peace and land. They did not ask for Lenin's Bolshevik revolution. But epoch-making events occurred in France and Russia. Take Gandhiji's movement. To how many people did the idea of Salt Satyagraha occur? But once Gandhiji started it, the whole country was fired by it. So, even though, in the beginning, there were few leaders like Nanasaheb, Rani of Jhansi, still, at a later period, the flames of the war of independence spread from the North West Frontier Province down to Maharashtra and Karnataka.; About three score reporters sat spell-bound while listening to the exposition of the events of 1857 by Savarkar. The late Mr. V. B. Gogate, who attended this function as a revolutionary, narrated the above incident to this author.

On May 28, 1958, Savarkar became 75 years old. So a reception in his honor was arranged by the Municipal Corporation of Greater Bombay at Kamla Nehru Park. Comrade Mirajkar, as Mayor, presided over this function. While expressing his gratitude for the reception, Savarkar said that "the Government was neglecting the policy of militarization. India's word would carry no weight in the councils of the world unless it was militarily strong. My heart-felt desire was to see India become as strong as Russia."

In November, Savarkar went to Poona. The Poona Municipal Corporation held a reception for him and presented him with an address. After thanking the Corporation for this honor, Savarkar said that democracy was all right. But on some occasions, military administration proved helpful to the country. If benevolent dictatorship became necessary for the country, then it should be welcomed as a beneficial thing. He expressed his sorrow that the defense was being neglected and great festivals of Dramas, Film Shows, and Tamashas were being held in Delhi. Finally he suggested that the Corporation should start a military school.

Savarkar, if he had not been released earlier, would have completed two life sentences of exile that is 50 years, on December 24, 1960. This day was celebrated in various parts of India as Mrityunjay Din (Victory over death day) the last function was held in Poona where Savarkar was honored. Speaking at this function he said that he wanted to see Maharashtra as the sword-arm of India.

Savarkar's charge that India was neglecting the policy of militarization was borne out on October 20, 1962. The Indian army reeled under the fierce attack of the Chinese army. India suffered great humiliation all over the world. In his talk on the All India Radio on October 22, Pandit Nehru said, "We are men and women of peace in this country, conditioned to the ways of peace. We are unused to the necessities of war." From such a person it was wrong to expect a powerful speech like that of Churchill. After the Chinese invasion, Galbraith notes, "Nehru's speech was a good deal less than Churchillian."[1] This was no surprise. If Savarkar was in the place of Nehru, Galbraith would have heard a powerful speech electrifying the country. But if Savarkar would have been at the helm of affairs, this humiliating event would probably not have occurred.

The Hindu Mahasabha session was held in December 1962 at Calcutta. Savarkar sent a message for this session. It would have been a wonder if it did not contain reflections of the events that had happened two months earlier. He said, ".... But remember that the boundaries of a state are decided by victory or defeat in war. If we are beaten, if our military strength is found deficient, if we are too weak to face the enemy, any suitable armistice may be made in the unfavorable conditions. But bear in mind that an armistice is no treaty. If our army can march from victory to victory without regard for the MacMahon or any other line or boundary, we shall march on to Peking."[2]

---

[1] J. K. Galbraith : Ambassador's Journal - p.466

[2] V. D. Savarkar : Historic Statmetns - p.241

In 1952, Savarkar had delivered lectures on the glorious pages of Indian history. The first part of these lectures was published on May 10, 1956 under the title of 'Six golden pages in the history of the Hindu nation.' The latter part of these lectures was published in April 1963. One is amazed to see Savarkar working so hard at the age of 80.

In November of this year his wife, Yamunabai died. Savarkar refused to perform religious obsequies of his wife. His reported remark was: Who would know the last wish of his wife he or the crow." But his son is reported to have performed the religious rites quietly. Savarkar gave donations in the name of his wife to some social institutions.

In December Barrister Chatterji was elected to the Lok Sabha. While congratulating him, Savarkar told him to lay stress on the following demands: "1. All Hindus in East Bengal should be allowed to come over to Western Bengal and at least an equal number of Muslims from West Bengal should be sent to East Bengal if necessary by force. 2. For every aggressive step taken by Pakistan, whether military or otherwise, must be met by prompt reprisals, military or otherwise, by the Hindustan Government, kind for kind, measure for measure. 3. Not an inch of our land should be surrendered to Pakistan without the consent of the Hindu public either on the Eastern Frontier or the Western."[1]

After his wife's death, Savarkar had said that in a year or two, he would also pass away. Before that an event happened that gladdened his heart. On September 1, 1965 a war between India and Pakistan broke out. When he heard that the Indian army was marching towards Lahore, he said, "Now let nothing stop our army in their forward march. Through fear of what others might say we must not retreat."[2] In the same month, his autobiographical piece 'In the Camp of the Enemy' was published.

Now slowly, his health began to deteriorate. From February 3, he ceased taking tea. He only sipped water. On February 9, there was a swelling in his leg.

On February 18, he felt very weak. Next day Dr. Sathe examined him and said that Savarkar's life was ebbing. On February 22, Balarao Savarkar read to him some excerpts from Mankekar's book 'Pakistan cut to size.' The Times of India was carrying daily news of his illness from February 22. On February 26 at 11:30 A.M. at the age of 83, he breathed his last. This warrior of epic dimensions passed into eternity. Messages of condolences poured in from all parts of India. The President and Vice President sent their messages. The Prime Minister of India, Indira Gandhi, in her message said, "Mr. Savarkar's death removes from our midst a great figure of contemporary India. His name was a byword for daring and

---

[1] V. D. Savarkar : Histoic Statements - p.243
[2] V. D. Savarkar : Histoic Statements - p.243

patriotism. Mr. Savarkar was cast in the mold of a classical revolutionary and countless people drew inspiration from him."

Next day, the funeral procession started. The Times of India said: "The most eloquent tribute to the reformer came from women. He had espoused their cause and they repaid him by marching in the funeral procession. The presence of so many women mourners was a phenomenon unusual in high-caste Hindu society." There were about 50 to 60 thousand people in this procession. At Bombay Central, 2,000 R.S.S. Volunteers stood to attention when the last post was sounded. When the cortege reached Chandanwadi, the crowd was estimated to be a hundred thousand strong. Finally, the procession ended and Savarkar's body was taken inside and put into an electric crematorium. At once the fire raged and the person who fired the minds of countless of his countrymen with patriotism, was consumed by fire. A great epoch in the history of India came to an end!

Savarkar: Some Vignettes

"Seek to perform your duty; but lay not claim to its fruit." [1]

I first saw Savarkar at close quarters in Baroda in 1938. He had come to preside over the conference of the Marathi Literary Society. He was staying at the Baroda State Guest House which was located on the west side of the Baroda railway station, while the High School was on its east side. The distance between these two was about a quarter mile. Our teacher had asked four or five of us to leave the class for mischief-making. At the entrance to the school, there was a huge tamarind tree. We were sitting under its shadow when one of us said, "Let us go to see Savarkar'"

I had heard some stories about Savarkar from my elders. But the most important thing was that I had read his book 'My Transportation'. The Bombay Government had banned this book. However, in Baroda, then a native state, the book was available in the Central Library. To read it was a thrilling experience. So when the idea of going to see such a great man was broached, we, at once, made a beeline to the State Guest House and were there in about ten minutes. There was a bearer in the waiting room. He went and told Savarkar that some boys had come to meet him. A few minutes later, he came into the waiting room. In my mind's eye I still see the picture of Savarkar as I saw him that day.

He was small in stature and was wearing a white shirt and a fine white dhoti. His skin was very fair. He was wearing a pair of golden rim spectacles and had a penetrating look. His forehead was broad and his brows were a bit knitted and a smile was playing on his lips - such was Savarkar's personality and he was standing before us. For a few seconds, he smiled and then asked us, "What brings you here boys?" All were tongue-tied. No one could think what to say. Finally I summoned courage and said, "We want your sahi - signature." "You mean swakshari." (Pure Marathi equivalent for the word signature) he said. "No. I want a message and sahi", I replied. He then said, "Yes, that is swakshari." Having said this, he wrote in our notebooks: "Write in new script - V. D. Savarkar."

I went to Poona for college education in 1940. Savarkar often came to Poona in those days. I had a few opportunities to see him talking in private meetings. Two instances stand out in my mind.

Savarkar was an ardent advocate of abolition of untouchability. It was an essential part of his movement for Hindu solidarity. The orthodox section approved of Savarkar's Hindu solidarity movement, but not his campaign against untouchability. The late Mr. Davare, who was one of the leaders of the orthodox section, indicated his dissent about it. Savarkar argued with him thus: "Our Hindu

---

[1] The Bhagawad Gita: Chapter 2 – Stanza 47

Sanghatan movement has just begun. We have to face three antagonists - the Congress, the Muslims, and the British. So why begin with differences amongst the Hindu Sanghatanists? First establish the area of agreement. It is quite vast. Let us work with one mind in that area. A lot of good will is achieved. We will go our separate ways when the real differences arise. Why waste our little organized strength in playing up the differences at the present moment?"

Once the late V. G. Deshpande remarked about a certain prominent worker from the state of Uttar Pradesh that he was a government man. To this Savarkar replied: 'We are so few that our number could be counted on fingers. Why drive away people from our fold on mere suspicion? It is no use wailing that the Congress has a horse and we have a donkey. You will achieve nothing by it. We must use our donkey and try to get a horse. But so long as we do not have a horse, we should not foolishly drive away our donkey.'

There are lessons in these instances for a person who wants to be an administrator or an organizer.

Savarkar came to Baroda in October 1943 for two days to attend his 61st birthday celebrations. At his behest, I worked as a liaison between him and the local organizers. During this period, I had an occasion to stay close to him for sometime. I had heard about his temperament. On the first day, after the evening function, we returned to the Brahman Sabha where he way staying. Then he went on the terrace and sat alone in a chair engrossed in thought. His figure in white apparel could be seen in the dim light that was coming from the adjacent room. Some local worthies came to see him. So I went up to him and said, "Tatya, some leading men of the city have come to see you." "What! Am I a machine?" I was a bit taken aback. I could not think of a way out. But Savarkar came to my help. Seeing me lingering at the door, he said, "I will meet them for a few minutes, but a little later." I went down and requested the worthies to wait for a while. Soon Savarkar came down and met them. He spoke to them in his usual delightful way and those worthies went back happy. It was a lesson to be learnt. A man in public life is like a machine. He must work like a machine till it stops irrespective of honor or dishonor, success or defeat, hardships, tiredness, pinpricks, and public misunderstanding.

The annual session of the Hindu Mahasabha was held in Amritsar. A procession that was taken out was lathi-charged. I received a few blows and was detained at the police station for a few hours. On my way back to Poona, I saw Savarkar. "You were much beaten, weren't you?" he asked me. "Well, I received a few blows, but my father has beaten me more," I said. His face lit up with a smile at my reply. He never guffawed like Dr. Moonje. Later I heard that he had playfully said, "I was a naughty boy."

I started reading books on nationalism in 1942. In the next four years I read considerable literature on that subject. I also read Savarkar's Hindutva a few times. Therein he has written, "It may be that at some future time the word 'Hindu' may come to indicate a citizen of Hindustan and nothing else." This clearly shows that Savarkar was ready to include Muslims and Christians in the family of the Hindus. In his concept of nationalism, loyalty to land and secularism had primacy. In 1946, Savarkar was staying in a hotel in Poona for some much needed rest and change. I met him there. While discussing the above point I said to him, "I do not understand why Hindu Sanghatanists are dubbed communalists?"

"I write for people. I cannot read for them. If my reading would have helped them to understand what I say, I would have done that," he said.

In 1948 news came that Savarkar was being implicated as an accused in the Gandhi murder trial. However vividly the picture of that time is drawn, its frightfulness cannot be understood today. In the first four months, though legally not guilty, the atmosphere was such that the Hindu Sanghatanists felt that socially they were out-castes. It was impossible to say at that time how many people would come forward to defend Savarkar. So a few friends in Baroda thought that I should go to Delhi and do whatever work that fell to my lot. Afterwards I met the late Mr. Bhopatkar in Poona and with his approval I decided to go to Delhi. But in the meanwhile, the defense was got up. I was not informed about it. So when I went to Delhi, I found that my presence was superfluous. Naturally I returned to Baroda immediately. After his acquittal I met Savarkar in Bombay. He asked me, "Why did you return immediately from Delhi?" "As you are aware of what really happened, I would rather not talk about it." I replied. Hearing my reply, he did not pursue the subject.

After a prolonged study of nationalism, I wrote a book in 1949 entitled 'Hindustanche Rashtriyatva.' I requested him to write a foreword to it. His son wrote to me that his father, being in indifferent health, would not be able to write it. The book was published in June 1950. Savarkar was then lodged in the Belgaum jail. A copy of the book was sent to him there. Then the matter slipped my memory. But on August 18, a messenger from the press where the book was printed came to me with an envelope. When I saw the handwriting on it, I knew it was Savarkar's. I could not bring myself to take the letter out of the envelope. What would be its contents? But once a writer has asked for an opinion, he should be ready to receive it. Convincing myself thus, I took it out. As I began to read, I could not believe that Savarkar had written that letter. At the end of the letter, there was an instruction: "Please acknowledge the letter." Later my friends gathered at my house and it was read aloud. Its language was eloquent. Those who had heard Savarkar speaking would get that feeling while reading it.

A few months later, I met him and respectfully expressed my gratitude. I had heard that he had spoken very highly of my book. But what he said during this meeting bowled me over. He said, "Your book is so good that my book 'Hindutva' need not be read."

In a few seconds, I recovered myself and told him, "Nothing of that sort. Your book does not lend itself to easy reading for a common man, mine does. My book is meant for school students while yours is for college students". This time also his face lit up with his usual smile. Then asking me to wait, he went into the adjoining room. He came back with a bagful of his own books and gave them to me. So I requested him to sign at least one book. He declined. I wondered then and I wonder even now why he declined. I felt a little hurt. I said to him, "Tatya, how much do I pay for these books?" Smilingly he said, "Make plenty of money in your legal profession and then send it to me." To me his appreciation of my book was important for another reason. It was a lesson how to energize a younger person by appreciating his work. This helped me considerably in my administrative career.

I had traveled in Spain in 1952 and had written a series of articles on it in a Bombay weekly 'Vivek.' Savarkar had read them. For he spoke about them to Mr. Desai, a friend from Baroda and said to him, "Joglekar did not see me." Later, when I was in Bombay, I went to meet him. But he did not see me. So I let be. On one of his birthdays, I went to his house along with other people. He spoke to us for sometime and then bid us good-bye. Along with the rest, I got up to go. But he pointed a finger at me and said, "You wait." Then he said, "I have read those articles about your tour of Europe. You visited Spain. What did you see?" The Moors (Arabs) had ruled Spain for about seven hundred years. They had built a fine Spanish-Arab civilization. Big mosques were built in Cardova, Seville, and Toledo. After the Spaniards defeated the Arabs, they turned the mosques into churches. For about half an hour he was asking questions about this and I was answering them. It was a sort of Viva Voce.

I don't quite remember if it was on this day or another birthday occasion. Savarkar was sitting in the small room on the ground floor. A group of people, who had come to wish him many happy returns of the day, were sitting around him. During the talk someone casually said, "You did not become President." I think he was sick of such remarks. A slight facial change indicated he did not like the subject. But his reply was unusual. He said, "Of what importance is the post of a president? You go to Ujjain and ask a man in the street who Vikramaditya was? He was one of the greatest emperors of India. But if people could forget him, then what of Savarkar?" I do not know what effect these remarks had on others. But they made a deep impression on my mind. If this is the fate of Vikramaditya and Savarkar, then what happens to a common man like me? Honor, admiration, criticism, jealousy, abuse, etc. really sink into insignificance.

In 1956, Dr. R. C. Majumdar, in his Nagpur speech, said that the 1857 eruption was not a War of Independence. This speech was reported in the Nagpur Times. He sent for me. So I went to see him one day. He gave me the newspaper cutting containing the speech and said, "You write articles refuting the thesis of Dr. Majumdar in the Bombay Chronicle." (It was an English daily, now closed, where I was then working) He made general comments on Dr. Majumdar's speech.

Then I left. But I was up to my eyes in my personal affairs and I could not find time to do those articles. Nor for many more years could I do them. It was only after 20 years I found time to write articles on the 1857 episode. In May 1981, I wrote an article in Bombay Marathi daily, with special reference to Dr. Majumdar's speech, and after 25 years the promise I made to Savarkar was partially fulfilled. Over the years I had written articles about 1857 eruption. These were published in book form in January 2000.

About five years later, that is, in 1961, my residential telephone rang. One Mr. Telkar, a journalist, wanted to meet me. He had earlier interviewed Savarkar. The interview had lasted for a considerable time. Savarkar had explained to him at length his political stand. This took a long time and tired him. When Telkar began to ask him specific questions, he declined to answer and said, "These are matters of detail. You see Joglekar and he will give you the information you want." So Telkar came to see me with Balarao Savarkar. I gave him the information he wanted. At the end Telkar said to me, "You use words like Savarkar." I replied, "This is Savarkar's interview. So I must use his words. I know them. That is all."

One morning in April 1963, my office phone rang. The late Mr. Sudhir Phadke spoke, then the late Mr. Appa Kasar spoke. A few days earlier my article, 'Once again Hindu nationalism' had appeared in a Marathi weekly 'Vivek'. I had tried to answer Prime Minister Nehru's criticism of Hindu nationalism. Savarkar had liked that article and had asked Kasar to inform me accordingly. That Savarkar should read that article and have his appreciation conveyed to me was a bit surprising.

A similar thing happened a year later. He had liked an article I had written. I do not remember which it was. But he had asked Balarao Savarkar to inform me that he had liked the article. Also, he had told him to give me the second volume of his book 'Six Glorious Pages', which Balarao did. It bears the date: March 3, 1964. Of course, I had many more passing meetings with him. But there was nothing special in them and so their memory has not stayed in my mind. The above reminiscences show something significant and useful. Also, they indicate the extent of my relationship with him. However, some people were close to him. Some were his blind followers. I did not belong to either category. For that one has to have a different temperament. I lack it. I could not have been intimate with him and it is also true that he would not have given such latitude to me. But I was deeply imbued with his philosophy and literature. And he also probably thought I had correctly understood his philosophy. If that were not the case, he would not have sent Telkar to me.

Having said so much, I must admit that mine is a distant view of Savarkar. I, therefore, could not describe his personal and private life. Like others, I was also curious about a few things. What were his reading habits? How did he read a book? How did he evaluate it? What paper did he prefer? How did he use a pen, a pencil, or a ballpoint-pen? How many hours did he devote to reading and writing? Did he rewrite his articles? Did he read Bernard Shaw, H. G. Wells, and Wodehouse? How much did he enjoy traveling and reading travel books? What were his food tastes? How much interest did he take in his children and grand-children? Answers to these questions would have been amusing and instructive.

I had spoken to Savarkar. I had also heard him in discussions in private meetings. But never did I see him get angry or excited. He spoke in a low tone. But while speaking, he would lay stress on certain words. In conversation he spoke sotto voce. In fact, anyone sitting in the adjoining room could have hardly heard him. It has been a permanent puzzle to me how Savarkar could talk in such a low tone or without getting excited. I am deficient in both these qualities and that may be the reason why I admired Savarkar's way of talking. The Andaman and Nicobar island authorities have made the following noting about Savarkar.

"He is always suave and polite but like his brother, he has never shown any disposition to actively assist the government. It is impossible to say what his real political views are at the present time."[1]

I had heard many of his public speeches and at a time when his eloquence was at its zenith. I have read the speeches of Cicero, Demosthenes, Fox, Burke, Churchill, Hitler, and others. At some point in the speeches, you feel the eloquence. And yet there is a feeling that something is missing. One feels that they are not instinct with liveliness. There is no rhythm, no stress on words. Printed speeches are like Greek statues. They look beautiful but are cold. The future generations will have this experience while reading Savarkar's speeches. We were fortunate. We heard some of his finest speeches. The late Mr. D. V. Gokhale, former assistant editor of Maharashtra Times, wrote an article on Savarkar after his death. He wrote therein, "Next day he gave a lecture in Shivaji Akhada. The subject was Hindutva. I do not remember even a word of the historical and social arguments he then advanced. But I was caught in the cataract of his eloquence. It is said that the chariot of Dharmaraja used to run a few inches above the ground. I remember that I felt a little elevated from the ground while listening to Savarkar's first speech. His personality and eloquence cast a permanent spell on me."[2] Gokhale's opinion, to a large extent, is a representative one.

Contradictory opinions are held about Savarkar's temperament. Some people do not find any fault in him. Others feel that he lacked the qualities of Tilak and Gandhi. I think both views run to extremes. Savarkar possessed both good and bad qualities. It is part of human nature. It is true that there was a wide gulf between Savarkar's way of working and that of Tilak and Gandhi. But there is nothing strange in it. Tilak and Gandhi were primarily leaders of mass movement.

---

[1] Source Material for a History of the Freedom Movement in India, [Collected from Bombay Government Records]: Vol II - p.464

[2] D. V. Gokhale : Vivek Weekly, March 6, 1966

It was only in 1937 when he became president of the Hindu Mahasabha that Savarkar entered the field of mass movement. His earlier life was spent in activities of the secret society. The impression gathered in one's youth molds one's outlook.

Savarkar had studied the lives of Russian revolutionaries. In 1909, his elder brother, Babarao Savarkar's house was searched when, among other things, a copy of Frost's Secret Societies of European Revolution, 1776 to 1876, was found. The book contains some information about the Russian Nihilist organization.[1] Mikhail Bakunin was a Russian revolutionary. He was the father of Nihilism. He wrote a book 'Catechism for a Revolutionary'. Savarkar either must have read the whole book or at least some parts of it. In the first section of the book 'Attitude of a Revolutionary towards himself' it has been stated: "... the renunciation of every interest, sentiment and personal bond; a break with the civilized world, its laws and convention; to know only one science, that of destruction; to despise public opinion; to hate accepted morals and customs; to be ruthless, expecting in return no mercy, but to be always ready to die and prepared to bear torture; to stifle in one's self all family sentiments, friendship, love, gratitude, and honor; to find no other satisfaction than that of the success of the revolution and to this end to destroy all obstructionists."[2] If Savarkar had absorbed one tenth of these ideas, then his behavior becomes understandable and one does not expect a conformist conduct from him.

There is some evidence throwing light on the character of the young revolutionary Savarkar. After Dhingra episode, Savarkar could not find suitable accommodation. On one day three housekeepers turned him out. Then he found some accommodation in a very poor neighborhood. Garnet probably often met Savarkar at this place. He has drawn the following word-picture of Savarkar at that time: "As a result I saw a certain amount of Savarkar and was more than ever struck by his extraordinary personal magnetism. There was an intensity of faith in the man and a curious single-minded recklessness which were deeply attractive to me. The filthy place in which he was living brought out both his refinement and also his lack of human sympathy, both characteristic of the high-caste Brahmin. ... In the room opposite lived an appalling slattern with four young children. .. Dutt often spoke of her and her children with horror and pity. But Savarkar was indifferent to her existence and indeed oblivious to his environment. He was wrapped in his visions. What was his vision then? I cannot say, but I believe it was that India was a volcano, which had erupted violently during the Mutiny and which could be made to erupt again, and that every act of terrorism and violence would beget further violence and further terrorism, until Indians regained their manliness and their mother country, her freedom. All the sufferings involved were but a fitting sacrifice to her."[3]

---

[1] Sedition Committee Report, 1918 - p.10

[2] Boris Souvarine : Stalin, A critical Survey of Bolshevism - p.23

[3] David Garnet : A Golden Echo - p.149

Savarkar had taken a pledge to bring about an armed revolution in India. So his temper became hard and devoid of sympathy. And yet his inner soul remained soft and sensitive. We get glimpses of it occasionally. In the last year of his incarceration in the Andamans, Savarkar was granted some freedom. Describing it, he writes, "Not only in the morning but at early morning I would be let out of my cell. I got an exhilarating experience of standing in the star-light after ten years! It was fun."[1] That these sentences have been written by Savarkar is rather difficult to imagine at first blush! But such was his complex personality.

Those who think that Savarkar was a paragon should be left alone. But those who think that because he lacked the qualities of Tilak and Gandhi, the Hindu Mahasabha did not triumph, are not correctly assessing the political situation. By establishing the Congress, the leaders of that time brought into being a new stream of public opinion. The generation of Ranade, Gokhale, Tilak, and Gandhiji by their sacrifice and by extra-ordinary qualities, turned this stream into a torrent. Muslim separatism had confounded Gokhale and Tilak. It had become an inevitable part of Indian political life. Yet the Congress was the only political party in India supported by Hindu Mahasabha leaders like Pandit Malaviya, Lala Lajapt Rai, N. C. Kelkar, and others. Such was the condition till 1937. It was only in that year that Savarkar propounded his separate political philosophy. But he had a very short time from 1937 to 1939 to propagate his ideology of Hindu nationalism. After that he devoted his time to militarization. How was it possible in such a short time to attract people imbued with the idea of Indian nationalism of the Congress to Hindu nationalism? As Savarkar once said that some tasks require generations to accomplish them. The work of propagating Hindu nationalism is such a task. It is, therefore, no wonder that Hindu Mahasabha was defeated as a political party in 1945-46 elections. The various political parties which broke away from the Congress met with the same fate. The fact is that the defeat of the Hindu Mahasabha was the cumulative effect of the movement of the past sixty years. Savarkar's temperament could not have made any difference to the final outcome and it did not. Now all this is academic. It has no relevance to the present time. But occasionally the question is raised and therefore I thought it right to deal with it here.

Of course, I am firmly persuaded that if power had come into Savarkar's hands, he would have effected revolutionary changes in India. He had the personality and caliber similar to Richelieu, Bismarck, Kamal Ataturk, Lenin, and Stalin. These leaders molded their nations and gave them a new character. If Savarkar were to get an opportunity, he would have performed the same miracle. He was fully conscious that he possessed the qualities of a nation-builder. One can find it in his literature. In his autobiographical piece, 'My transportation', he wrote about himself thus: "Your capability is like a high powered machine which can

---

[1] V. D. Savarkar : Samagra Savarkar Wangamaya, Vol I - p.654

regenerate a nation."[1] It was because of this capability that he could overthrow the small Pathani Kingdom which was reigning in the Andamans before his arrival there and established in its place a Hindu Kingdom within ten years.[2] As he was aware of his immense strength, he could tell his orthodox opponents, "If there was Peshwai, who could say that Gangabhat would have become Peshwa? Why could I not have become Peshwa or at least Nana Phadnavis?"[3] Also in one of his speeches in Poona he said, ".... If you vote, I might become President and within two years I will make India more powerful that Khrushchev's Russia ... yes, yes, in two years' time..."[4]

Savarkar's personality was that of a nation-builder. But his administrative capacities never got a chance to flower. That he had administrative instincts could be seen from the following wire he sent to Pandit Nehru: "Hearty appreciation of and support to your courageous step putting our Eastern borders under military charge. Punitive and prohibitive military reprisals in kind and measure can alone restore our lost prestige."[5] But one has to admit that it was not fated that Savarkar should be at the helm of affairs in India.

After Savarkar's death, London Times wrote an obituary. The first paragraph runs thus: "Mr. Vinayak Damodar Savarkar, who died in Bombay on Saturday at the age of 83, is a reminder of a period of Indian politics that now seems distant and faint, the period of sporadic terrorism against the British which was largely extinguished as Gandhi's influence took hold of the independence movement. But Veer Savarkar, as he was called (Veer means hero) stood for something far more lasting; he was among the first and most influential articulators of Hindu nationalism and could be called the father of Hindu Communalism as a political force. His slogan was 'Hinduize all politics and militarize Hindudom."[6]

The estimate of 'The Times' that Savarkar's life stands for something far more lasting than the terrorist movement is absolutely correct. The far more lasting thing is the ideology of Hindu nationalism.

---

[1] V. D. Savarkar : Samagra Savarkar Wangamaya, Vol I - p.374

[2] V. D. Savarkar : Samagra Savarkar Wangamaya, Vol I - p.644

[3] V. D. Savarkar : Samagra Savarkar Wangamaya, Vol III - p.422

[4] V. D. Savarkar : Samagra Savarkar Wangamaya, Vol VIII - p.504

[5] V. D. Savarkar : Historic Statments - p.239

[6] The London Times : February 28, 1966

Appendix A

JAIL HISTORY TICKET OF V. D. SAVARKAR[1]
Convict No. 32778
No of corridor - Top
Class 3 C.
No of Block 2

Date

30th August 1911	6 months solitary confinement until further orders.
14th August 1911	Letter from Secretary to Government, Educational Department, to the effect that the Degree of BA conferred on him has been cancelled.
30th August 1911	Petition for clemency.
3rd September 1911	Petition rejected.
15th January 1912	Removed from solitary confinement.
11th June 1912	One month's separate confinement for writing letters to others without sanction.
11th July 1912	Removed from separate confinement.
10th September 1912	Seven days standing handcuffs for having in possession a letter written to another convict.
29th October 1912	Petitioner to be released from Cellular Jail because he has been in 16 months and that his conduct has been better.
4th November 1912	Petition rejected.
23rd November 1912	One month's separate confinement for being in possession of a note written by another convict.
18th December 1912	Informed of his brother's address : 98 Premchand Burat Street Bow Bazar, Calcutta.
23rd December 1912	Removed from separate confinement.
30th December 1912	Refused to eat his food all day.
1st January 1913	Refused to eat his food all day.
2nd January 1913	Ate his food this morning.
14th November 1913	Permitted by the Hon. Member of Home Department to write a petition: Petition made and sent to Medical Superintendent.
16th December 1913	Absolutely refusing to work.
17th December 1913	One month's separate confinement without work or books.
17th January 1914	Removed from S.C. Rope making.
8th June 1914	Absolutely refusing to work. Seven days standing handcuffs imposed.

---

[1] Source Material for a History of the Freedom Movement in India, (Collected from the Bombay Government Records) , Vol II 1885-1920, Bombay Government Publication pp 478-481

15th June 1914	Completed S. H. Cuffs.
16th June 1914	Absolutely refusing to work. Four months chain gaug imposed.
18th June 1914	Absolutely refusing to work. Ten days cross bar fetters imposed.
19th June 1914	Asks for work in Rope making.
29th June 1914	Removed fetters.
16th July 1914	Convalescent gaug.
10th September 1914	Asks to make out a petition to C. C. granted.
14th September 1914	Petition forwarded through Medical Superintendent.
16th October 1914	Chain gaug fetters removed.
1st December 1914	Government rejected prisoner's proposals in the petition.
18th May 1915	Convalescent gaug (Discharged on 11th June 1916 on admission to hospital).
5th July 1916	Brothers address: N. D. Savarkar, Goregaonkar's 1st Chawl, ground floor, Girgaum, Bombay.
28th October 1916	Promoted to 2nd Class with effect from 2nd November 1916.
2nd October 1917	May write a petition to Government of India
1st February 1918	Informed that Secretary has placed his petition (in which he prays that a general amnesty be given to all political prisoners) with the Government of India.
1st January 1919	To continue as a hospital patient for purposes of diet and treatment.
30th May 1919	Interview with wife and brother Dr. Savarkar – one hour.
31st May 1919	Interview with wife and brother Dr. Savarkar – 1 ¼ hours.
24th January 1920	Petition to Jails Committee.
6th April 1920	Petition to Government of India, forwarded to C. C. for disposal, forwarded to Government of India.
14th July 1920	May do some clerical work in his Verandah
19th August 1920	Reply received from Government of India "The Viceroy is not prepared at present to extend to him the benefit of amnesty.".
28th September 1920	Savarkar desires either to be made foremen or to be given definite clerical work. The former is at present not possible. The latter should be granted as far as possible.
4th November 1920	Appointed a foreman on probation in charge of oil godown.
10th February 1921	Recommended to be made a pucca.
2nd May 1921	Embarked on SS Maharaja for transfer to join Bombay Presidency.

Appendix B

The following quotations are printed with one purpose only. It would enable the reader to judge Savarkar and his political opponents Gandhi and Nehru

"Nearly a thousand miles away from Delhi and its tarnished imperial splendors, living in a decaying mansion in Calcutta slum, the Mahatma was trying to reduce the religious terror – and succeeding, though the scale of the tragedy was too large even for him. Thirty-two years of struggle had, he said, come to 'an inglorious end'." – Michael Edwards: The Myth of the Mahatma p. 13

"Dr. Bonn, who met Mr. Nehru at Teen Murti House a few days before his death on May 27, 1964, found the once energetic Prime Minister walk with 'a slow halting gait.' 'The paralysis was very evident. He walked as if he was on the edge of a precipice. His shoulders were bent as if under a heavy burden. But his eyes were clear,' recalls the author in the book. 'You have before you a statesman who has failed,' Nehru said with a smile as he sat before Dr. Bonn" – Times of India : October 12, 1992

"In 1959, Nehru had reportedly described Gandhiji as 'an awful old hypocrite' in a conversation with the visiting Canadian statesman. Lester Pearson who was 'shocked' as he says in his memoirs. This from Nehru who 35 years earlier described Gandhi as 'a great and unique man and a glorious leader." Gandhi and Nehru, an ambivalent relationship. – S. C. Gangal, Indian Express, March 29, 1993.

Appendix C

Frontline published an article under the caption 'Far from Heroism: The tale of Veer Savarkar' in its issue of April 7th 1995 vilifying Veer Savarkar. I prepared a rejoinder to it refuting all allegations made in it and showing their hollowness. Thereafter it was sent to Frontline. The magazine did not publish it. Pundit Bakhale, Secretary, Swatantryaveer Savarkar Rashtriya Smarak, personally handed over a copy of this rejoinder to the Frontline Office. Yet it remained unpublished. Shri Shastri, the editor of Dharmabhaskar, published it in his Marathi monthly. Mr. Bakhale published it on behalf of the Smarak under the title 'Veer Savarkar Vindicated' to help students and researchers to know the true facts of Savarkar's life. Here it is reproduced to show how time and time again some writers, despite contrary evidence, enjoy vilifying Savarkar as a pastime. It also throws a floodlight on the liberalism of the Indian Press.

The Editor,
Frontline,
Kasturi Buildings,
Madras 600 002

Sir,

This refers to the article under the caption 'Far from heroism: The tale of Veer Savarkar,' written by Messrs Dubey and Ramakrishnan, which appeared in the column 'Reappraisal' of Frontline dated April 7, 1995.

The article is an attempt to denigrate Savarkar and thereby condemn Hindutva. It therefore calls for a rejoinder.

After Veer Savarkar's death, a great many leaders issued condolence messages about him. Mrs. Gandhi, the late Prime Minister of India, said, 'Savarkar's death removes a great figure of contemporary India. Describing his name as a by-word for daring and patriotism, she further said that he was cast in the mould of a classic revolutionary and countless people drew inspiration from him.'[1]

I think these few lines are sufficient refutation of three-page colossal effort of your research scholars to denigrate Savarkar.

Bur for enlightenment of your readers I will give information about Savarkar which throws light upon his life and shows how illustrious it was.

---

[1] Dhananjya Keer : Veer Savarkar – p. 548

The authors have quoted Savarkar's letters to show how unnerved he became, how his spirit was broken, and how he made an abject surrender. If this was really the position, revolutionaries themselves would have turned their backs on him. This does not seem to be the case. Mr. Sanyal, Mr. Parmananda, Mr. Aiyar, Bhagatsingh, Rajguru, and others, specially came to see him in Ratnagiri where he was interned. The authors of the article are not aware that two followers, who remained devoted to him till the end, were involved in terrorist activities. One was Mr. Wamanrao Chavan, who shot a sergeant in Dhobi Talo, and was jailed for 7 years. It is to be noted that after this shooting incident, Savarkar was detained in jail for 2 weeks as Mr. Chavan hailed from Ratnagiri. The other was Mr. Gogate who shot at the Acting Governor of Bombay Mr. Hotson. Mr. Gogate was sentenced to imprisonment for 8 years.

Bhai Parmananda was sentenced to death. But later his sentence was commuted and he was sent to the Andamans. Mr. Ashutosh Lahiri was also sent to the Andamans. Both were in the Andamans at the time Savarkar was there. Your readers would be interested to know that Bhai Parmanand became the President of the Hindu Mahasabha and Lahiri was its General Secretary and both were valued colleagues of Savarkar during this period of his Hindu Mahasabha Presidency from 1937 to 1942.

Incidentally Mr. Achyut Patwardhan of '1942 Quit India' fame and Mr. S. M. Joshi, leader of the Socialist party, met Savarkar, when he was released from the internment in Ratnagiri in 1937 and requested him to join their Socialist Party. Strange that Patwardhan and Joshi should have felt that Savarkar, whose spirit, as your learned authors say, was broken, should join their party!

Your authors have made a wonderful discovery. They write, 'One warning from the Government, and his concern for the so-called welfare of the Hindus had disappeared into thin air.' Your readers should read the chapter 'Social Revolution' from Keer's biography of Savarkar or Balarao Savarkar's volume Hindu Samaj Sanrakshak Swa. Veer V. D. Savarkar (Ratnagiri Parva) to find out for themselves what tremendous social transformation he effected in Ratnagiri during his internment there and thereby earned encomiums from several reformers of Maharashtra. The great social reformer Mr. Shinde was moved to say that God should give the remaining years of his life to Savarkar. And it be noted that Gandhiji, always hard-pressed for time, found it worthwhile to meet Savarkar to discuss social problems with him in 1927 when he was on tour of Ratnagiri. He also praised Savarkar's sacrifice and patriotism. And yet your authors have the temerity to pen the above words. Only blind hatred could have produced these words.

In the same article, in a box item, under the caption 'contrasting approaches' the authors have mentioned Motilal Nehru's 6 months sentence. This should not have been done. No one denies Motilal's sacrifice. But can 6 months in jail in 1930 be compared with 50 year's sentence in 1911? In 1930 the Government had become mellow. Provincial autonomy was 7 years away and Swarajya was 17 years away. But in 1911 the British Indian Government was harsh. When Savarkar was jailed, Gandhiji was in South Africa, Jawaharlal Nehru was in London. Motilal Nehru was more with the liberals than with the extremists of the Congress. What kind of life Savarkar had to face in the jail in the Andamans? The History ticket of Savarkar tells the story. Here are a few notings'[1] :

i.   6 months solitary confinement.
ii.   Seven days standing handcuffs.
iii.   Absolutely refusing to work, ten days cross-bar fetters imposed.

How many top leaders of the Congress had to suffer such punishments?

There is a following noting on page 464 of the above book. 'He is always suave and polite but like his brother, he has never shown any disposition to actively assist Government. It is impossible to say what his real political view is at the present time.'[2]

Your authors write, 'What is clear from a study of these documents, many of them available with the National Archives, New Delhi, is that Savarkar sought his release from British prisons not merely by giving an undertaking, not to engage in political activity but also by acknowledging that he had had a fair trial and a just sentence.' Now, one does not have to go to the archives to read the contents of these letters. Savarkar in his book 'My Transportation' has narrated on various pages what talks he had with Sir Reginald Craddock in 1913, with members of the Jail Commission, and with the Governor and what restrictions he would accept for his release from the Jail.[3]

Savarkar did not believe in Satyagraha. So jail going was not an important part of his political activities. If he was caught, he thought it was legitimate to give any undertaking to secure his release. He was a disciple of Shivaji. One should read Shivaji's letter to Aurangazeb. To secure his release, Shivaji made many promises in that letter. But when he escaped, these promised evaporated into the thin air.

Why judge Savarkar by Gandhian principles? We may, if we want, judge him by Leninists standards. Did not Lenin accept the offer of 'Sealed car' from the Kaiser's German Government – a capitalist government? He came in that train to lead the Bolshevik Party and to seize power in Russia. Stalin made a pact with Hitler, his arch enemy. But what is laudable in Lenin and Stalin becomes condemnable in Savarkar. To a jaundiced eye everything looks yellow.

---

[1] Source Material for a History of the Freedom Movement in India (Collected from The Bombay Government Records) Vol II; Bombay Government Publication – pages 478,479

[2] Source Material for a History of the Freedom Movement in India (Collected from The Bombay Government Records) Vol II; Bombay Government Publication – p.464

[3] V. D. Savarkar: Samagra Savarkar Wangmaya, Vol I – pages 448, 620, 690

'In contrasting approaches' your authors write, 'The desperate telegram from Haily, in which he explained the old man's determination and character in some detail, forced the issue and Motilal Nehru was released on September 8, 1930 unconditionally. He died 5 months later, on February 6, 1931 in Lucknow, with Jawaharlal Nehru and Gandhiji at his bedside.' How could Gandhi and Nehru be at his bedside? Because 'On January 25th Viceroy, Lord Irwin, ordered the unconditional release of Gandhi and the members of the Congress Working Committee, including Nehru.'[1]

Mr. Nehru's wife Kamala went to Europe for treatment. Mr. Moraes writes, 'On September 4, 1935, Nehru was suddenly discharged from Almora, five and a half months before his term was to expire... On the same afternoon he set out by Air for Europe.... On the evening of September 9th he reached Badenweiler.[2]

No one grudges this sympathetic treatment given to Nehru. One only wishes that people should know that Savarkar brothers met their family members only once in the Andamans. And in this meeting Savarkar's elder brother came to know that his wife had died earlier. Here are real contrasting approaches.

Now how was Savarkar treated in the jail in the Andamans? The following 3 excerpts show it.

1. 'Bombay Government do not recommend any remission of the sentences passed upon Ganesh Damodar Savarkar and Vinayak Damodar Savarkar'[3]
2. 'Government of India agrees that the Savarkar brothers should not be released under Royal Amnesty.'[4]
3. 'The Government of Bombay by their letter No. 1106/36, Home Department, dated 29th February, 1921, informed the Government of India that the Governor in Council was not in favor of the transfer of the Savarkar brothers from Andamans to a jail in the Bombay Presidency, as that would lead to a recrudescence of agitation in their favor.'[5]

Your readers should carefully read the marked lines. They showed the Government's worry and public sympathy for Savarkar.

---

[1] Frank Moraes : Jawaharlal Nehru – p. 171

[2] Frank Moraes : Jawaharlal Nehru – p. 246

[3] Source Material for a History of the Freedom Movement in India (Collected from The Bombay Government Records) Vol II; Bombay Government Publication – p. 467

[4] Source Material for a History of the Freedom Movement in India (Collected from The Bombay Government Records) Vol II; Bombay Government Publication – p. 469

[5] Source Material for a History of the Freedom Movement in India (Collected from The Bombay Government Records) Vol II; Bombay Government Publication – pages 477, 478

Your authors have said that Savarkar and his family showed an increasing tendency to mollify the British authorities. What was wrong in that? Any family would do that. It is natural; moreover, the British Government was not sympathetic, tender, accommodating to the Savarkar brothers, as it was with Gandhi and Nehru. I will illustrate:

While sentencing Gandhi in 1922 to 6 years imprisonment, Sir Robert Broomfiled observed: 'I should like to say that if the course of events in India should make it possible for the Government to reduce the period and release you, no one will be better pleased than I.'[1]

Government on medical advice released Gandhiji in 1924.[2]

The same consideration was extended to Mr. Nehru. Mr. Moraes writes, ' On the night of August 11th Nehru was brought from Dehra Dun under police escort to Allahabad and there informed that he was to be temporarily released in order to see his ailing wife. He was to be at liberty for eleven days.'[3]

Mr. Moraes further writes: 'Nehru had given the Government no undertaking when he came out of jail, but he felt it would be improper to engage in political activities during the respite they had allowed him.'[4] The Government was sure that he would not take part in politics and hence did not impose this condition. However, in Savarkar's case, the Government imposed the condition that he should not engage in political activities. How can it trust a man who jumped the ship at Marseilles?

Your authors have written about Savarkar's surrender, etc. It would have served the cause of history better if they had inquired into what was happening in the Congress camp. Writing about the settlement, Gandhi-Irwin pact, Mr. Moraes writes,

'Glancing at it, Nehru noticed that Gandhi had accepted the principle of self-government with reservations or safe-guards. He was numbed by the discovery, being literally shocked into silence.'

'As Nehru lay in bed that night, his mind traveled back to the saga and sacrifices of the non-violent movement. Were all these sacrifices to be frittered away in this temporary provisional compromise? How could Gandhi have brought himself to surrender the position when victory seemed within his grasp? Were all their brave

[1] Tendulkar: Mahatma, Vol II – p. 134

[2] Tendulkar: Mahatma, Vol II – p. 163

[3] Frank Moraes : Jawaharlal Nehru – p.237

[4] Frank Moraes : Jawaharlal Nehru – p. 238

words and deeds to end in this? Nehru wept. He was distressed beyond measure, and his grief and embitterment found vent in tears...'[1]

Comments are superfluous!

Your authors have labored hard to show that Savarkar's spirit was broken. They should have read the following paragraph from 'The Struggle for Freedom'. Dr. Majumdar writes, "By that time the individual Civil Disobedience 'was dead like a door nail.' Referring to the commencement of the New Year, 1934, the official history of the Congress records: 'The progress of events in the line of Civil Disobedience was none too satisfactory. The prisoners who were released were fagged. The provincial leaders who had promised the Poona Conference to lead their provinces if Mass Civil Disobedience were given up and individual Civil Disobedience continued, did not carry out their pledges, except in a few cases. Those who were released from jails found themselves unable or unwilling to face another conviction.' Slowly and silently the movement faded away, and during the upheaval caused by the great earthquake at Bihar on 16th January, 1934, it passed away unnoticed into the limbo of oblivion."[2]

This should show whose spirit was really broken.

In 1937, when all restrictions imposed on Savarkar were removed and Savarkar became free, Subhashchandra Bose, Jawaharlal Nehru, and M. N. Roy welcomed him to full freedom. Your authors say, 'Although Savarkar's conditional release was not much of secret at the time, when it occurred it was criticized by sections of the press.' And yet Bose, Nehru, and Roy thought it wise to welcome him. Who is more sensible? Bose, Nehru, and Roy or your authors?

Your authors have stated, '... Vinayak Damodar Savarkar who was one of the founders of the Hindu Mahasabha and is considered to be the father of the Anti-Muslim Hindutva ideology....' This statement reveals their colossal ignorance. For Hindu Mahasabha was founded in 1915 when Savarkar was in jail. According to Dr. Majumdar, 'The great leaders of Hindu Mahasabha, to begin with, were Swami Shraddhananda, Pandit Madan Mohan Malviya and Lala Lajpat Rai. Rajendra Prasad, too, presided over the special session in 1923. Then came Dr. B. S. Moonje and Bhai Parmananda, and last of all the great revolutionary Veer Savarkar, who gave it a militant character. During the whole of this period the Hindu Mahasabha really constituted a political organization to fight for the interests of the Hindus to which the Congress leaders were indifferent and even hostile.'[3]

---

[1] Frank Moraes : Jawaharlal Nehru – p. 181

[2] Dr. R. C. Majumdar : Struggle for Freedom,Bharatiya Vidya Bhavan Publication – p. 525

[3] Dr. R. C. Majumdar : Struggle for Freedom, Bharatiya Vidya Bhavan Publication – pages 988,989

As regards the charge of anti-Muslim Hindutva let me quote a few lines from Savarkar's Hindutva. He says, 'It may be that at some future time the word Hindu may come to indicate a citizen of Hindusthan and nothing else!' Does this not show that Savarkar visualized that a time would come when Muslims would be included in the fold of the Hindus? If this is so, how can Hindutva be anti-Muslim? But when ignorance parades as research, it becomes limitless.

The last heroic thing that Savarkar did was to give up his life voluntarily. No man who has lost his nerves can do this. How many leaders, except Vinoba Bhave, have shown this courage? Any way, Savarkar has departed from this world in 1966 with his reputation unsullied. No amount of research will tarnish it. He was the father of Hindutva-Hindu Nationalism. Now Hindutva has gathered its own momentum. No denigration of Savarkar will stop the growth of Hindutva.

It would have served the cause of National integration better if your authors had done research to find out why Indian nationalism failed and why Pakistan was created and why Muslim separatism still persists.

J. D. Joglekar

Appendix D

Savarkar worked hard to end the evil of untouchablility in Ratnagiri where he was interned. Chapter 8 of this biography narrates what he did in this connection. Yet his war on untouchablility is purposefully igorned but Gandhiji's toiling in the same cause is lauded. How deep was the effect of his drive to end untouchability? The following quotation gives at least a partial answer to this question.

Dr. Dhanagare writes, "Gandhiji was certainly aware of the limitations of his campaign against untouchability. When he had first selected Bardoli for launching a no-tax campagin in 1921-22, he had doubted whether his staunch upper-caste Hindu followers in Gujarat had really removed untouchability, and whether they were really treating antyajas as social equals. What leaders preached in public differed from what they practised in their private lives; 'those who met (or hugged) untouchables in public meetings before Gandhiji bathed with their clothes on when they returned home.' The hiatus between morals and private conduct was so large then, that there is no reason to believe that the new politcial enthusiasm, unleashed by the 'constructive programme', had narrowed it or had altered the status of the untouchables in Bardoli even at the time of the 1928 satyagraha. It is of interest in this context that until 1936 not a single untouchable student had been admitted to the ashrams and hostels run by the Patidar Mandal in the Bardoli area. This reflects on the superficiality of the entire campaign against untouchablility."[1]

---

[1] Dr. D. N. Dhanagare : Peasant Movements in India, 1920-50 – pp 102-103

Index

61302230R00110

Made in the USA
Middletown, DE
18 August 2019